The Hurt Artist

The
HURT ARTIST

My Journey from
Suicidal Junkie to Ironman

SHANE NIEMEYER

with Gary Brozek

Thomas Dunne Books
St. Martin's Press ☙ New York

THOMAS DUNNE BOOKS.

An imprint of St. Martin's Press.

THE HURT ARTIST. Copyright © 2014 by Shane Niemeyer and Gary Brozek. All rights reserved. Printed in the United States of America. For information, address St. Martin's Press, 175 Fifth Avenue, New York, N.Y. 10010.

www.thomasdunnebooks.com

www.stmartins.com

Library of Congress Cataloging-in-Publication Data

Niemeyer, Shane, 1975–
    The hurt artist : my journey from suicidal junkie to ironman /
Shane Niemeyer ; with Gary Brozek.—First Edition.
        pages cm
    ISBN 978-1-250-00908-1 (hardcover)
    ISBN 978-1-250-02109-0 (e-book)
 1. Niemeyer, Shane, 1975–   2. Triathletes—United States—
Biography.   3. Drug addicts—United States—Biography.
4. Ex-drug addicts—United States—Biography.   5. Ironman
triathlons.   I. Brozek, Gary.   II. Title.
    GV1060.72.N54A3 2014
    796.42'57092—dc23
    [B]
                                                        2014008829

St. Martin's Press books may be purchased for educational, business, or promotional use. For information on bulk purchases, please contact Macmillan Corporate and Premium Sales Department at 1-800-221-7945, extension 5442, or write specialmarkets@macmillan.com.

First Edition: May 2014

10 9 8 7 6 5 4 3 2 1

A Note to Readers:
The names and identifying characteristics of
a few individuals depicted in this book have been changed.

This book is dedicated to all the lost and broken souls struggling to find a way out from the darkness.

For all those who have left us before their time: may they rest peacefully.

Though it does not come easy, true and lasting change is possible, and with it, happiness follows.

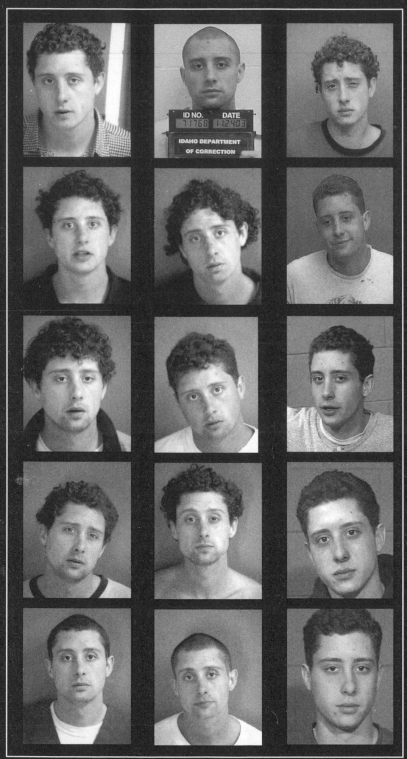

The Hurt Artist

Introduction

The cement floor felt cool against my forehead. My chest was heaving and my guts felt knotted with nausea. My triceps throbbed with the effort to push myself up one more time. I quivered and felt on the verge of collapse. I had no more to give. I tried to slowly lower myself; my vision narrowed, and the ringing in my ears rose to a crescendo. I thudded to the floor, unable to support my own weight any longer. I lay there trying to fight against the dope-sick symptoms that washed over me, gulping for air like a landed fish. I blinked my eyes to clear them of my stinging sweat.

After a few minutes more, I rolled onto my back, raised my feet onto my bunk, clasped my hands behind my head, and started to do my sit-ups. My abdominals, buried under a layer of fat inches thick, burned. I grit my teeth and pushed past the pain, gutting it out before surrendering to my brain's urgent shouting to stop. When my heart rate steadied, I stood up and went to my notebook and recorded day one's totals.

Eight push-ups.

Fifteen sit-ups.

Day one was complete. I was glad that I'd have another chance the next day.

The clamor of voices coming from the other inmates of the Ada County Jail, an asylumlike assemblage of laughs, shouts, and freakish screams, reminded me of where I was. Not that I needed to remember. Not that I wanted to remember. But I also knew that it was important to never forget this day. I also couldn't forget seventy-two hours earlier, three days to the minute, I imagined, and another moment I spent sprawled on the floor of that same building.

I remember every bit of the hurt like a fever dream.

I watched my fingers quaking from fear and the early onset of heroin withdrawal as they tied off the other end of the extension cord to the railing. I bowed my head and looped the noose around my neck. I shivered as the cold plastic coating of the cord licked my sweat-slimed skin. I stepped over the barrier keeping hold of the top rail with both hands. The metal felt cool against my clammy palms. I leaned out and away, held myself like a figurehead on a ship's prow, felt my body's weight tear at my shoulders.

A minute passed.

Another.

My calves burned, my toes clenched the concrete ledge, fighting involuntarily to maintain their grip.

Tears and snot ran down my face. Blood and bile rose in my mouth. The taste of salt and acid nearly gagged me. My pulse throbbed at my temple, neck, and groin; my balls contracted.

Twelve feet below me, the concrete floor of the Ada County Jail's intake unit glistened in the fluorescent light.

It shouldn't be this way; unless this was the final act, some kind of western frontier justice hanging at high noon. I shouldn't be hearing the voices from the yard, the faint static on the public address system overpowering the sound of my blood roiling in my veins.

It should be dark. Everything should be dark when you're about to murder yourself. It should be silent.

Fuck the *should*s and the *would*s.

Get your brain to just shut up and do it, already.

At least for once in your life you fucking idiot, do this one thing right.

I stood there, my legs trembling, the sinews in my arms vibrating like plucked guitar strings. Did I have what it took to do this, to really finish this thing off?

Forty-eight hours before that, I had woken up in the back of my van and struggled against my painfully spasmed muscles to get onto all fours. I rooted through the dumpsterlike contents of my life—a few articles of dirt-crusted clothes, dozens of fast-food bags and wrappers, newspapers—and found what I was looking for. I took a long pull and felt the pleasantly astringent taste of vodka rinsing out my mouth mucous. The alcohol flickered a tiny flame in my belly, a meager attempt at warming me. I slapped my hands against my upper arms and rubbed my legs, trying to get the circulation going. A few more swallows, a couple of prehypothermic shivers, and I was good to go.

I patted the pockets of my lone pair of cargo pants and everything I needed was there—my baggie of black tar heroin, my rig, and a small bundle of cash left over from my last grab and dash. I rushed over to the Albertson's on South Vista in Boise and picked up a few things to bring back to my friend Grace and her kids.

Once I brought in the groceries and watched her kids go at their breakfast with delight, I looked over at Grace. Our eyes met for a second, and I smiled. I nodded my head toward the hallway that led to the bathroom.

"Sure. Help yourself." She folded her arms across her chest and shrugged.

I went into the bathroom and sat on the toilet. The room reeked of mold, mildew, and Dial soap. The bile rising to my throat nearly gagged me. I leaned into the tub area and cranked open the window inside. I looked down and the shower curtain was crusted and flaking. I looked up at the shower's ceiling, the white tile mottled with orange, red, green, and brown splotches, an Impressionist's apathetic canvas.

I hadn't showered in days, and my junkie funk, a slightly sweet cheese gone bad odor, mixed with the sour tang of pickle brine, could only have gotten worse if I'd bumped against that science project of porcelain and tile. Even in my twisted state, I recognize the irony of my high-handed hygiene ethics.

I rolled up my sleeve, and looked down at my pockmarked forearm—mottled with blue, green, yellow, and violet bruising.

I laughed ruefully as I tightened the worn belt around my arm.

Pot. Kettle. Black. Tile. Arm. Who was I to criticize anybody's housekeeping. First, I didn't have a house to keep, and second, what passed for a house, what passed for my life, was anything but in order.

I watched my blood swirl lava lamp–like in the syringe for a moment and leaned back as the rush began. My head rested against a pair of pristine monogrammed hand towels. I quickly shifted positions and felt the cool tile against my skull. My world of hurt slipped away.

An hour later, I was in the hot grip of an Ada County sheriff, being "processed" at the jail. Photos. Prints. She held me by the wrist with her gorilla's grip, and I felt one of the abscesses just above my wrist pop and the putrid smell of my blood and pus reached my nostrils before my eyes saw its ooze spread across the flatbed scanner's glass. What should you expect from a junkie who'd tapped into nearly every vein in his arms for the last decade and more?

Her disgust was apparent. I didn't give a shit what she thought. Just get this over with, let me lie down someplace. Let me enjoy this last bit of being comfortably numb.

Truth was, I was still feeling something. Despair mostly. Exhaustion certainly. I was so tired of all the *never*s coming true. I'll *never* drink and drive. Done that. I'll *never* do cocaine. Ditto. I'll *never* inject. I submit as evidence these tracked-up arms, a relief map of resignation to what had come to feel like the inevitable decline.

And I was scared—not about being arrested, this was one of more than a dozen times for that. I had another kind of prison in mind.

No addict wants to be dope sick. That's why we do all the fucked-up shit we do to land us in places like the one I was in. And how did I know what dope-sick looked like? Because for the last few years I associated myself with the biggest dirtbags on display, and I was worse than any of them.

I had no job. I had no possessions other than a pair of pants, a couple of shirts, a pair of shoes. Worse, I possessed no sense of who I was or who I wanted to be. I was a mindless machine, singular in purpose, solid in a state of high and wasted. But that machine was breaking down. I was exhausted. I just wanted to shrivel and disappear and end the struggle. Strung out and stretched thin, tired of hitting the ground running to a hustle or a visit with the dope man, I was dissipating what little energy I had left, passing out at the end of every day and pissed off to be waking up the next.

I was also angry about this: how I could let the product of some chemical processes so completely overpower me?

Why the fuck couldn't I just quit?

Worst, I was out of control, drugs ruled me completely, and the only thing that I thought I might be able to control is whether or not I lived or died.

I chose to die. How much worse could that be compared to being a homeless addict?

For years, I knew I'd never make the transition from addict to former addict. At that point, I didn't even want to contemplate trying to make that conversion. I knew I only had a limited amount of time and energy, and I had to best utilize those resources in the service of accomplishing one task—murdering myself. I'd completely wrung myself out the last fifteen years, leaving behind a trail of broken promises, rehab programs entered, failed, booted out of, DUI convictions, possession charges, so many second chances given and gone up in so much crack smoke, wrecked cars, broken bones, riots incited, assaults committed.

I wanted to end a life that I never expected to last beyond thirty years anyway. I'd fucked up every relationship I ever had, had woken up in hospitals after overdosing and wondered why the fuck anyone had bothered to call 911 and wished to God they hadn't. I'd not held a job in years, was a leech sucking on society's blood, and the one good deed I could finally do was to check out permanently.

I knew what I was going to do, and unlike my sometimes haphazard, catch-as-catch-can efforts to get drugs for myself, I was going to plan this motherfucker meticulously. I silently thanked Becky—it was clear that she'd ratted on me—for helping me finally put an end to all this bullshit.

I got off the bench, walked over to the closet, and checked the door. The janitor had locked it, but there was something fucked up with the mechanism. The knob would turn just a bit, and I could hear the dead latch (and believe me I noted the irony here) moving inside the strike plate. Timing is everything, and if I could just twist the knob and pull on it simultaneously, I'd be able to get the door open. Two attempts and it was done. I closed the door and tried it again, realizing that I needed to build up some muscle memory. Access gained.

That was the easy part.

Next, I lay back on my rack and did something I'd never contemplated doing before. I planned my last conversation with the person who I'd hurt the most in my life, the woman who'd stood by me and supported me the best she could, even in the face of me pushing myself so far down and out of my life, that it proved impossible to reach me, let alone help me in any meaningful way. She could, and frequently had, reached out. I either let that hand hang there flapping in the breeze or bitten it so fiercely she had no choice but to pull it, flesh torn and bleeding, away.

Planning over, I executed the call, just a few hours before taking my leap of faith.

"Mom. It's me. It's Shane." A cool drop of my perspiration ran down from my armpit and I shivered.

"Where—"

"No. Please. Mom. Don't. It doesn't matter. I don't want you to talk. I don't need money. I don't need you to come and get me. I don't need another stint in rehab. I just need you to listen."

I swallowed and I tasted a bit of blood from the inside of my cheek where I'd bitten down on it. The phone's mouthpiece smelled like an unfiltered Camel, and my saliva thickened. I tried to talk, but it felt like my tongue had a hard-on.

"Listen. I just wanted you to know that I know what my problem is, and it's me. I'm causing all my problems. Always have. And I'm sorry. Please tell Dad, and tell Trent, I'm sorry. It must have been so tough for that kid having an older brother like me. I wish I could have made it easier for all you guys."

Struggling to breathe, I felt like somebody had taken a pair of vice grips and clamped them onto my voice box. I tried to hack up a lung cookie, something, anything, to either clear the blockage or lubricate those cords. I felt like I'd swallowed a handful of those little sandbag type things manufacturers put in some packages to keep moisture out. I wondered for a minute if that's what it would feel like later.

On the other end of the line, I could hear my mom sobbing, and that just tore me up. I went from dry and choked up to fairly drowning in my own fluids. All I could manage to say every couple of seconds after another heaving exhalation was, "I'm okay. Don't worry."

I knew I had to change tacks a bit, that the plan I'd formulated wasn't really working for her or for me. "Remember when I was growing up, the time I took Dad's Cherokee and wrapped it around that telephone poll? I was so fucked up, I went to a Chevy dealer, the phone line and concrete mesh and rebar dragging behind me. Told the guys there that it wasn't my car. When the cops came, Mom, I pushed the lighter into its socket, heated it up, and then mashed it into my palm. I needed to sober up. I needed to punish myself for fucking up again. Eight months for that heal, Mom. And I did it all to myself. You guys did nothing wrong. It was all on me. All me. I'm sorry for everything I ever did to hurt you guys."

"Shane—" my mom's voice was a toad's croak from a pond, a distant sound evoking another time and place, a reminder of the dislocation I experienced and later enforced.

"Mom. No." I knew she was going to tell me again, for what would be the thousandth time, that it was okay.

But it wasn't.

"Mom. I've gotta go. But before I do, there's one more thing. I told you that story, and I said it happened when I was growing up? Well, the thing is, I could say the same thing about two years ago, two minutes ago. I still haven't grown up. I still haven't taken responsibility for things. That's going to change soon. There's things I have to take care of here. You take care of yourself, okay? No matter what. Do that for me, please? I love you, and I am so sorry for everything. I couldn't have had asked for a better mom."

I set the phone back in its cradle, watched the coiled cord dance and contract. Somehow, on jelly legs, I weaved my way back into the unit, leaving behind me an oozing trail of despair, regret, and longing.

Afternoon's "recess" came in what seemed an instant. To avoid suspicion, I joined everyone outside for exercise, squinted painfully against the sun's assault. With my hands tucked in the pockets of my jumper, I walked around the "yard," a sterile patch of concrete. We had twenty minutes out there. I figured I'd need twelve, so I started counting each step, circling the concrete pad, nearly feeling the bottoms of my shoes being worn away.

After 480 steps, I headed back inside. The dorm was quiet, except for the buzz of the lights and a moth butting its head against one.

Jimmying the door took longer than I'd expected. I was confident that the rest of the guys would stay out for the duration and beyond—doing anything they could to extend their time out in the air.

The tying done, the climb onto the ledge complete, an image came to me. A young woman from our high school. A nothing-special kind of girl, dishwater blonde, an anvil-shaped face. Mary Beth Olinger had hung herself. None of us understood.

Coward.

Act of weakness.

The easy way out.

We all had our heads so far up our asses. We couldn't have known what it took for her to do that, what kind of pain she must have been in. She had felt like I felt, that there was no other way except to make the pain stop. We were wrong. She wasn't weak at all, she was in more anguish than any of us could have known then, but I knew now.

I stood there teetering on the edge, wondering if I had the strength, if I could finally grow some hair, be a man.

One last thought. I didn't want to piss and shit myself, but I knew that was inevitable. Poor fucking janitor. Not only might he catch hell for the door lock and my scamming the extension cord, but he'd have to clean up my mess.

Same old, lame-ass Shane. Some things never change, I guess.

No need for a deep breath now. Just do it.

I jumped.

ONE

I was born in Loveland, Colorado, in November 1975, but in a lot of ways, I could say I was born in the Ada County Jail in Boise on June 23, 2003. When I came to after the extension cord snapped and I survived my suicide attempt, I was in a world of hurt; my neck was stiff and abraded and my head was pounding and I was nauseated from not having done any dope or having a drink of alcohol since my arrest two days before. Worse than that though, my feet were throbbing. I'd fallen a good twelve feet or so and landed shoeless on a hard concrete floor. Birthing pains are tough on everybody.

Opening my eyes for the first time after I'd jumped—my ears ringing, my head pounding, and the anguished tears that I'd been crying moments before as I'd let go of the railing and let go of life still coursing down my cheeks—I was surrounded by a few people, including someone in hospital greens.

For the longest time, I'd assumed that I was going to die well before longevity statistics suggested that I should; either I would be

killed by one of the dealers I had robbed, not wake up from an overdose, or perhaps another car wreck would end things. However, having somehow come through that jump, something inside me changed.

As soon as they determined that I hadn't snapped my spine or sustained any life-threatening injury that necessitated me going to an
off-site hospital, they took me to the medical unit. I was stripped down
to my skivvies, examined, and then placed in what's called a "security
blanket," a Kevlar garment that strapped my arms tight to my torso.
They were trying to prevent me from doing any more damage to myself.

The thing is I didn't need that. At some point in those moments
shortly after I was reborn (no religious overtones implied or intended),
I had a passing thought about being such a failure that I couldn't even
end my life successfully. I'd spent so much of my life thinking that I
was a fuckup—and hating myself for that—that I couldn't be completely free of self-loathing about another monumental and spectacular failure. This time instead of wallowing in that muddy sinkhole of
self-incrimination and subterranean self-esteem, I let go after a minute of berating myself. Those negatives were immediately replaced by
an overwhelming sense of gratitude that I was getting a second chance.
Hell, I don't know if I can calculate the number of second chances I'd
received previously. Though I was very sick, hurting, and in a world
of shit, I felt enormously unburdened. It was an intensely freeing experience to have come through that attempt alive. In a strange way, I
had passed a test, endured a skewed rite of passage that only someone
with my train wreck of a past could have seen as a positive.

That's not to say that I wasn't still dejected. The one feeling I wasn't
experiencing was fear. I had been scared shitless standing on that
ledge and about to jump. Now, I wasn't afraid at all. I felt like I no
longer had anything to lose, and I didn't. I had no personal belongings,

no girl, no job, and no real future plans. I couldn't and didn't really long for the halcyon days of my golden past that I'd let slip through my fingers and could no longer return to. I had a blank slate of a life in front of me. If that metaphorical door had been opened, there was not a single thing I could see on the other side of the threshold.

That was such a liberating place to be. I didn't hit bottom; I fell through its fucking floor. I got past that critical moment of despair. I had come to see in the hours and days that followed that I had come through so much that should have ended me. Once I lost my will to live I came to look at things completely differently. I had lost my freedom long ago and now I had lost my physical freedom as well. There was nothing left to lose; instead I came to think of things in terms of what I had to gain. It forced me to reframe my perception of things, and immediately changed my perspective. I was down at the bottom looking up at the infinite possibilities. My life could be a blank slate, and this was my point of origin. Freedom was mine. In that goddamn cell I vowed to myself that this was it, it was time to start living and cramming it all in because I had pissed away twenty-eight years of my life to this point, and the clock was ticking.

Fear holds us back from attempting so many things. I'd attempted what I think most people are extremely afraid to do. I'd done it, and regardless of the results, I could look at that suicide attempt and say one thing: I'd gone through with it; I'd pushed past the fear.

If I was experiencing some dread, it was rooted in something more immediate. I'd been dope-sick for a few days a couple of times during my various rehab stints or when I tried on my own to quit using or when my pipeline had somehow temporarily run dry. Detoxing and withdrawal were like having the absolute worst and most unrelenting flu symptoms you've ever had for hours and hours on end. I wasn't looking forward to enduring those days. But even in those first moments when I woke up the next morning alone in that tiny cell, still in my less than comfortable restraints, with the red light of the surveillance camera and the bare cot and a black-bound Bible the only things breaking the monochromatic haze of white I was fogged into, I knew immediately that I was done with doing drugs.

I had to be.

For a long time I thought I had two options—quit drugs or die. I had tried to quit many times over the years. I'd just tried to die, so that left me with one choice. No choice really. I had to do this thing. I'd actively struggled for years to control my drinking and usage to no avail. Suicide was a way of both taking control and surrendering it. Now, I figured it might be time to do the same thing about my addictions, to just release them, stop being so attached to whatever pains and pleasures they brought me.

Also, I no longer wanted to kill myself. I knew all the things people said about a "cry for help," but that wasn't what I had been up to that previous afternoon. Without a doubt, I did want to end my life that day. The thought of death gave me so much comfort in those hours after my arrest. Life had become unbearable and I had completely lost hope. The moment I hit the ground after the extension cord snapped, I no longer wanted to end my life. In trying and failing to end my life, I'd given myself hope.

I'd spent years doing the worst possible things to myself, and then I'd attempted the ultimate act of self-destruction and I'd come out on the other side of it alive. That jump had shaken something loose inside of me, something that I had tried to kill with chemicals, and it had proven stronger than them. It was as if I'd done everything destructive I could possibly think of, and somehow the life force inside me hadn't been defeated. I'd tried to kill myself, and the self-loathing, pissed-off-at-the-world part of me had survived, barely. I realized that now it was up to me to consciously take the steps to finish the job, to really lay that old self to rest.

I wanted the pain of my new injuries to end, that's for sure. But I even took some comfort from them. They were visceral signs that I was alive, active reminders that I was still kicking, in a better place than I had been before the jump.

In that medical unit, I literally and figuratively came to my senses that next morning. I don't know about divine intervention, God's plan for us all, or anything like that. Maybe those things serve as an explanation or as a comfort. I do believe that all along in my life—through all the addiction issues I had, all the crimes I committed, all the general mayhem I manufactured for myself, my friends, my family, and society at large, even when things were the bleakest—there was still a tiny part of me that wanted me to pull it together and do something productive with my life. Eventually, I'd come to accept that there was more of a connectivity and confluence to our life circumstances and our choices than I had before when randomness ruled. That was going to take some time and a lot of work to get there. For once in my life, I wasn't going to ask myself why it was that something had happened to me. I don't know if I could say that I'd cheated death; all I knew was that my heart was pumping, my kidneys were producing piss, and my neurons were still sparking.

There was something to be said for just accepting that, establishing some kind of homeostatic balance for the moment and just respiring for a few moments, taking it all in.

I still had a lot of anger in me; some I directed toward myself for the horrendous choices I'd made, some at other people and circumstances that I thought had led me to the point I was at. As long as I was alive, it was okay to be angry. I'd figure out some way to deal with that. I had so much to sort out, and I was grateful that I was looking at doing a stretch in prison down the line. That would give me some time and space to figure out what it was I was going to do with the rest of my life, how I was going to manage to not waste another of the many opportunities I'd been given.

My time in the medical unit was the same as it would have been if I'd been put in solitary. Twenty-three hours out of the day I was alone in that closet of a room, constantly under video surveillance. If I knew one thing about myself it was that even though my body was so sore and damaged I could barely make the walk to the shower I was allowed during my sixty minutes outside the confines of my cell, my mind was going to be on a feverish walkabout. I needed something to keep myself from going crazy. My request for something to read was ignored. Of course, the medical staff had done their part to help, putting me on a low-dose antipsychotic/antidepressant called trazodone. For the next seven or eight days I would remain on it, mostly to help me with my physical detox. I would continue to do the Trazodone Shuffle throughout, a stooped-old-man-stiff gait that you might see a Parkinson's patient use to get around.

That dosage may have calmed me a little, but it sure wasn't doing much to help me unwind from all the neurological wind sprints I was doing. Each time I lay down on that cot, it was like time stood absolutely still. Because of the camera and the county's need to surveil me, the lights were on all the time. The dope-sick was getting worse, and one moment was just another ghastly and ghostly white reproduction of another. It was as if a Xerox machine were spitting out blank page after blank page, filling up the room.

For the last several years, my entire life had revolved around thinking of ways to get money to buy drugs, procuring them, doing them, and then cycling through that constant preoccupation for years on end.

Day after day. Hour after hour. Twenty-four seven. I was an animal, primal in pursuit of what I needed to survive.

What was I going to do with my brain now?

I couldn't just sit there with nothing to do but wait for the dopesick to get worse. I couldn't just sit around for the rest of my life being a drag on society. Something had to give.

The surveillance camera's dead eye never blinked, never acknowledged my presence.

The next morning, Deputy Freeman and another CO walked me to the shower. I know what a water closet is, and I know that describing this thing as a water closet might make you think of a bathroom, but really it was about the size and shape of a closet with a dripping nozzle poking out of the ceiling. A whore shower, I remember someone else calling it.

On the way back to my private accommodations, I asked again for something to read, this time adding, "What am I going to do? Paper cut myself to death?"

A little while later, I heard footsteps outside my cell. Next, I heard and then saw something slide under the door. I scooted along on my ass, pissed as hell that I had to use my already aching heels for traction, to see what had been delivered. The reading materials that lay there courtesy of Deputy Freeman consisted of a single magazine.

Being bound up and muscle sore like I was, it wasn't easy to flip through that thing. I'd received a dog-eared copy of the June 1, 2000, *Outside* magazine. I scanned its cover and saw that the issue contained an article called, "Could This Be Love?" Given my desire to find anything to occupy my mind, I scrunched my toes across the glossy paper until I got to the one piece that had initially caught my eye. A photo of a very fit-looking man dominated the opening page.

The first thing that arrested my attention was the writer stating that guys like him raced in competitions that consisted of a 2.4-mile swim, a 112-mile bike ride, and a 26.2-mile run. Besides the numbers, the other thing that struck me, so much so that I can still quote the words today, was that they accomplished all this, "like Zen masters, enclosed in bubbles of unremitting effort." The crazy dude pictured was Dave Scott.

As I read on, I got more caught up in what was involved in pushing yourself to complete such a grind in a single day. All the hours of training. All the obsessing about what to put into your body to fuel it. All the planning you had to do in order maximize your performance so you could physiologically peak at a precise moment.

After I finished reading, I sat there thinking about all those questions I'd been asking myself about how I was going to occupy my time and my mind if I wasn't doing drugs. The guys in that article seemed to be as obsessive about their routine as I had been about mine.

I also thought about the abuse that I had heaped upon my body. Not only was I a twenty-eight-year-old drug addict and an alcoholic, I smoked a couple of packs of cigarettes a day for years, and if it weren't for the security blanket, I would have been oozing rolls of fat out of my clothes. It didn't take a genius to figure out that I was a physical wreck as well as a moral, spiritual, and emotional one.

Looking back on it now, I can see that my decision to pursue the sport that Dave Scott had reigned over made absolutely no sense logically. I'd never really been an athlete. I'd had to run from some Honduran drug dealers (we'll get to that), enraged security guards, and a few police officers in the last ten years, but that was the extent of my physical fitness regimen.

I do think it's possible to be both lucid and delusional simultaneously. I may have only been a few days free of drugs, and I was suffering from the aftereffects of a kind of hangover that no one should ever have to experience. But I was completely lucid when I set my sights on the first worthwhile outcome I'd had in years—to qualify for and eventually compete in the Ironman World Championship in Kona, Hawaii.

I had to ignore the fact that I faced a significant hurdle right out of the starting blocks.

I was in jail and headed for prison.

I was likely to be behind bars somewhere for an as-yet-to-be-determined but probably lengthy amount of time. Boise ain't Kona, and I'm all for purposeful delusion, but even I could see these initial environmental limitations. I had no pool. I had no bike. I had no roads to run.

For at least the previous ten years or more, my future had consisted of getting the drugs I needed by any means necessary to get me through the day. Those days mostly involved me being a drag on society, on those who I came in contact with directly, and generally tearing myself and the world down. Post-suicide attempt, I was looking for something to achieve, some way to make a positive move. For years and years, I'd been in a kind of static state at best but mostly regressing. I wanted to move forward, to push myself, to finally after all the years of just being a complete energy suck to test my mettle and see what I was really made of. I knew that this would be a case of self-denial and discipline to the extreme. Extremes were something that I was good at. I always wanted to be the craziest motherfucker in the bunch. I had to drink more than anybody, take the most risks, defy most fervently whatever strictures those in authority placed on me.

For me, there never was a middle ground. To borrow a cliché, it was always go big or go home. Trying to kill myself was just another example of that. If you're going to punish yourself, then that was as big a way to do it as there could be. Now I was going to punish my body to the extreme, but with a critical difference. I was going to achieve something, make some kind of positive contribution.

I finally had an outline for myself and my future that didn't include winding up as another in a very long line of dead junkies.

TWO

Despite a long history of promising myself that today was going to be the day that I was going to quit, that this was the absolute last time I was going to drink, snort, or inject and failing to follow through, I kept at my new fitness program. Like most people, I had a complicated relationship with the notion of quitting. I was used to abandoning things that were painful as well as refusing to give up what gave me pleasure but ultimately led to my suicide attempt. I'd been in and out of five different rehabilitation programs, done my time in AA, crafted my own "no more/never again" efforts to quit using and drinking, but always, every time, sooner or later the siren song of substance abuse proved more powerful than my will. I understood this at the time, and in those days after my failed suicide attempt I drove the point home with every basic exercise I did.

I'd given up on myself, had wanted to kill myself because I was too weak to overcome my addictions. My life was no longer in my control; chemicals ruled me. Post-suicide, I knew that I had to get stronger in so many ways. At the time, getting more capable physically seemed the easiest and most essential phase of my overall rehabilitation.

Anyone who knew me, any betting person informed of my track record, would have laid their money down against my succeeding, taken the over and under at somewhere between five and ten days. I don't blame them for being doubtful. I didn't have much of a past that I could draw from. Empty optimism is a fragile thing, but with each day of sobriety and each day's work-out totals exceeding the previous one, I built a framework to support the "what the fuck do I have to lose" mentality that defined those earliest days of my transformation. Desperation sometimes makes us cowards and sometimes makes us courageous. At least I was making a good choice by trying.

It's funny to think of it now, but I did have one thing in my favor: I was used to hurting. I'd been experiencing those painful sensations for most of my life. I wasn't used to doing the kind of hurting that would pay positive dividends down the line, but that was an easy switch to make.

Even though in those first few weeks as my cells screamed at me to feed them what they'd grown so accustomed to, I listened to their complaints, tried reasoning with them by telling them that the pain would eventually go away, shouted at them to shut the fuck up when they wouldn't listen, and generally waged a war of attrition on my body. It was as if I was telling myself, "If you think this withdrawal hurts, how about the sting from another set of prisoner squats?"; like that parental old school mentality of telling kids, "You're crying now; how about if I really give you something to cry about?"

I had been killing myself slowly. It was the slow and yellow death of a coward suspended between conviction and apathy. Working out provided me a way to "build myself" up through discipline and self-infliction. It was a way to whip myself into some form of self-respect. It was a way to finally experience a sense of achievement through work and discomfort. For way too long I'd chosen the easy way out. No more of that for me.

As random as my decision had been to choose triathlon as my post-Lazarus vision of my future might seem, in some ways, I wasn't so much counting on the emergence of a new self but a return to a previous one. I hadn't always been an addict and a criminal, and I did have some experiences being an active kid who loved the outdoors, played in some youth sports, and who, when doing something I loved, exhibited a form of the maniacal drive required in endurance athletics. Tapping into those traits and experiences wasn't going to be easy.

Most people have their Garden of Eden, and for me, and for my father, that place was outside of Loveland, Colorado, where I was born and raised.

The Big Thompson River flowed past the house. Compared to most places, Colorado is arid. Though the spring melt in the high country can raise the water level several feet in the late spring, by most standards, this tributary of the South Platte River is pretty benign. We lived on the outskirts of the town of Loveland, down river from where the Big Thompson had carved out a fairly narrow canyon of the same name.

I didn't know anything about the river's history at the time we were living there, but the Big Thompson wasn't always so benign. I've moved back to the area after more than twenty or so years have passed. Only now do I understand why there are signs posted all along the

Big Thompson Canyon, and in the other canyons I train in, warning of the danger of flash floods.

DANGER: SEEK HIGHER GROUND.

I wish now that I had heeded that warning as a kid instead of choosing to sink so low.

In 1976, the year after I was born, the Big Thompson lived up to its name. In late July, a thunderstorm dumped more than twelve inches of rain in four hours in the upper section of the canyon. A flash flood that produced a twenty-foot high wall of water killed 143 people, destroyed 400 cars, 418 houses, 52 businesses, and a significant stretch of the ribbon of pavement winding through it. Those twelve inches of rain in that short four-hour period represented 75 percent of the amount of rainfall the area normally receives in an entire year.

How's that for a bit of excess wreaking havoc? Mother Nature sometimes doesn't know when to quit. Maybe it's from her I picked up my tendency.

In some ways, I find it odd that no one in my family ever spoke about the flood, the horrific storm that caused it, the later devastation that left lives and property in ruins. In other ways, their silence on the matter seems perfectly natural. We tend to keep things to ourselves.

My father was like the river we lived on. Quiet most of the time, explosive at others. No warning signs were posted. Much of what must have caused his deluge of anger was left unspoken, unaccounted for.

I remember what I remember.

Life on the Big Thompson was ideally suited to someone of my disposition. There was room to roam outside, and my father, Ralph, a rural Iowan who made his way out to Colorado, found something magical about the place. My mother, Lynne, worked in nearby Greeley for the State Farm Insurance Company in some managerial capacity; while Dad was a facilities manager, moving from job to job not out of necessity but due to his promotability, his skills and work ethic. We were solidly middle class, and by the time my brother, Trent, came along four years after me in 1979, we could have certainly afforded to live in town, on one of those cookie-cutter developments with a house that the Brady Bunch would have envied.

We didn't. Too crowded. Too noisy. Too many people knowing your business.

That's what I've been told.

My dad grew up dirt poor and less, and though as far as I can remember I never asked him about why he chose to have us live a more redneck-blue-collar kind of life than their combined salaries might have earned them, I suspect now that our home on the river was some approximation of what back in Iowa he'd envisioned as an idealized existence. Rather than rolling fields of corn, we had a river, high desert plains to the east, and the highest peaks of the Rocky Mountains just an hour's drive to the west. Colorado was his escape from what I would later learn was a childhood that made my pain seem like nothing in comparison.

That's not an excuse for what he did to me and vice versa. I can't say that his verbal and mild physical abuse caused me to fuck up my life so completely. I can't say that my hatred for him was a direct result of how he treated me. The headwaters of his anger and frustration with me and the world were a distant trickle of a stream that went back eons, something more suitably measured in geologic time. Fathers and sons. Epic battles for dominance.

It often feels that way to me now, as if the tensions between us predated both his and my time on earth. We were just carried along in a current more powerful than either of us knew.

I can't say with any certainty that I remember more or less about my childhood than other people do. I don't know if that's attributable to all the drugs I took, the general fallibility of memory, but I do remember some things with a clarity that startles me.

I remember my dad taking me to the playground. My mom and my brother, Trent, weren't there. It was just him and me. Him pushing me on a swing, me gliding away and then returning. Later that day he was gone for a while and then back again. What pushed him away I don't really know.

Like a drop of some catalyst placed in a solution, a few things crystallize. One of the earliest pictures I remember seeing of my dad and me is one of him squinting fiercely into the sun, a crooked grin splitting his face, a can of Budweiser hoisted up alongside his cheek, condensation running down it like sweat and tears, my freshly squeezed head resting under his other.

Things were tough between them for a time. Early on she saw signs, she knew, but she chose to wish them away. They met one night when, breathless and panicked, he came storming into a friend's house where she was visiting. The cops were after him and he needed some place to hide. He immediately tapped into the wellspring of my mother's essential nature. Here was someone who needed help. It didn't hurt that he was good-looking and charming, that despite his desperation he managed to be both polite and dangerous. One thing led to another and they were dating and married; he did a stint in the army and that discipline and order seemed to tame or at least put to good use the rampant spirit that coursed through him. Who knows how his tour of duty in Vietnam might have twisted or straightened him out? He wasn't about to share his feelings with anyone.

I couldn't have articulated this then, but as a kid I always sensed that my dad was willing himself to stay within some boundary. To me, he was like an electrified fence, wires strung taut between two poles, emitting a faint hum and a hair-raising pulse of energy that you could detect only when you got too close. From a distance, you wouldn't know that danger existed.

I remember for the weeks that my dad was gone not feeling or hearing any of that audible and inaudible static crackling through the house.

My mom said that I have the same energy he did, only instead of it being contained, it spilled out all over.

I pictured one of those kid's toys, the popcorn popper like gadget with the plastic bubble, the wheels, and the wooden T handle. I imagined myself toddling around the house with that thing, loving the racket it made with its riot of balls spitting around. I also imagine my father seething at the disquiet I created, reaching into the refrigerator for another cold one to drown me out. I do know that until he went into rehab, my father drank every day, and I can't remember a time from those early days when he didn't have a beer can in his hand or nearby.

God bless Mom, but she couldn't bring herself to elaborate too much on what I was like as a preschooler, other than that I was a handful, a kinetic presence who, instead of being stilled when a hand is placed on the thigh, transfers the energy to the party hoping for calm. I was a human stadium wave, a perpetual commotion machine. I was released into the outdoors temporarily, as if I was some semidomesticated pet, a squirrel or a raccoon or something like that, who was still feral enough to be destructive, but cute and cuddly enough to be kept as a fond oddity not without its charms and value.

As bad as things could be with Dad, I hated the idea of being without him. He seemed to sense that, and like the ultra-loyal Labrador retrievers he bred, bullied, and occasionally beat, I always came back for more. Worse was when I shrank from him like the runt of the litter. He grew up hard, and he wanted me to be the same way. If I shrank from him or flinched before he slapped me, it seemed to piss him off even more.

One incident sums up what it was like growing up and the worries that nearly consumed me. I was eight and a half and my dad was taking us with him to the grocery store. I must have asked one too many questions. He slammed on the brakes, yanked the wheel so that we wound up on the shoulder. He flat-sided me just behind the ear, and with his eyes bugging out, he leaned in really close, his face growing larger as I pressed myself against the door to escape, "Shut up you dumb fuck. Keep it up and you're going to drive me to drinking again."

Message delivered. I was the cause of his anger; I would be the one who drove our family apart. In time, I grew to hate him, found unfathomable his demand that I, at the age of five, drown our peahen's newborn chicks, while he stood over me watching with a glazed look of pride and perverse pleasure. "You've got to be a man," he seemed to be saying, and that meant suffering and causing others to suffer.

Eventually, I'd learn what demons possessed him, but until that revelation when I was thirteen, he was a mysterious and fear-inducing force in my life. He was smart, too. Around my mom, he exhibited little of his rage and seldom directed any of it toward me. My little brother, Trent, was spared his wrath almost entirely.

I could only come to one conclusion about my circumstances: It must have been me. I must have been what tore my dad up so badly that he had to retaliate and treat me so horribly.

Later on as a teen when I was really acting out. My buddies and I used to laugh at someone falling down or doing whatever to hurt themselves and say, "That's going to leave a mark." Well, for better and worse, that's what my dad's anger did to me. Whatever confidence I might have developed in myself was stillborn in that toxic environment.

I lived in a confused world of pain and pleasure and love and hate. In time I'd find a way to numb myself to that world of hurt; as a young adolescent, I was merely along for the ride. As a teen, I'd find refuge in drugs and alcohol. I became intent on hurting my father.

One solution my mom and dad discovered for my agitating presence was to open the door and let me outside—I could do less damage out there, be less of a pest. To be honest, I didn't mind being turned loose into the outdoors. While I wasn't actively involved in any kind of sports, being able to ramble around the woods and along the river gave all my energy an outlet. My buddy Tom Howie and I spent hours wandering around, hunting with our BB guns, fishing with our dads, and generally living a Huck Finn–Tom Sawyer kind of existence, him with the kind and loving family, me always on edge with a volatile father. While fishing required me to sit still, something I was loathe to do most other times, I did it because when my dad was enjoying himself, he was a pleasure to be around. Fishing seemed to soothe whatever ailed him, and I was always happy to be around him when our two energy fields matched.

In 1986, when I was eleven, we moved to Mission Viejo, California, when my mom accepted a transfer there. I was sad to leave Tom and the rest of the boys back in Loveland, and at first I hated life in a planned community with its uniform rows of houses and no place to really roam and explore, but I soon discovered a couple of other passions. The ocean seemed to have a magnetic pull on me, and I couldn't get enough of bodyboarding. In that activity, I found another release for my abundant energy. The first time I saw people paddling out into the surf and riding those waves back in, I was enthralled. The first time I tried it, I was hooked.

I befriended a Korean kid in the neighborhood by the name of Kwang-Sun. Kwang (no one called him Kwang-Sun but his parents) and I frequently rose before dawn on weekends and caught the bus to Newport Beach and "The Wedge" or to San Clemente and T Street, the best surfing beaches in the area. I was one of those kids who was undisciplined at school and earned decent but not exactly exemplary grades, and after just about every parent-teacher conference my mother reported back to me that my teachers thought that I needed to focus better and work on disciplining myself. In the sixth grade, I was diagnosed with attention deficit disorder, and from that point on considered myself a marked young man. Having to march down to the nurse's every day to take my meds, my earliest experience doing a "perp walk," tore me up. Everyone knew where I was going and what I was doing, and I might as well as have been asked to wear a sign saying TROUBLE around my neck while I did it.

I hated, viscerally hated being labeled with that "disorder" and everyone and everything to do with it. I associated every authority figure—teachers, doctors, school administrators, and even the police with whom I'd had a few early encounters—with a vast conspiracy to deny me the right to be me. Yes, I was full of energy, but instead of helping me find ways to channel that energy, they tried to medicate me into a dull and lifeless little droid. Yes, I'd flipped off a substitute teacher and gotten sent to the principal's office but the guy was a douche bag, I was the new kid, and I was just trying to impress everyone and make a few friends. It was a fucking joke and not worthy of a suspension. Yes, I couldn't stop talking in class, but did any of them ever get sick and tired of sitting in a confined space for hours a day being beaten on with words?

In 1988, when I was in the sixth grade, my parents took me in for my first psychological evaluation. Angry, impulsive, inattentive, low self-esteem are the highlights of that initial diagnosis.

Before the drugs and the alcohol, bodyboarding and surfing provided me with a purpose and a direction. I could go to The Wedge, my preferred locale because it was a bigger thrill, and spend hour after hour working on perfecting a move. I didn't stop for lunch. I didn't stop because my arms ached from all the paddling. I didn't stop when my failure to kick out soon enough found me thrashed onto the beach and then sucked back out by a riptide. I had focus. I had discipline. I just didn't exhibit those traits when and where everybody else said that I should demonstrate them.

In hindsight, I can see that bodyboarding fed another of my personality traits. I was a bit of an adrenaline junkie from early on. The Wedge was formed by a jetty that ran about a quarter mile out from the shore. Because of how it sits, its angle to the swell, it could pitch up pretty quick. By Southern California standards it was a really thick wave, and the bigger and dicier the surf, the more I liked it.

Just as in Colorado, when either I became too much for my family to handle, or my energy threatened to overspill its boundaries, I'd find refuge outside. One day in particular in 1990, I needed that kind of release and relief. I'd been told that we were going to have to leave Southern California. Mom had been transferred back to the home office in Bloomington, Illinois. I looked at a map and about puked. There was the ocean, there were the Rockies, and then there was this vast blankness at which, to my geographically impaired mind, sat Bloomington, Illinois. Tensions were high in the house, mostly stirred up by me, but my parents tried to assure me that things would be even better in Bloomington. All I could focus on was the fact that it had a twin city by the name of Normal. Who the fuck would want to live near Normal?

Normal didn't work for me. I always wanted to go my own way. That included how I handled the few chores I was given. As my time in Southern California rapidly drew to a close, my patience for the mundane order of life in our house shrank into something about the size of a BB. I was also getting pretty sick of my dad being on my ass about everything.

Ralph Niemeyer had very high standards that he expected me to meet. I don't know if it was his time in the army that drilled into his head the idea that anything worth doing was worth doing right, and that good enough is never good enough it has to be your best. I'd heard words like those my whole life. I had a paper route, my parents seemed to be doing okay financially, so I didn't have an allowance strictly speaking, but I did have to do some chores. One of those was washing the cars. My dad had his method: a cool rinse to begin, a hand wash with warm soapy water (dishwashing liquid and not, and I repeat NOT clothes detergent) administered with a terry cloth towel, followed by another cool rinse with the hose—and goddamn it, keep that nozzle at least six inches away from the car's body panels and paint—and then a hand dry using a chamois cloth specifically made for automobiles, a dried bit of leather that had to be wetted in order to dry the car and not scratch its surface. No drying in vigorous circles that might produce whorls in the glossy topcoat either. Straight lines and frequent rinses and rewetting of the chamois.

My father might have had the patience and luxury of time on Saturdays to spend the hour or so it took to do a single car. I didn't. In addition to having other chores to do, I had places to go and people to hang out with to whom I was not genetically linked.

So, I'd do what I considered to be a thorough job of washing the cars. None of the easily visible surfaces showed any signs of dirt. My dad got down on his hands and knees, looked at the area beneath the doors and shook his head.

He showed me a finger smudged from the rocker panels and said, "Do it again."

I don't know what it was about that particular Saturday, but when he told me that I had to start over, I lost it. I don't know if it was because earlier he'd said that my scrubbing of the bathroom, and the toilets in particular, wasn't good enough, and this latest failure to meet the International Ralph Niemeyer Cleanliness Standards was just one more outrage I couldn't endure, but I said to him, "No. I'm not doing it again. I did it. It's done. I'm done. You want it better, you do it."

He came back out of the garage, tugging at the waistband of his blue Dickies work pants and wiping his hands on a red shop rag.

"You think you've got it tough here, don't you?"

"I do. It sucks." My dad shook his head and let out a heavy sigh. He spread his feet apart a bit and settled into an arms-folded-across-his-chest stance that had him rocking back and forward on his heels and toes for a minute. I saw the tiny muscles and tendons in his jaw quiver and then settle. He glared at me. He didn't say anything, and I stood there thinking of my friend Tim and his mother. When I first moved and met him, he showed me a small dresser-drawer filled with cigarettes and condoms he said his mom provided him. And he wasn't the only one with parents like that. There were lots of single moms and divorced dads with partial custody who'd indulge their kids every whim. Greg's mom and John's mom would throw them parties while my dad was on my ass if I left my wet suit, that I'd paid for with my own money, out in the backyard to dry without rinsing the salt water off it. He'd ream me for not taking good care of all the shit I had. And I was at an age when I was hanging out with a lot of kids with a lot of different backgrounds, and not a single one of them had a dad who was as strict as mine. He was better about not hammering me with his name-calling and ego deflating, but he was still on my ass all the time about doing better.

My dad and I were still engaged in a kind of stare down. My heart was pumping pretty good, but I wasn't really scared. I was jonesing to get the fuck out of there and go to the beach with my best friend Kwang, and the longer this went on the less time I knew I'd have to ride the best waves of the day.

But I didn't give in, instead, the little arsonist in me woke from his Saturday morning sleep in and said, "Some of the shit you do to me would be child abuse if I went to the cops and told them." I thought of the few slaps to my head he'd delivered over the years.

My dad's initial physical response caught me off guard. He laughed.

I looked away for a second, watched a neighbor's automated sprinklers rise up and sputter to life, as if they sensed the fire that I'd started.

"No, son. You don't know a good goddamn about anything. You haven't had a man more than twice your size come after you and pound you in the face and literally kick your ass so that you couldn't sit for days."

He stopped and then it was his turn to look over at the sprinklers and their prismatic display.

"And all that was on a good day. On a bad day, your uncle would come after you." He swallowed hard a couple of times and chewed at his lips. His next words were stillborn strangled things that died nearly halfway to me but whose spirits carried the gap, "That's another kind of thing, and I hope you don't know what I mean by that."

I forced myself to not think about what that meant.

"So go on, then. Get the fuck out of here if you think you've got things so bad."

My dad turned and walked into the shade of the garage. I heard a few tools rattling around.

I stood rooted in place. When my dad came out again, he appeared startled to find me there.

"Just forget what I said and get on out of here. I don't need your help."

"I hate you."

I said the words, expressing something that I thought and felt was genuine and those words were never truer than in that instant. As I stood there listening to my dad reveal to me the abuse he'd suffered as a kid, I was fucking pissed off.

At him.

At a world where shit like that went on.

At him for telling me these things. For making me fucking feel like I was the one who should have told him that I loved him, that everything was going to be okay, that he was a good man, that I saw and appreciated how hard he worked. I did want to do some of those things, and I did appreciate him for how hard he worked and how demanding he was. I just wanted him to not be so relentless about it all.

Then I thought, he'd never really done or said most of those things to me. He was the adult. I was fucking fourteen years old; yeah, not a little kid anymore, but not an adult, and just what the fuck was it that I was supposed to do with this knowledge? What did he expect of me? He'd had to carry that burden around all his life, and now he was offloading a bit of it onto me.

I stood there numb and overwhelmed. Part of me was grateful that what I'd experienced with my dad's various forms of discipline paled in comparison to what he'd endured. What were a few "stupid shits" and a couple of slaps in the head compared to that? Still, the damage had been done. I felt inadequate even before he told me these things and now even more so—I couldn't help him.

Over time, I'd learn a lot more about my dad and his completely fucked-up early life—the physical and sexual abuse, homelessness, early entry into the military, having to threaten to shoot his stepfather to get him to stop abusing his brothers and sisters. Knowing how bad my dad had it only fueled my hurt and anger.

Eventually, I punched holes in walls and in all the "rules" my parents imposed. I smashed things. I cut and burned myself. Mom and Dad couldn't control me, so they sent me to Linden Oaks—an adolescent psych unit in Chicago. My time there paid off. I came out a new person. He didn't live very long.

Very soon, I picked up exactly where I left off, and my tolerance grew and so did my appetite. I found something I was good at—drinking more than anybody else I knew, fucking up in the same proportion. All of it earned me a reputation and attention, things I craved. If my dad had drilled into me the idea of being the best at something, then that was what I was going to do. I was going to eventually outdrink every motherfucker I encountered, out crazy even the most rebellious and risk taking of my peers.

My behavior became more erratic—a couple of DUI convictions, expulsion from one school, a brief stint at an alternative school, transfer from public to private school (and getting bounced out of there two weeks before graduation for more drinking-related offenses), and finally completing high school through a correspondence course.

All that corresponded with an escalation in my consumption and risk taking. I also discovered the ecstatic high of cocaine and started stealing shit from friends' houses and committing other petty crimes in order to get the stuff. Eventually, I'd be arrested for the twenty-fifth and last time. I quit doing the things that got me thrown into prison.

Quitting and not being able to quit have always played a part in my life. Even now, the temptation to walk off a course when things aren't going well is still great.

Old habits die hard.

That day, after my father's "confession," Kwang and I went to the beach. I could tell by how the surf was thundering onto the shore and against the jetty that this was a day on which I would be wise to be cautious. That wasn't my nature, and maybe after dealing with my dad and all that other shit I'd been dealing with for a while, I paddled furiously out, determined to ride every wave I could, just thrash myself to the point of exhaustion. At one point, as happened frequently, I did get caught in a riptide and drifted out farther and farther from the shoreline.

Also, my leash had failed and my board and I had gotten separated. I was a decent swimmer, but the swells were far too big for me to surmount, and so I was treading water, trying to conserve my energy for one kick-ass run for the beach. In my haste to get out of the house, I hadn't grabbed any food, a Gatorade, or any water. I was hungry, a little dehydrated, and muscle tired. I have no idea really how long I was out there, bobbing up and down like a surface lure. I started to cramp up, my hamstrings tightened from all that kicking, and I had to relax them in order to ease the pain. Each time I did, I sank below the surface, my suit's buoyancy not enough to compensate for my lack of motion. Holding my breath and then clawing my way back up was more exhausting than treading water, but I had little choice.

After a few more descents, I was cashed. I couldn't get back up to the surface. I remember thinking very clearly that I was going to drown, that it was really going to suck to have to take in all that salt water, feel its corrosive effects on my mouth and nasal passage, gag it down and into lungs that had no way to turn it into anything usable. All I had to do was just surrender to it, and it would be over in a few minutes.

After expelling the oxygen in my lungs, I was even less buoyant than before, and I drifted down. The water was colder, the light dimmer, the water nearly opaque. I was calm, my heart beating a steady unrushed rhythm. When my feet made contact with something solid, slick, and impenetrable simultaneously, it was like someone had injected my heart with a shot of adrenaline. I bent my knees into a squat position and then pushed myself up, once again using my arms and legs to propel me toward the surface. I don't really know how, I can't explain the hydrodynamics of it or how the ocean's currents work, but when I surfaced, I was a few hundred feet from the shore, a good quarter mile or more south of the jetty where I'd been riding. I didn't question my good luck. I just stretched myself out and did a slow crawl back onto the beach. I sat there just past the edge of the tide, gathering myself for a few minutes before I made the walk back down to Kwang and where a couple of other buddies were hanging out kicking a Hacky Sack.

"Seen my board?" I asked.

Kwang nodded down toward the water where he'd secured it to a rock. The board flipped and helicopter-bladed in the rough surf.

"Where you been?" he asked. "I was getting worried."

I just shrugged. How could I explain?

"You wanna go home?"

I shook my head and retrieved my board and retethered it. I only paused for a second before I plunged into the surf and paddled out again, wishing briefly that I'd bummed some water or some food from one of the dudes we were with. Still, tired, hungry, and thirsty as I was, I knew that this was where I belonged and this was what I needed to be doing. There'd be plenty of time to nod out on the bus. The sun was still above the horizon, the waves were still lining up and then marching in, doing their slow processional before exploding.

Kwang had joined me. We agreed that the sets of waves were still solid and even though there wasn't anybody there to tell me that on my last ride I should have kicked out sooner and if I ever wanted to be any good at this thing I had to do it again, I did it again anyway, time and time again, until I was satisfied that I'd done the best I could, and that I'd done everything in my power to beat back against those forces that seemed so intent on drowning me.

It's funny that I chose the triathlon and how its three disciplines—the run, the bike, and the swim—make up the event. It's clear to me that I was doing a lot of literal and figurative running as a kid, how I used drugs and alcohol as a way to escape from the pain and confusion I felt. The swim, my love of the ocean and the water, my nearly quitting and nearly drowning, needs no more elaboration.

Oddly, for a while, riding a bike was something that brought my father and I together in a way that nothing else really did once we left Colorado. In the Rockies, we had hunting and fishing, things that he loved to do and I accompanied him on. In this instance, the order was reversed. I was the one doing the activity and he took on a more supportive role. If boarding was a California thing to do, then so, too, was BMX racing. Like the origins of most sports, it's difficult to trace exactly who was the first person to take a bicycle off pavement and ride it over a series of hills and jumps. Just about every guy I know, and a few women, have told me tales of their youthful exploits going over homemade jumps and ramps. One thing is for certain, BMX racing's roots, as a more formal endeavor, date back to California, some time in the seventies.

"The Gully" was a stretch of land that the construction companies had dug out of the hillside and flats as a drainage ditch for the infrequent rains. In my sixth-grade mind, it was a huge ravine shaped like a bowl at a Colorado ski resort. Perfect for hucking a BMX bike off of. I loved the sensation of flying. In addition to The Gully and its series of jumps and whoop-de-dos, Kwang and I built all kinds of contraptions that we could launch ourselves off of and land safely on after enjoying those all-too-brief escapes from gravity's pull. It ain't bragging if it's so, but I was pretty good at doing that kind of ballsy, stunt riding. Something about escaping gravity, going fast, and later, getting high, escaping the bonds that threatened to drag me down, anchor me to the solid earth, drove me to take huge risks.

If the measure of a young man's courage is the number and severity of his injuries, then I was one brave and fearless little bastard. I had crashes like the rest of the kids in the neighborhood did from trying to bunnyhop over garbage cans and that kind of thing, but I don't think anyone sustained the level of injury that I did.

Kwang and I were at The Gully and along with the natural incline/decline of the retention area and other excavations, we decided—well, okay, I decided—and Kwang helped—to construct a six-foot-high ramp at the bottom of that area. We also built a landing ramp, both pieces from "discarded" lumber that was sometimes legitimately lying around and other times sourced.

I was the first to test out this hellacious jump, and I can still remember a bunch of other kids all sitting on the seats of their bikes, their arms folded, their heads shaking. One of those cloned doubters said, "You're nuts. You're going to pick up too much speed going downhill."

Taking those words as a gauntlet thrown, I tore off down the hill pedaling fanatically. The kid who spoke must have been a psychic to be because he said "You're nuts." He wasn't quite right about what part of my body was injured on that failed landing. I remember doing a tank slapper, nearly smashing my teeth on my handlebars in the process, when the force of the landing collapsed my knees and brought my crotch in painful contact with the seat. I'd gotten so much air that my spindly little legs couldn't deal with how mass, acceleration, and the gravitational constant all conspired against me.

I managed to not do a complete yard sale in the dirt; the adrenaline rush was so great that at first I didn't feel any pain. I felt something warm and wet running down my leg. First thought was I'd pissed myself. Then when I looked down, I saw a tiny little rivulet of blood ran down past the hem of my Ocean Pacific cord shorts. I don't remember the number of stitches it took to sew up my nut sack; all I remember was that I'd solidified my reputation as a crazy kid, capable of doing just about anything.

It seemed I was missing some essential component that allows most people to stop after they've had the crazy thought and consider the advisability, consequences, and nearest emergency room location before acting on that impulse. I know there's the temptation to chalk this up to a kind of boys-will-be-boys mentality and we were all lucky to survive our childhoods and adolescence considering the stupid shit we did; however, I'm looking for patterns here, trying to figure out how it was that I got to the point where I'd wrecked myself in so many ways that I so badly wanted the commission of stupidities and crimes to end.

The truth is my reputation as the craziest kid in the neighborhood mattered to me. I wasn't the biggest. I wasn't the fastest, couldn't fart the loudest, spit the farthest, cram the most Ho-Hos, Ding Dongs, or Little Debbies into my mouth, but I could wreck it up with the best of them, get up, dust myself off, and try it again better than any of them. In time, the metric by which kids judged one another changes as the years go by. It may become that instead of consuming large quantities of sugar and preservatives you can down more beers, do more bong hits, and puke your guts out and keep on drinking that your standing among your peers is determined. Some kids resist the tidal pull of public opinion and the dreaded peer pressure.

I couldn't.

I wanted to ride on the crest of that wave of popularity no matter what it cost me in blood, sweat, and my parents' tears. I don't recall feeling too sorry for them or myself. In fact, my parents were to a certain degree complicit in my acts of youthful mayhem. Even though life in Southern California made it possible for me to be outside so much, I still must have had an excess of energy. That made it difficult for me to sit still, to calm the rampant urges to get up and do something that coursed through me like blood and oxygen. At school I remained more than a handful, frustrating teachers and counselors who tried to reason with me. At home, I was much the same way, bouncing off walls to the point that my parents were constantly telling me to go outside and run around the block, hop on my bike and go for a ride, do *something*, just get out of here. Those directives were my golden ticket in a lot of ways, and it entitled me to be *that* kid in the neighborhood, the one in the summer who was up and outside as you were backing out of your driveway to go to work, pedaling furiously to keep up with you as you drove out of the subdivision, and who was there doing laps around the cul-de-sac when you came home that evening.

My parents did attempt to channel some of that energy I used in taking on the challenges of The Gully, by getting me involved for a short time in organized BMX racing. They'd tried and failed with other organized sports. Baseball was too static for me. Too much standing around waiting for something to happen. Soccer was better. I got to run my ass off, but my coaches wanted me to stay back or come forward when they wanted me to and not when I felt the urge. Eventually that sport felt too confining.

BMX racing required that you stay on the course if you wanted to win, but there was enough of an adrenaline rush that came from flying down that starting ramp and barreling into the first turn fighting for position that offset any sense of restriction I might have felt. My lack of stature helped me, too. I was small enough that everyone underestimated my physical abilities. They had no way of knowing how driven and reckless I was. My internal motor was wired to go fast and my brain was constantly telling me to take more chances. I can summarize my BMX career like this: Win or wreck. I either got the trophy, and I won more than a few of them, or wound up in a cloud of dust and a ground-level view of the other racers leaving me behind.

Today, I can see that that kind of racing was perfectly suited for me. They were short, incredibly intense sprints, where not a whole lot of thought went into strategy. Balls out all the way was the only real option I saw.

Through it all, my parents were incredibly supportive, particularly of my BMX-ing. My dad never made any attempt to coach me, but he was my ace mechanic, helping me take apart the hubs, repack the bearings, truing the spokes. He was good with tools and objects, and seemed most at ease when he was doing something useful. Idle hands and the devil's workshop and all that.

Maybe my father, despite all my thoughts at the time to the contrary, really did understand me well. He knew that I needed to keep myself occupied. At the age of twelve BMX racing and bodyboarding seemed to fit the bill. Still, there were those other moments inside and outside of school when that nervous energy that possessed me took over. Kwang and I became experimental chemists, and a mix of WD-40 (a lubricant that was supposed to help keep the drive train of my bike in good shape) and a bit of gunpowder from the shotgun shells my father kept around the house, set fire to vacant land in the neighborhood. Every kid is an arsonist at heart, I suppose. Just combine the right chemicals, a lack of impulse control, and a love of thrills into a volatile mix and you've got yourself a scorched-earth policy that will eventually leave little undamaged.

THREE

Humans are bundles of contradictions wrapped in flesh. I think I'd known that for a long time, even in the middle of the shit storm that was my adolescence and young adulthood, but only now with the clarity of nearly a decade of sobriety and the maturation of the new, post-suicide Shane, am I able to articulate just how the contradictory nature of existence played out in my life.

Along with struggling against being labeled as an ADD kid, and hating every other attempt to have me placed in any other category, I had a tortured relationship with control. Labeling, and in particular the ADD diagnosis being slapped on me and having doctors, school administrators, and my parents all conspiring to medicate the energy out of me, pissed me off to the extreme. I can see now that those people were, mostly, well intentioned and their desire to help me control my behaviors was a worthwhile end goal. At the time, and still to a certain degree today, I see it as an attempt to annihilate the essential qualities that made up me. They were trying to kill off that Shane who they felt was overexuberant and too often out of control.

In a way then, my suicide attempt was part of a larger pattern. When you can't control something by any other means, then the next logical step is to kill it. At that point in April 2004, I'd known for more than a dozen years that my major problem was that I couldn't control my alcohol and drug intake. At their height, my habits consisted of a daily dose of a fifth of vodka, a twelve-pack of beer, and two grams minimum of black tar heroin (and as much as I could get my hands on other days) that I'd inject. My addictions had total control over me. As I saw it, the only way that I could break their grip on me was to break me. Very often suicidal people express their belief that killing themselves is the last effort they can make to seize control of a life that has spun wildly out of their grasp. I believe that statement to be true. While this might sound a little too twelve-step-ish for my taste, since Alcoholics Anonymous helped me but wasn't the be-all and end-all of my sobriety, but I'd admitted that I was powerless against my addictions a long time before I tied that makeshift noose around my neck. Who knows, maybe I was just replacing one noose for another, but I also believed for many years prior to my failed attempt to kill myself that I was going to die young, had come close several times in car accidents and overdoses, so as I saw it, all I was doing was bringing things to a more hasty conclusion. It was as if I was tired of watching this show, weary of its repetitive nature, and just fast-forwarded it to the end, skipping all the commercials and redundant scenes.

As human beings we all want to believe that we are in control of our fate, and it's no accident I chose an individual sport to be my salvation. As much as I found baseball and soccer boring, I also chafed against the notion that my winning and losing were tied to the efforts of other people. I couldn't control how they performed, and yet the outcome of the game was almost wholly dependent upon them possessing the skills, desire, and savvy that were equal to or greater than my own. BMX racing was not like that, and when I read that article about Dave Scott and the kinds of effort he put into training, how it didn't just occupy one part of his life but subsumed all else under a kind of umbrella, I knew that was what I needed in order to stay clean and reform my life.

I knew that, for me, no middle ground existed. I was either going to continue to be completely out of control or demand of myself almost perfect self-discipline.

In certain ways, prison was both the ideal environment for me to be in as I began my training and the worst possible place. I had none of the facilities that I would need in order to swim or cycle, and only a very limited space in which I could run or work out. Prison did help in that its daily schedule exerted some influence over my behavior. In another of those contradictory phenomena, I had all the time in the world to concentrate on my new fitness regime, but I was also living in a highly structured environment that dictated to me when I could eat, when I could be out of my cell, etc. Obviously, I can't say how things might have turned out, but it's unlikely that outside of prison I would have been able to initiate and then follow through on my program.

Those first few weeks were incredibly hard, schedule and facility issues aside, simply because I had long since lost the discipline, the self-control, that I'd had as a kid when bodyboarding and BMX racing were so important to me. I can see now that one of the reasons why I lost control over myself was that I felt that there were forces working against me that were even more powerful than my own desires. That sounds a bit overdramatic when you consider that in 2011, 200,000 families relocated due to work transfers. Those numbers didn't matter to me back in 1990 when my parents told me that we were leaving Southern California for the Midwest and Bloomington, Illinois. My parents cited that 200,000 figure and I could have given them 200,000 reasons why I didn't give a fuck about those other 199,999 cases. All I cared about was me and what this meant for me.

My parents tried to paint a rosy picture. A return to their Midwestern roots. A chance for me to have a fresh start in a new school where all my disciplinary problems, my less than stellar academic success, could all be wiped away and I'd have that proverbial blank slate from which to begin again. All I saw was what I was going to lose, as I had lost when we moved from Colorado. I was being displaced from an environment that I loved. I'd lost the mountains and forests, and I now was going to lose the ocean. I'd lost one place where my father and I experienced something approaching communion, had found a form of that in California, and now that was being taken away from me. I pleaded with my family to let me stay and live with Kwang and his family. What was an adrenaline junkie like me going to find there that might compare with the ocean—a cornfield?

Eventually, I would find my thrills in Bloomington, but they mostly were found, initially in liquid form, eventually herbal, and then chemical in nature. Imagine this: we lived on a golf course and that was my chosen sport for a while. Compare hitting a drive off the first tee into the fairway to the pleasures of riding a wave, and you have some small measure of understanding of how far I'd fallen on the excitement scale. In retrospect though, I can see how golf might have helped me. It is a game of concentration and discipline, but my high-energy nature couldn't appreciate its benefits back then. I had to control golf and turn it into a game that suited my temperament. That meant that eventually playing the game wasn't enough. Sneaking onto the course at night, stealing golf carts and drunken joyriding around the course, off-roading and abandoning the vehicles in sand traps, doing donuts in the fairways, became par for the course.

And, of course, the fuel for that fun was alcohol. When I lived in Mission Viejo, I knew kids who drank, and my best friend Kwang and I agreed that consuming alcohol was stupid and not something we'd ever do. Who needed it? We were having enough fun without it, and when you're sober and you see someone who's fucked up, they seem like idiots. Eventually, I'd be the idiot and not the observer.

Inevitably, I would combine alcohol and drug consumption with my search for an adrenaline rush. I was the kid in high school who had to climb out of the car window and Spider-Man myself across the windshield while my admirers drove along at 40-plus miles an hour. I loved the idea that I could outdrink and out crazy every one of my peers. So what if my playing chicken along Illinois Highway 51 three years after we moved resulted in me sustaining a broken leg and a fractured skull—neither of which prevented me shortly after my discharge from the hospital with a Day-Glo orange cast on my leg stealing a case of beer from a local gas station. Then confronted by the police, stating with a straight face, if not a straight blood chemistry, that it must have been some other dude with an orange cast on his leg who had committed the offense. Then there was the incident I told my mother about in what I thought was my last conversation with her. The car wreck, the lighter pressed to flesh, the months the wound took to heal.

I hated Bloomington-Normal. At first, I was glad to be the fish out of water, the California surfer dude with the nonfarmer tan and the glint of mischief in his eye. I got attention immediately and that was cool. I kind of bought into my mom's notion that I was going to be able to have a fresh start there at Parkside Junior High. Nobody told me about transcripts, that my past wasn't really my past, but an extension of my present and the perceptions my teachers had about me.

Some kids have a highly refined sixth sense. They can walk into a classroom for the very first time and spot the kids they're going to hang out with; it's as if those other kids emit an aura that lets you know to which group they belong. All kids want to fit in, and I desperately wanted and needed to after having moved halfway across the country, but being the alien that I was, I struggled those first few days to get a good read on what niche I would fit in. Not all kids possess that innate belonging-recognition ability, and if they don't possess that keen instinct, life can be pretty harsh until they figure it out.

My status as an outsider and a novelty earned me attention, but not always positive attention. Even in the first few days of school, I'd picked up on a vibe as I rode the bus in. There seemed to be a territorial distinction between kids like me who lived along the country club and those in an adjoining newly constructed subdivision. Apparently, country club living and all it connotes rankled those kids in that neighborhood and touched some inferiority nerve that forced them to overexaggerate the economic disparity between the two areas. We were all pretty solidly middle class and white, so the whole thing seems ridiculous now, but some jerkoff country-club kid was on my ass immediately the first weeks of the new school year. Apparently, I was dragging our group's reputation down.

I put up with his shit for a couple of days, but I knew that this was a situation that required bud-nipping before it grew out of control. I had been in a couple of schoolyard/neighborhood scuffles, nothing more than shirt-collar grabbing and chest shoving really, but I felt like I had to do what I had to do. Both of us got off the school bus at the same stop. Our encounter started with name-calling and then escalated to punches and face grinding into the dirt and grass.

To be honest, I don't know who won the fight. Mostly what I remember is someone coming up afterward and sticking his hand out to help me back up, "Hey dude. That was awesome. I'm Brian."

I knew Brian Krull from school, or rather, I'd see him and recognized something about him that I liked. Brian had this big wedge of hair that fell in a sharp angle across his face and that hid one eye. It wasn't his looks that struck me, it was his I-don't-give-a-shit-about-anything demeanor that I picked up on immediately. When called on in class, Brian had the disarming and infuriating habit of saying almost immediately, "No thank you," to the teacher. His mix of being polite and a prick intrigued me. I was all kamikaze frontal attack in my classroom disruption techniques, and Brian seemed stealthier.

Brian and I became friends very quickly and I learned equally fast, that his mastery of the subtle ran deeper than just being a classroom dipshit. Brian lived near me and in no time we were at each other's houses after school. We would wander the neighborhood together, and eventually Tommy, Ryan, and Pat would join our little group. One night Brian suggested that we head over to a new subdivision. I'd had my own experience with construction sites, and most of what Kwang and the rest of that crew did was lob dirt bombs against the plywood sheathing, or through the spaces where the windows would eventually go. Brian raised that ante considerably. Today, I'm surprised that the construction company developing that area did this, but after the workers went home at night, they left behind air compressors. They were chained to the 2×4 studs, but still, we could fire them. They also had locked boxes of power tools. Brian broke into one of them that night and powered up a pneumatic nailer and fired off a bunch of rounds. We all got into that action, and I can still hear the coughing and rattling sound of that nail gun echoing through the semi-occupied streets. When a porch light went on, we'd duck for cover, flattening ourselves against the framed walls and onto the sawdust-covered floors.

Rap music was popular among us suburban white boys, and we fell under the sway of the "gangsta" lifestyle portrayed in some of those songs. Eazy-E's and MC Ren's "Ruthless Villain" was one that we listened to all the time, and it became inspiration for Brian in particular. I guess he got tired of messing around on the golf course or in the homes under construction. One night, Brian said, "Boys, I gots me a plan."

He laid it out for us, and I immediately thought there was no way I was going to join him in breaking into people's houses. My face must have betrayed my anxiety.

"Hey, Homes, don't be playin' the pussy on us. You can't be scared of doing this shit."

Brian's eyes had a way of bugging out of his head and twisting his face into an expression of disbelief and mockery that would later remind me of the actor Jim Carrey as the Riddler in one of the Batman movies.

Pat immediately said that we were nuts and went home. Why Brian was so bent on breaking into people's houses wasn't clear. He had moved to Bloomington from somewhere in the South and hated the new place almost as much as I did. He also had very strict parents, like mine tried to be, but his were super-religious. It was clear that he was rebelling against all that.

I hated the idea of sneaking into someone's house, and every time I did it with Brian, I had this queasy, "this is not right," feeling in my guts. I'd done my share of shoplifting and in my obviously very skewed sense of morality, I saw that as being okay. I wasn't taking anything from an individual. I was taking it from a company, a corporation, some nameless, faceless someone miles and miles removed from my locality.

Our little on-and-off crime spree lasted a few months. I didn't always go with Brian, he and his brother seemed to be really determined to make this their after school jobs or something. The local paper reported on the incidents; kids around school, some of whom we had victimized, started talking about it, and, of course, the police were involved. By the time word got out the police figured it was schoolkids and not some "real criminals," I was out anyway. I finally had the nerve to tell Brian that I was not going to do it anymore. He agreed that since so much heat was on us, we should cool it for a bit. My reasoning was different, but I didn't explain that to him. I couldn't deal with the guilt. I tried to imagine what it must have been like for those people to come home, how violated they felt when they learned that a stranger, a criminal had been lurking around in their house. Even later, when my criminality reached a much higher level, I told myself that I wouldn't resort to residential burglary, wouldn't steal from a "civilian" and I didn't.

I had to use that twisted sense of right and wrong a few weeks before school let out. The police had been coming by the school to do some investigating. The gossip machine had let us know that the Bloomington Police had made a cast of a couple of pair of boot prints they found in the dirt underneath a window of one of the burgled houses. This was a Cinderella and her glass slipper situation. They were going to go around and check on various suspects, hoping to match the boot print with an actual boot.

Sure as shit, a few days after the cops were first seen at the school, there was a knock at the door, and two members of Bloomington's finest, eyeing me menacingly and asking to see my mom and dad. I let the cops in and went into the family room where they were watching television. As soon as I said the word *police* my dad's face froze. He shut his eyes and shoved himself out of his La-Z-Boy recliner. I watched him walking away with his stiff-legged gait all the while hoping that as he rubbed the back of his neck, he wasn't thinking about how he'd like to wring mine.

I had to go down to the police department headquarters in Bloomington to be "interviewed," but I never gave up my buddies or myself and neither did any of the others. We all simply claimed that we didn't know nothing about anything to do with anything.

Later, out in the car, my dad said, "Well, finally there's something you're good at. Playing dumb suits you."

I ignored his putdown, mostly because he was right. I was in too much pain from clenching my anal sphincter for so long. I hated that feeling of knowing that every syllable I uttered could spell doom or glory for my sorry little punk ass. Still, a tiny voice inside my head let me know that I'd done good, that I'd passed the test, that the crew was still intact. I'd managed to take control of a situation that threatened to spiral into the ground. I'd pulled out of the dive and lived to fight another day.

I do understand now how twisted this all sounds, but back then I was hooked on something maybe even more powerful than the alcohol and drugs I would begin to consume. All my buddies kept telling

me how smart I was. This flood of positivity soaked into and nour-
ished the scorched earth of self-worth that my father had left behind.
I suppose that the reason why our friends are our friends is because
they make us feel good about ourselves. In Brian, I'd found someone
with whom I could commiserate about being hauled out of an environment I loved and thrived in.

That first year in Illinois, I was spiraling into the ground. The
break-ins were just one part of that. Some of this might have been just
the usual adolescent hormonal maelstrom, but I got angrier and angrier and became impossible to live with. I remember being in my
room, listening to Pink Floyd's *The Wall* for probably the twentieth
time that week. I know I wasn't alone in feeling that the double
album was an anthem to my personal sense of isolation, of being a
rootless and wandering soul buffeted around by forces large and small
and completely out of my control. I'd always loved music, but during
my school years in Bloomington, I craved its comforts, and *The Wall*
spoke to me in its soothing and discordant tone.

That particular day, my mother walked in on me. "Would you
please turn that down?" was only half-formed on her lips before I
started in on her. "What the fuck do you want? Get your ass out of
here." My mom would almost visibly shrink, as if she was a boxer on
the ropes.

I can't say why I acted out that way, but I can say that for a lot of
that time, I felt like I had a fever. I saw events taking place through a
kind of haze, much like I would later when I was in a drug-induced
state. Other times, it was as if the camera through which I was view-
ing my actions and other people's responses came into hyperfocus,
sharp edged and with prominent highlights and shadows as if my
brain was Photoshopping every image. Depending upon my mood, it
would either leach out the color leaving everything dark and gray or

hyperbright and gaudy. But mostly it was lifeless and dull. Compared to the weather and the terrain in Southern California and Colorado, with their dazzling sunshine and crystalline blue skies, Bloomington was gray, and my emotional weather matched it.

When I wasn't out with friends, I moved like I was underwater.

The one constant was that I was angry, angrier than I had ever been, especially around the house. Even though the major irritant in my life had been my father and he wasn't there, I was still pissed off. My dad had taken a job in Chicago, working at the Museum of Science and Industry, and he was away during the week. This was another of those contradictions. His being gone gave me the freedom I craved but still I didn't like the idea of him being away, of how that set me apart from my peers, and of how when he was around he ratcheted up the discipline to make up for his absence. How sad I was that my life had changed so much from what I'd enjoyed in Southern California. I was a bundle of confused emotions and my poor mother bore the brunt of it.

Some define *depression* as sadness manifested as anger turned inward. I'm not sure I was ever formally diagnosed during this period as suffering from depression, my inner anger spilled over the levy of my personal boundaries and ravaged the lives of my family, washing away whatever peace there was in a torrent of angry retribution. They tried to snag whatever branches they could to avoid being carried downstream. Little did we all know that we were then presently navigating relatively calm waters, that the rocks and severe rapids were several bends beyond our vision.

My dad and I had begun seeing a counselor in 1990 to help us resolve some of the issues that we had with one another, and then, in April 1991, the whole family was in treatment. I don't recall much of the specifics of any of these sessions really. I did not want to be there, though I did pick and choose my times to air my grievances against my dad. He had grown so tired of me and my shit that, out of sheer frustration, he started to threaten me whenever I made some outrageous statement about doing harm to my mother and my brother. Those were idle threats, but even as the words were coming out of my mouth, I knew it wasn't in any way acceptable to be saying them. Telling your mother and brother that you're going to kill them, especially when you live in a house where guns are located, and where I'd written large my lack of control in a series of fist holes punched through drywall in various rooms around the house, had to be taken seriously. I had sustained "boxing fractures" to each of my hands without having taken a swing at another person. I can see that now, but back then, my mother and father's every effort to de-escalate the drama and the threatened violence just made me ratchet up the threats and the acting out. They each had a foot on my throat trying to crush my spirit; everything they did to try to help me was just another brick in a wall that would inevitably—a design failure of my own devising—come crashing down.

I do recall sitting in Dr. Mel French's office one day in 1991, still during my freshman year at Normal Community High School. This was toward the end of the school year, and administrators had already made it very clear that I wasn't going to be welcomed back for my sophomore year. My options were to be placed in some alternative education program the district offered or to go to private school. I couldn't believe that my family was conspiring with the fucktards at Bloomington to make me leave another place when I'd just started to settle in and make friends.

A few weeks after that, Brian came by, and something else took control of my life. We'd gotten into the habit of sitting on a hip roof that jutted out from beneath my bedroom window. The configuration of the house's rooflines put us in a blind spot for anyone looking out of any of the other upstairs windows. We sat there looking out across the fairways to where his house and the others in that part of the development were Lite-Brite blocks of yellow illumination.

"Lighten up, asswipe. Nothing can be that bad."

He handed me the bottle of Boone's Farm. I took a drink, not for the first time, and felt the Green Apple adhere to my tongue and cheeks.

"I just want to get the fuck out of here. Go back to Colorado or California."

"Quit your bitchin'." Brian's mocking tone wasn't what I really wanted to be hearing. "At least you've got cool places to miss. I wish that I could be in South Carolina. How fucked up is that?"

I'd started to drink a bit, but never to the point where it penetrated my angsty anger.

That changed.

When the new school year rolled around, I was at Central Catholic High School (CCHS) in Bloomington. Another few pointless words about fresh starts. Another chance for me to make some nice friends, not like those nasty kids at the public school who were such a bad influence. Little did my parents know that the kids at CCHS and its wonderful Christ-centered education was actually its own little Sodom and Gomorrah.

Just as I had at school my freshman year, at CCHS, I immediately glommed onto kids whose main focus of their studies was how to violate as many of the Ten Commandments in as many creative ways as possible. I don't recall exactly how I met Ryan Hornby, but we soon became best buddies. Ryan had already turned sixteen and was driving to school, a real POS Honda Civic hatchback the shade of a chlorine-faded blue-green diving board, and I was able to bum a ride off of him—if not to school, at least back home.

Instead of taking me home that day, we stopped at his place. I don't recall there being any special reason why on that day we decided to break into his dad's liquor cabinet. Ryan said that his dad didn't drink anymore and he wouldn't notice if anything was missing. He grabbed a bottle of Wild Turkey and said, "Let's roll." We drove out beyond my folk's house into some of the surrounding farmland. We pulled over on one of the dirt roads that bisected that area, one set of wheels in a small ditch, the others still on the roadway. Ryan twisted the top off the bottle and took a swig, the liquor sloshing around and then making that gulping sound as it settled back in.

I took the bottle and did as my buddy had done. Back and forth the bottle went, the two of us not talking, just sitting there with the world tilted 20 degrees off of center, the lines of barb-wire fencing and utility poles and wires like a blank musical staff receding into the distance.

After four or five hard pulls on the bottle, the bourbon was having its effect, and for the first time, I really felt I understood Pink Floyd's "Comfortably Numb." I was right there in that sweet spot. Not quite numb, but certainly comfortable. The alcohol made me feel warm. I was pleasantly buzzed and after a few more swigs and another half hour or so, I was wasted. I felt so calm, cocooned is the best way that I can think of it. Nothing else in the world existed except for me, the front seat of that Honda Civic, and what felt like warm honey that coated my esophagus and heated my belly. I was still seated, but I wasn't aware of my ass against the velour and vinyl. I was disembodied, just a brain and a few sensory receptors. For a lot of my life, I realized in those moments of initial intoxication, I'd been hearing a bunch of white noise and a high-pitched whistling, like when you're driving at high speed with your car windows down for a long stretch. You only notice that sound when you raise the windows, hear that little suck belch as the glass seals, and then the pleasant stillness.

I've heard it said that male adolescents are just a bundle of anxieties covered in skin. Alcohol is a cure-all for that hyper-anxious state they live in. It emboldens the weak and the strong, and relaxes inhibition. It set me free from all my worries and insecurities. I simply didn't care about anything, and I felt wonderful.

Very quickly after that afternoon with Ryan and the Wild Turkey, I was drinking every day, frequently sneaking off of campus to grab another two or three of the beers we'd stashed somewhere nearby. Getting alcohol was seldom a problem. If we couldn't get it through a fake-ID connection or a legal-aged aider and abettor, we stole it. From our own houses, from liquor stores, gas station mini-marts, or wherever.

Whether it was the classic rock we listened to or grunge, we heard plenty of songs sung in praise of the liberating effects of drugs and alcohol. In short order, I couldn't get through a day, much less a boring school day, without some help. Every morning, Jason would pick me up along with this kid I only knew as D. We instituted what is known as "wake and bake." We'd get stoned before school just to make those hours in the classroom bearable.

I developed the habit of keeping a bottle of Johnny Walker Red Label in my room at home. I'd drink a third to a quarter of that bottle every night, just to offset the tense vibe that fucking house had seemed to absorb into its very paint and woodwork. The best way that I can put it is that alcohol was like a magic elixir, producing an I-don't-give-a-fuck-about-anything-in-the-world sensation. The effects it had on me were so powerful that I wouldn't have traded those substances for the secret to transmuting lead into gold. Pot on the other hand, made me more introspective.

I'm sure that I did my share of puking, but I don't really remember any of those occasions. I do know that I had no stop mechanism in me—except when the keg was dry, everyone was broke, and all the stores were closed and, while shoplifting the shit was okay burglary wasn't—I could never drink just two or three beers or do one or two shots of alcohol. I was somebody who hated boundaries of any kind, so how could I expect me to limit myself.

I didn't see it that way back then, all I knew was that if a buzz was good and wasted was better, then drinking until I passed out was the best. Beer was okay, but that was for the kids with the cups at the parties that were a regular fixture of every weekend in Bloomington. That was for the quarters playing, beer bong, and buzz amateurs who needed a fucking *game* to keep their epiglottises bobbing. Not me. This was no game. This was my life and don't you fucking get in my way of living it. You can have your Miller Lite, your Bud Light, and you can shove that Heineken shit up your heinie, I was only interested in the Mad Dog, Old English 40's, Colt .45 malt liquor. Liquor and none of that pussy drink those sad sacks of shit will blow chunks with later.

I did have one resolution in those early days of my excess. No powders or anything else that could be snorted. No-no. Not me. I'm a drinker. I'll fire up a spliff, but that just means that I party. Nothing more. Everybody does this shit. I just happen to do it longer and better. If my dad thought my playing dumb was my only real ability then why wasn't he proud of me when I came home wasted after drinking everybody under the table? I was keg master at many of the blowouts not because I wanted to be the good host, the center of attention, but because that keg was my fucking lifeline, and extension of my digestive and alimentary canal.

I loved, loved, loved, the way that alcohol made me feel. I liked not having to be so self-conscious and hyper self-aware all the time. When I was drinking, I didn't have to wonder if I was some kind of psycho killer to be who threatened his mother and father and brother.

If I believed what my parents and others told me, then I was a Jekyll and Hyde fucked-up little dude whose behavior could vary from moment to moment and transform from the good little Catholic schoolboy doing well in his classes into the drunken and out-of-control piece of shit who started stealing from his friends' families in order to get alcohol and later drugs.

Lie or tell the truth?

Do someone a solid or fuck them over?

What difference did it make?

And to make all those complications disappear, along with my self-loathing and all the various *them*s who had it out for me in a variety of ways I imagined or incited, I just had to open that bottle or can and they would all just go away. When I let alcohol or drugs take control of me, I was in complete control. I could make all the hurt and the anger and the confusion go away.

Unfortunately for me, at least as I thought about it then, not everything could go away all the time. In fact, my acting out at school and at home got so bad that my mom had no choice but to make me go away for a while. So much for my being the one in control.

Linden Oaks was my first experience at being put under lockdown against my wishes. I'd crossed the line one too many times, my mother told me. More than that, and she would only tell me this later, she was just as fearful that my father was going to cross the line with me. The two of us antagonized one another so often and so vindictively that my mom feared that violence was inevitable.

I have the intake evaluation and patient history that Linden Oaks provided my parents. What it doesn't describe is how they had to wait until the middle of the night, when I was in a drunken and sleep-induced stupor before they could haul my ass out of bed and into the car. Things didn't go as they planned, and my dad had to subdue me with a couple of punches to the face. More than him hitting me, it was my mother's look of terror, her anguished and guttural wailing, and chewing on her knuckles as she sobbed and bowed watching us go at it, that convinced me to just submit.

The bright penny taste of blood in my mouth, wearing nothing but my jockeys and a T-shirt, I climbed into the Hyundai and laid myself down on the backseat. If I was going away somewhere—my parents had threatened me with this before so I knew what was happening to me if not specifically where I was going—then I wanted those people to see me in my natural state, show them the blood on my face, how my parents had mistreated me, so no matter what it says there on the page and all the little details that they go into about my and our history individually and collectively, let this be a red-letter fucking–red flag reminder to you all of why I'm *really* here.

FOUR

One of the other major contradictions that I had to deal with was that while I was in control of the long-term vision that I had for myself—becoming an Ironman triathlete, transforming myself into a more highly developed and contributing member of society—my immediate future was also under the direct control of the Idaho Department of Correction (IDOC). I'd been arrested a bunch of times before, but this was the first really deep felony trouble I'd been in, and I was now facing serious prison time. What was also different was that I was determined to take responsibility for those past actions, particularly as it applied to the outstanding charges against me in Ada County, Idaho.

Some of my previous arrests had occurred in Boise, and I was represented in those instances by a lawyer named Brett Fox. He'd helped me out when I had a string of misdemeanor offenses, most of which were dismissed with a fine or probation. These ranged from a DUI, Reckless Driving, multiple Driving on a Suspended license charges, probation violation, dog at large, dog without a license, petty theft, battery, transporting open containers of alcohol, and drug paraphernalia possession.

To be honest, looking at my record prior to arrest in October, my final 2003, I was getting away with another crime when the state only charged me with possession of a controlled substance, possession of drug paraphernalia, battery, and a number of counts of business burglary. I was extremely fortunate that the Boise Police Department's efforts to tie me to a theft ring had failed. The truth was that I wasn't part of any kind of organized group of thieves, but I had been supporting my drug habit for a long time by grabbing and dashing (CDs, videocassettes, video games, and the like) from various retail outlets around Boise for a number of years. I'd also stolen cash, dined and dashed from restaurants, perfected the art of the complaint about poor service and unsatisfactory meals to earn myself and friends complimentary meals, and generally been a leech sucking the life blood out of the economy. I have no way of totaling the amount of goods and services I stole during those years, it had to be in the six-figure dollar amount, and if I had been convicted of theft in addition to those drug-related charges, I would have been looking at a sentence in the 20–25-year range. Eventually, I would face some of those charges in a separate case from my drug arrest, but the authorities certainly didn't account for all the crimes I'd committed.

While I was willing to privately accept accountability for those other crimes, I wasn't about to confess to things for which I wasn't facing any charges.

Since being arrested, I had to attend a few hearings, sometimes with counsel present and sometimes without. My attorney, one of Brett Fox's associates by the name of David Manweiler, had taken my case knowing that I wasn't exactly asset laden. My parents had been informed of my suicide attempt and incarceration. I'd only been in communication with them sporadically over the last few years. We never talked about the failed hanging, but we did a bit about my being in jail. They were relieved I was in jail. It meant I was safe and likely to stay that way. They had agreed to pay Manweiler to see me through the process. There wasn't going to be any heavy legal lifting in this case. I was going to plead guilty. I was guilty, and I didn't see any point in trying to fight that truth. I would also be taking control of the situation and not prolonging things. I wanted to get on with my life and my plan. I was still thinking strategically, however.

One thing I could hope for was the judge would look at me in the same way I was looking at myself. I was worth saving, despite all my repeated past efforts at proving to everyone that I was beyond redemption. The other thing I could hope for was to have my case handled by anyone but Judge Thomas Neville. He had a jailhouse reputation for being the worst of the bunch in Boise. Nobody wanted to go in front of Neville the Devil. The thing was, as I later realized, the reason no one wanted him to be their judge was because he was absolutely no bullshit fair. He also liked to deliver his judgments with a lecture, and that wasn't something that most inmates wanted to hear.

On August 4, I was arraigned and learned that Judge Neville would be presiding over my case. On August 25, 2003, I entered a plea of guilty in the District Court of the Fourth Judicial District of the State of Idaho. Kendal McDevitt was the prosecuting attorney. Judge Neville handed down his sentence in mid-November. Seven years, consisting of a fixed term of eighteen months and an indeterminate term possibly lasting as long as five and half years before I could be paroled out. Judge Neville retained jurisdiction over me for six months and recommended that I be placed at the North Idaho

Correctional Institution and entered into what the state called a "New Directions" program.

The judge also retained the right to resentence me if I wasn't assigned to that program. Essentially what that meant was that he wanted some control over me and my disposition within the criminal justice system. He was a hard-ass in a lot of ways, but in reality was really doing me a big favor. If I toed the line, completed the program (something called a "rider") he wanted me enrolled in, I could be paroled out in a relatively short period of time. It was a classic carrot-and-stick situation, but I didn't care. I wanted to be held accountable for what I'd done, and was extremely fortunate to have this "one-shot" opportunity.

One lesson was carrying over from my efforts to rehabilitate myself physically: I had to take personal responsibility for my actions. Just as no one but me would know if I skipped a day's workout, cut short by a few reps the number of pull-ups I was doing, or cheat by not going through the full range of motion on a push-up or a pull-up, how long I was going to remain in prison was almost entirely on me. Yes, Judge Neville would be the one to decide whether or not I met his criteria for release, but for the first time in my life, I felt like an authority figure was going to be as fair and impartial as it was possible to be.

Later, I'd understand this on a different level. My times in Ironman competitions were a kind of trial, and I'd be exposed—had I done the work necessary to achieve a solid result or hadn't I? Of course, as I also later found it, the equation relating training effort and reward wasn't quite that simple, but at least I wasn't scheming and trying to figure out ways to cut corners to get the best result. I was going legit and trying to accomplish things honestly. That hasn't changed since my early days doing prison workouts until today—an honest effort no matter how bad I was feeling beats a dishonest effort anytime.

I had developed a kind of discipline when I was an addict, but it was a warped kind of do whatever it takes mentality that didn't serve me well. If I couldn't hit a lick or get my hustle I would rob the dope man with a gun. If I didn't have a gun, I'd use a knife. If I didn't have a knife, I'd smash and grab. I was willing to go to great lengths to get what I needed. When I sat in my cell and thought about what I'd committed to doing, I knew the exact lengths that I would have to swim, run, and pedal. I found some strength in knowing that I'd done whatever it had taken before. In those early days, I wasn't completely certain just what I would have to do to complete the race, only that I was capable of figuring out what resources I would take advantage of. I would figure it out. I was capable of doing the work and making the sacrifice.

Most of that change in attitude and behavior was attributable to something Judge Neville had said to me at an earlier hearing. He'd obviously read the pretrial reports and knew about my suicide attempt. After all the court business was taken care of, Judge Neville looked up from a document, his eyes not completely visible through the lenses of his glasses that reflected the overhead lights. From my angle, that made him almost look blind. He cocked his head to one side, and still looking as brow-furrowed stern as he'd been throughout the hearing, said to me, "Take care of yourself, young man. You have a lot to offer yourself and your family. I need to know that you're not going to hurt yourself again."

Judge Neville's words stuck with me, the fact that he didn't find me irredeemable was another of those hands offered to me to help me get up and steady myself.

I had also gone up in front of Judge Weatherall on separate but related charges, pled guilty, and gotten ten years that were to run concurrently with the seven Judge Neville had given me. Weatherall didn't say much at my sentencing hearing, just processed me through. I appreciated that Judge Neville had said those words to me, and I always wondered why he bothered with a dirtbag like me.

I didn't bother to explain to him that I was already hurting myself, this time in a more productive way, a way that as Ernest Hemingway would say, would allow me to be stronger in the broken places. I became familiar with Hemingway in prison when I realized that if I was going to succeed at transforming myself into an Ironman triathlete, I was going to have to work on more than just my fitness. I was going to have to take a hard look at and develop other components of my new self, the self that I aspired to be. That meant working at my spiritual, mental, and emotional sides as well. Control was certainly an issue, as was my anger and depression, but I'd have to really lay myself bare and become a better person if I wanted to become a better athlete. Prison was going to give me the time to focus on all aspects of myself.

71768.

I won't ever forget that number. The Idaho Department of Corrections christened me with it following my sentencing. Every day, three times a day, for eighteen months I had to answer, "Here" to it when roll call was read. Their use of that number instead of your name stripped you of your humanity, reminded you that because of what you'd done, you weren't deserving of anything but the most cursory of human interactions. It reminded you three times daily that you were in prison.

But I chose to look at it another way. The guy who was 71768 was me, but just one facet of me, a version of me that was in transition changing out of the gear useful in one event and putting on the equipment I would need to get me better prepared for the next.

After sentencing, I was transferred from the Ada County Jail to the ISCI, or the Idaho State Corrections Institution in Kuna, Idaho, about 20 miles southwest of Boise. There, in addition to being given my new identity as 71768, I was tested for various potential health issues, and evaluated as a security risk. If I had a record of violent crimes, for example, the IDOC might have disqualified me from the New Directions program that Judge Neville had insisted upon. Fortunately, there wasn't going to be a need for any battle between the judge and the IDOC.

Even more fortunately, my tests of hepatitis C and HIV came back negative. I was never a needle sharer, at least that I know of, when I was lucid. I always had a clean bag of ten in my pocket. A few times my rig was on a counter within a foot of someone else's but that was it. I always knew which was mine, but I still worried that somehow things could have gotten mixed up. Just because I was disease free didn't mean I was healthy—I was so overweight and out of shape that I was issued a waiver that stated that I should always be given the lower bunk. That way I didn't have to heft my fat self up top and potentially injure myself in the process. I was also told my liver function was extremely compromised.

The ISCI was a state prison, and there are some pretty hard-core cats in there, and I was glad that I was assigned to go to another correctional facility, the North Idaho Correctional Institution (NICI) in Cottonwood. NICI was about 200 miles north of Boise, and though it was a state prison, it had the barb-wired fences and everything you might imagine surrounding it, it felt more like a boot camp than ISCI ("The Yard") had. Because I wasn't considered a high-risk individual according to the IDOC's guidelines, I lived in a dormitory-type environment. I was there to do what was called my rider, the New

Directions program, for three months. After that, I didn't know what was going to be done with me.

My bunk mate there was a tweeker of the toothless variety, so he spoke with a lisp tinged with a twang, like he was a character out of some R-rated version of a Hanna-Barbera cartoon. He was smart—both street savvy and intelligent—but with his disfigured mouth and his dentition-impaired speech, it was hard to take anything he said seriously. In fact, very little of what he said could be taken seriously. He had a skewed sense of the absurd. As cellies go, he wasn't so bad, if you could put up with his habit of using "son of a bitch" (which came out sounding like "thon-oth-a-bith") as a modifier for every third noun. Levi was an AB, a member of the Aryan Brotherhood, and called himself a "Wood"—short for peckerwood—and like many other inmates had a 5150 tattoo on his forearm that he constantly scratched: 5150 used to be code for criminally insane. Levi wasn't that, but he was a piece of work that had been rejected as unfit for distribution.

Nearly everyone at Cottonwood that I encountered was in there for some drug-related offense. The sex offenders (I was shocked to learn what some of the twisted shit these dudes had done and how lenient the state had been on them) were housed in a segregated area from the rest of us. For three hours a day, we were all subjected to what was called "programming." It reminded me of being back in school with the lamest of teachers who used an out-of-the-box self-directed learning "experience." Basically what that meant was that the IDOC had purchased a "program" from some publisher of materials for use with substance abusers. This particular program was a series of five workbooks whose pages of information you had to read and a series of questions to which you had to respond. The system provided a facilitator for the coursework, a man who seemed less thrilled to be in Cottonwood than the inmates, a white guy who went by the Native American named "Lightfoot" who was an overeager and oversharing drug counselor.

As painful as it was to sit through those "lessons" every day, I knew that I had to develop the mental discipline necessary to endure those hours. I knew what the consequences were if I quit or fucked up—my rider would be revoked, Judge Neville's sentence with the five years' minimum would go into effect. I also realized that much of what is required of an Ironman is the mental tenacity to compete, to endure long hours at a stretch. I couldn't really replicate the physical demands of my chosen sport while in prison, but I certainly could the mental ones. Focusing on the lessons, letting my mind drift to other places to allow the time to pass more quickly without resorting to drugs or alcohol, were all things I needed to learn and practice before I got into the real world.

The New Directions program was a huge waste on many of the inmates. Most were playing along in exchange for reduced sentences. They couldn't wait to get out and resume their lives of fucking around. There were a few, like me, who wanted to get their lives moving in a different direction. But what troubled me most about the program's emphasis was this notion that I had a "disease."

Just like I'd recoiled at being diagnosed as ADHD, I didn't like the idea of laying all the bad choices I'd made on my being a victim of a "disease." I can't discount entirely the genetic propensity that I might have had to metabolize alcohol in a way that was different from other people, but just like those lame notebook exercises I had to do, that answer felt far too simplistic. Part of the reason I rejected that disease model was because that it took out, to a great degree, the possibility of human action/choice as an agent of change. When you have a disease, you become a victim; you place responsibility for your actions on someone or something outside of your control, like your genes for instance. If I was going to stay sober, if I was going to get out of prison and pursue my dream of qualifying for and competing in the Ironman World Championship, then I had to be the one in control. I had to be the one to take responsibility for my choices and the outcomes those decisions produced.

During those early stages in my rehabilitating myself, I was convinced that the only program that would really work for me was one that I designed and executed myself, drawing upon resources and ideas that intuitively appealed to me. That wasn't because I was more knowledgeable than anyone else, but I sensed that nothing but inner-directed and managed modifications of my own behaviors would ever be effective in getting me to stop fucking up my life. I'd valued autonomy my whole life—no one can tell me what to do—and I had always gone in the wrong direction in rebelling against those who wanted to control me. How could I give up that value? What I needed to do, what I had decided was best for me, was to remain autonomous but use that power to better myself. I didn't need to alter my personality as much as I needed to make better choices and add new thoughts and processes into the equation.

Now that I was no longer using, I could see just how flawed to the core, how aberrant/pathological my prior thinking had been. I knew that being in prison was not the norm. I knew that being homeless and suicidal was the product of my being broken. I knew that I needed to mend myself and I had to develop a better program for doing that than what the state was offering me.

In the past I had made a choice to drink and abuse drugs. Now, I had made a choice to stop drinking and abusing drugs. I was always going to be faced on the "outs" (outside of a prison environment) with choices about how to act, whether or not to cave into temptation to drink, get high, or shoot up. If I bought into the disease model, I'd have another kind of out. If I gave into temptation, that meant that me, being a sick individual with a disease, a victim of a chronic illness, really shouldn't be blamed for my actions. I wanted and needed to accept full accountability for all my actions. My rationalization factory had been working overtime for a decade and a half producing all kinds of excuses for myself. I wanted to be in control and produce a blueprint/methodology that would keep me clean and sober and send me toward a better life.

I'd also taken enough psychology courses and had started reading enough works of Eastern philosophy to know that control of outside factors is an illusion. However, control of the self is not illusory. We always have the capability to control our thoughts, feelings, and responses to factors outside our control and ourselves. I couldn't control the environment in prison, the constraints placed on me, the schedule. What I could control is how I viewed prison—as a place of punishment and denial or a place I could utilize to my advantage in my efforts to change. Again, taking what I learned in prison and applying it to an endurance sport would prove very useful. Control what you can in your training and racing and let go of the rest. That was easier said than done for me, but at least I had a lot of exposure to those concepts and contradictions.

I had begun reading Jiddu Krishnamurti's book *Freedom from the Known,* which I discovered in Cottonwood's library. I don't know why I was drawn to it. I'd never heard of him prior to that, but something about the book's title intrigued me. I'd always struggled with what I saw as the hypocritical/exclusive/dogmatic Catholicism we practiced at home, which I followed out of a sense of hopeless obligation. I felt powerless to do anything about my mother's desire that I be baptized, catechism-ed, communion-ized, and terrorized by a belief system that seemed to place great value on adhering to a set of demands more out of fear and illogical, purposeless tradition, than any real desire to attain any kind of transcendent humanity.

Krishnamurti believed that there is no truth but our own. That we must make our own way through life based on observations we make ourselves. We could look to others as a guide, but could not rely completely on their models, we cannot blindly rely on organizations or individuals to give us the truth, because the truth is uniquely our own. This ideology influenced me to become critical of many methodologies and organizational views. I could use and draw upon various elements of thoughts or ideas—but I needed to apply them in a way that made sense to me, for my unique situation. Blindly following religious dogma, philosophies, etc., have led to most of the world's violence. Furthermore, it creates "separateness." If I so strongly identify with the Republican Party (or any group, concept, organization, etc.), then I inherently put myself in line with the thoughts and attitudes of the party and naturally "separate" from and feel superior to (in philosophy) the Democratic Party. Instead, it would behoove me to observe the thoughts and ideas of each entity and find my own truth.

Krishnamurti played no part in any particular religious organization, and he really didn't espouse any beliefs that conformed strictly to any single ideology. It seemed to me that he defied, purposefully, categorization. I liked that about him. I always hated being codified/categorized, boxed into a set of expectations based on someone else's construct of what someone who was deemed to be "X" should think, behave, and aspire to. In looking at my life, and again I don't blame anyone but myself for the choices I made in response to how I was treated, I could see that I'd been living down to expectations for most of my life. If it was known that I had ADHD, anger issues, an antiauthority streak, or that I was an alcoholic, drug addict, and criminal, then I proscribed my choices based on those assessments of myself.

Perhaps I bought into the idea that I was doomed to die some day of a violent or horrific or meaningless death because my existence fit into one of those neat categories—criminal, addict, alcoholic, etc.

He also seemed fairly pragmatic, trying to address the human condition as it existed in his time, and offering insights into our shared human connectedness to one another. As a result of reading his work, I decided that I wanted to become a personal trainer. I wanted to compete in an Ironman Triathlon, but I didn't want to become a triathlete. That distinction was crucial to me. The swimming, running, and pedaling were a means to an end and not an end in themselves. By becoming a trainer, I could be of use to other people. I could connect with others and become a part of a community. By focusing on helping other people, I could get out of my own head, and focus on other people's problems. I also looked at it from a pragmatic point of view—I would need to make a living somehow. An added bonus would be that I'd work in an environment that would help reinforce my athletic ambition.

Granted, my understanding of Krishnamurti's work was basic at best, but in reading his words for the first time, I was able to reconfirm what I'd suspected about my suicide attempt. By surviving it, I'd busted out of that set of known conclusions that are associated with someone like me. I'd been living according to a set of guidelines established very early, even before the days when my school counselor had announced to my parents that I was one of those kids likely to have turned out very much as I eventually did.

In my time as an addict, I'd created an endless feedback loop that produced nothing but negative results for me and for other people. Krishnamurti's work helped me to better understand how we are constantly shaping our world and our reality through our interactions. When I spent all my time associating with other addicts and criminals, if I was constantly on the prowl looking for ways to take advantage of other people or remaining hypervigilant to prevent myself from being robbed or assaulted, then all my interactions were negative. I could turn that around in ways that might seem simplistic but I believed were actually very powerful.

I was going to be positive and upbeat and friendly with guards and my fellow inmates. If I could just be pleasant in greeting people, and not in some happy smack insincere way, but be genuine about it, I believed that I could effect great change in my reality. Over time, I saw the results of that change in my attitude. Just as my physical workouts produced tangible results, so did this attitudinal outlook. I wasn't angry. I wasn't depressed. I was grateful for the opportunity I'd been given, and I was going to make the most of it.

I also liked Krishnamurti's view about human's overreliance on reason because it reconfirmed my choice to pursue my goal of qualifying for and racing in the Ironman World Championship. Rationally, there wasn't a reason in the world why I should expect that to be a reasonable outcome of my efforts to change. I was nearly thirty years old. With the exception that brief flirtation with BMX bike racing twenty years prior I'd never competed in any kind of sporting event even remotely close to the three components of an Ironman. Yes, I had loved the ocean and boarding, and I'd had to develop a pretty good paddle stroke to propel me beyond the breakers, but I hadn't swum in at least a decade. Hell, I was so unfamiliar with water, that I don't think I drank much of it at all during my decade and a half as a drunken drug addict.

When I entered prison, I stood 5 feet 10 inches tall and weighed 208 pounds. Today, I know my ideal weight is 155. When I walked into Cottonwood in November 2004, I was more than 50 pounds over my ideal weight. My body mass index, had I even known what that was back then, would have calculated out to be 30.8, putting me in the obese category.

Despite those "facts" about myself, I chose to ignore that outer-imposed reality to pursue my Ironman wannabe program.

At Cottonwood, I was able to not just expand my mind through reading and journaling; I was able to work on my body. At the Ada County Jail, in addition to my basic calisthenics, I'd added stair climbing and running to my exercise regimen. There, I ran in a tight circle in a space no more than eighty feet long, and shaped like a Trivial Pursuit wedge. Considering that at first I could barely shuffle around that space at no more than a two dozen laps an hour, barely above a walking pace, the size of my track didn't matter. Up north, I was able to use the weight room. I had a lot of respect for the power lifters and bodybuilders in prison. They had their goal; I had mine. Strength training was a means to an end for me, however, and as another form of movement, it had its utility and benefits, and I loved the emotional release it provided.

After those first six months or so of being incarcerated, I'd shed maybe twenty pounds, and the days when it was a struggle for me just to haul my lardass into a top bunk were now far less frequent. If it was a battle to get up there, it was mostly because of exertion induced soreness as my fatigued muscles shouted at me and longed for the good old days of lethargy and laziness. Buoyed by my reading and grateful for a break from imposed and self-imposed moments of stillness and restraint, any physical outlet was something I craved. I was also, as the weeks turned into months, appreciative of the fact that my efforts were producing measurable results. I kept track of my accomplishments in another notebook, and tallying the quantity of exercises and repetitions I did and going back through that notebook's early pages to see my progress produced a satisfaction in me that I'd once taken

in topping my own personal record (PR) for downing a case of Budweiser. I wasn't that far removed from the days when I couldn't climb
a flight of stairs without feeling crushed.

I was reminded of the transient nature of, and the illusory quality
of control, when I was nearing the end of my third month at Cottonwood in January 2004, when I heard one of the COs say, "71768, roll
'em up."

I quickly rounded up all my gear, the few books that were my
possessions, mainly ones that my mom had sent, my notebooks, and
other things, and boarded a bus for the miserable five-hour ride (in
full shackles) that lay ahead. Of course, no one would tell me exactly
what the nature of this trip was, but I was quietly hoping that I was
going to be in front of a review panel to determine if I'd done enough
in my programming to get released well before I was parole eligible.
That was a possibility, based on how rider programs like the one I was
on worked, but unlikely. What I wasn't expecting was to be told that
I was no longer going to be incarcerated up north at Cottonwood;
instead, I was going to be doing my next stretch of time, of indeterminate duration, back at the Idaho State Corrections Institution.

I was still going to be in the state's custody, but I could say good-
bye to dorm-style living and the comparatively relaxed environment
of Cottonwood. I was going to be doing my time in what inmates
called "The Yard." That meant living in a locked and barred cell instead of bunking in a dorm. Worse, for a reason that wasn't clear to
me yet, I was going to be denied access to that prison's work-out facilities. I was going be kept under stricter control.

I couldn't figure out why all this was going down, but eventually a
call to my attorney revealed that the state of Idaho and its legal system might not be done with me. Apparently, some of the other stores
that I had ripped off had continued their efforts to press charges and

to see me tried and convicted of additional counts of business burglary. Even though I'd already been sentenced in two courts on several matters, one of which was for crimes similar to the possible new
charges, no double jeopardy was attached. These were new cases, new
accusers, and to keep the folks at the corporate offices happy, a very
real possibility existed that I could be brought to trial again and sentenced to longer terms. It would be up to the discretion of the judge to
determine if those sentences would run concurrent with the sentences
already handed down and for which I'd already been serving time.

This was not the news I wanted or needed to hear. In the past, any
kind of bad news, any setback at all in any area of my life, was an excuse to get drunk or high or angry enough that I would do something
to make the situation worse. None of those really happened. I did get
upset, and I did lash out, but this wasn't me acting on impulse. I was
purposefully angry and got into a fight at the ISCI as a way to signal
to the inmates there that I was not be fucked with. For the most part,
if you conducted yourself decently and showed respect for your fellow
inmates, the COs, and the rest of the prison staff, you weren't likely to
be hassled. The ISCI wasn't a hard-core maximum security place with
a reputation like San Quentin, but it was definitely not as laid back a
place as Cottonwood. The usual mix of drug offenders was there, but
so were a lot more violent criminals. The worst of them, of course,
were segregated, but still, a few of those in the more secure (read: high-
risk) units would be moved out of them into the general population
and those boys didn't always do so well after their promotions.

So, as a preemptive measure, I took on a menacing asshole named
Curtis in a fistfight. I was hoping that my out-of-nowhere attack on
him, he was a chomo (child molester) so I did have some justification,
would earn me the "crazy fucker" reputation that might keep me safe.
That fight also earned me some time in "the hole," and I remember

being escorted there by a CO who knew me and whom I had treated with nothing but respect.

"What got into you?" he asked.

"I don't really know," I lied. I knew exactly what I was doing and my calculated in-control-out-of-control display of violence against a verbally abusive convicted child molester did the trick. No one wanted to fuck with me after that.

This wasn't exactly Krishnamurti-like, but at least I was making a conscious decision to act out with violence and anger. The old Shane would have simply given into impulse. This was a calculated choice of self-preservation. I wasn't naïve enough to think that a peace, love, and understanding approach was going to help me survive in prison. Describing a fight in prison doesn't really qualify as a shining example of someone turning his life around, but I saw that as progress. Before, I was all impulse. I can't tell you the number of times I wanted to get in somebody's grill or throw down with them, but I didn't. I thought about what the negative consequences would be and decided against taking action. This time, I did a cost-benefit analysis and made a determination to go. For me that was progress.

After doing a few days in isolation, I was allowed back into general population. The only thing that made me angry about having to do that was that my fight went onto my record. If I was going to get out on my rider, I couldn't afford too many black marks against me.

In looking back on my years on the fringe, being an addict and homeless and a criminal, I could see that I was living by accident. I was opportunistic and shortsighted, letting external factors direct me, instead of being self-directed with a clear sense of where I was headed. I was like an atom acting randomly and being acted on randomly. Then, something jumped orbit. I was trying to kill myself willfully and intentionally and by coincidence I survived. I had read some of Deepak Chopra's work, which taught me that seemingly random and unpredictable events are in fact connected on a deep level. They are also important messages that we can and should use to guide our own destiny, or what he called "SynchroDestiny." In that regard, what might have happened to me if a guard had brought me a copy of *Mechanix Illustrated* or *People* or something else instead of that copy of *Outside*? It doesn't matter really because the right thing was placed in front of me at the right time. Once I recognized the pattern, that triathlon fit my need for physical exertion, my temperament, and my obsessive nature, the rest was up to me to take control of.

While in prison, I also read the psychiatrist Viktor Frankl's classic work, *Man's Search for Meaning*, and it was enormously moving and influential. Frankl lost his mother, father, brother, and pregnant wife in a Nazi concentration camp. He worked in four death camps himself, including Auschwitz, and tells the story of how he and others managed, and in some cases failed, to survive such a horrendous experience. I will never compare anything I went through to those horrors, but Frankl wanted to show people that no matter the kind of suffering we endure or imagine we endure, we can overcome it, cope with it, find meaning in it, and move forward in a more productive way. In a sense, he contradicted Freud who thought that humans were primarily motivated by pleasure; instead, he believed that our primary motivation as a human being was to find meaning and purpose. That I latched onto the idea of competing as a triathlete was in some ways immaterial. That was a means to an end. My real goal was to become a more productive human being, to stop being a sucking vortex of negativity, dragging down myself, others, and burdening society at large.

I also read several of the Buddhist monk Thich Nhat Hanh's works and Lao Tzu's *Tao Te Ching,* each in an attempt to better understand my behavior and essential nature. Hermann Hesse's *Siddhartha* taught me that experience would be the best teacher, and I realized that forgetting completely about my past, pretending as if it had never happened, would be foolish and unproductive. Those days had been wasteful, but they weren't a complete waste, they only would have been if I didn't try to learn something from them about myself or about the nature of existence.

Ernest Hemingway's style was very different from these writers, but I found some parallels that proved to be useful and insightful. I suppose that what I learned wasn't anything that anyone who had taken, and not passed out during high school American Literature would have known, but the way that Hemingway wrote, the sparseness of it and the descriptive powers he possessed amazed me. I wanted to be a Hemingway hero, that in control, that composed, and not the fidgety, excitable, and run-amok spaz that I had been for so much of my life. I wanted to be as self-possessed as Frederic Henry in *A Farewell to Arms,* and if I had to walk out of a hospital after my wife died in childbirth, then I hoped that I could let people know that those broken places in me would heal.

For a lot of the same reasons, I admired Cormac McCarthy and especially *All the Pretty Horses,* and identified with its hero John Grady Cole and his lonely isolation in prison. That point of identification wasn't entirely justified, but McCarthy's writing about it, and Cole's relationship with his horse as an anchor in his life, suited me in my self-pitying and past-wallowing moments.

All the reading I was doing was designed to accomplish another goal—to slow me down. One of the great appeals of Eastern philosophy was its emphasis on appreciating the moment. I'd gotten to the point in my life as an addict that I can't really say I enjoyed the high.

There was the temporary relief of having given my body what it craved, but my mind was always focused on the next high, the next fix I had to get, the next bump I could do to allow me to go, the next pill I could swallow that would slow me down. Doing and attaining drugs was all consuming. I had been leading a hollow and bleak existence—a painful and dirty autopilot.

It naturally occurred to me that if I was going to become a different person—I mean really and truly change—it wouldn't happen spontaneously. Clearly, I was broken in every way. Mentally, physically, emotionally, and spiritually, I would need to add something new or different into what had become my warped and twisted closed system. I had to seek out change. I had to acquire resources so I could draw on new thoughts and ideas that would promote growth and change. Many of these thoughts and ideas came by way of the authors and works I've mentioned plus a whole lot more reading and thinking.

I journaled every day because my thoughts were broken; this is clear even from the letters I wrote at that time. I needed to observe myself. All of this would culminate in the development of the plan. A picture of what my life would look like in a perfect world.

My exercise routines, mental and physical, were crucial in showing me that I could live a life that wasn't so one-dimensional. I certainly had been a pleasure seeker/pain avoider, but body, spirit, and mind were all getting better about seeking and enjoying meaning in the activities themselves. That element, becoming more process than product oriented, would take the longest amount of time to evolve. I was still very much goal attached and quantity obsessive. I can't say that I got to the point where I enjoyed my workouts completely for the sake of their being an expression of animal nature and the joy of movement. That was part of it, but I wasn't about to stop keeping score.

Another of my teachers was a cat from, ironically enough, Hawaii, who everyone called Pineapple. A very large pineapple, as tough and spiny as one, and as intimidating to contemplate how to get at its center. I don't know why Pineapple took an interest in me. He was in the ISCI pretty much as a lifer; even though parole was possible, it wasn't likely. Even in prison, he was a prickly prick, and maybe it was because of his Samoan heritage and his status as a complete outsider in Idaho, that he was constantly on edge. Given the large presence of the Aryan Nation and its skinheads, I couldn't blame him.

Pineapple saw me working out, and he was as jacked as anyone I'd ever seen, though he didn't go to the weight room all that much. One day, I was in my cell alternating crunches with declined triceps push-ups, when I noticed him standing outside my door. We weren't in lockdown, so he was free to roam the unit. If I could get past the 6 foot 6 inch wall of sculpted flesh in front of me, that is.

"Let me show you something, bro'."

Pineapple tore the sheet off my bed. For a second I wondered what was up, but Pineapple sat down on the floor opposite me, his tree-trunk legs slightly splayed open in front of him. He wound the sheet around his two fists like a corner man or trainer getting a boxer ready to put on the gloves. He left a trail of about three feet or so of sheet.

"You do it." He nodded his massive head to indicate the sheet and that I should wrap my hands up as he did.

Once I did, he said, "Pull."

Before I could react, he had pulled me nearly face first flat onto the ground in front of him.

"You have to put up some resistance," Pineapple said. "It's kind of like tug of war. Great workout."

For the next few minutes I strained my arms trying to pull that hulking guy toward me. The effort was intense, and the veins in my arms were hyperdilated, standing out against my pale skin like rivers on a relief map.

Eventually, Pineapple and I were work-out partners for that portion of our routine. The variable resistance stuff we were doing was great, didn't necessitate going to the weight lifting area (which for some reason I was banned from) and was as effective as a several thousand dollar Cybex or Nautilus machine. I was surprised by how many variations and muscle groups we could work on with just a sheet. Pineapple knew a lot about strength training, and I was an eager pupil. I'd like to think that our relationship was a symbiotic one, with me being the little remora that attached itself to the shark's dorsal fin and fed on scraps and kept him healthy. I can't say how much Pineapple benefitted from our workouts, and I didn't talk to him at all really about the reading and thinking I was doing. For one thing, I wasn't sure if he would be receptive, for another, I didn't want to come across as a jailhouse preacher.

Pineapple wasn't the only source I had for information on working out. I started to read issues of *Men's Health* and *Men's Fitness* and even read a copy of what is still considered a gold standard or Bible in the fitness industry—*The Essentials of Strength Training and Conditioning*. It was a busted-spine old war-torn version of the classic, but that didn't matter to me. I poured over that book as a regular part of my day.

Part of the reason why I didn't talk to Pineapple about the other part of my program was that so few of the people I spent time with in prison seemed like they would be receptive to any of it. My cellie was a guy who I'd heard about months before from my toothless tweeker of a roommate my first go around at NICI. Levi had been there long enough to hear the story of a guy who was now known as Hambone. Hambone had earned his new name about eight months before he and I were paired.

I'm going to put this delicately here. One afternoon while working in the kitchen, Hambone seized a moment when he was alone. He carved out a little opening in a canned ham, unzipped, and inserted himself into the pork cavity. Someone walked in on him as he was engaged in bestiality after the fact with what had once been a living breathing pig. Surveillance cameras also caught his little show. There was a lot else not to like about the Hambone, but to his credit or as a sign of his complete depravity, he seemed to take his nickname in stride and answered to it as if his dear mother and father had given it to him.

I don't mean to suggest that everyone in jail is like that or worse, but the sad truth is that most people in prison don't just deserve to be there, they *need* to be there. That included Russell, another chomo who so relentlessly picked on another weaker inmate that I had to step in. Another week in isolation, another possible reason for Judge Neville to not release me, but a few points earned with my fellow inmates and the guard who let me know the incident report would go down in my favor. Also, after that fight, more guys started asking me about what I was doing with my workouts and what was with all the books?

I wasn't going to preach to anybody, but I answered them as best I could. I didn't want to go back to being the way that I was in the past. I had a bunch of time on my hands and I wanted to make use of it and also to just make the time pass as quickly as possible. All of that was true. The rest—reading Eastern philosophy, classics of Western literature—was just a part of the process of distancing myself from that former life. I didn't say a word about my decision to train for an Ironman when I got out. That seemed like something to keep on the down-low.

Maybe it was because despite all my fuckups, I'd managed to graduate from college. Consequently, I was somewhat of a rarity in the prison environment. That allowed me to see things from a different perspective. I'd had a lot of advantages over many of these guys. That didn't make me better than them, but it did give me a leg up on them in some respects. I may have sunk to a level lower than most of them during my addict days, but fortunately for me, I could draw on my memories and experiences of being around a group of people whose aspirations far exceeded what many of my fellow inmates could envision for themselves.

There was no magic to it. You didn't have to belong to some special club and know the secret password in order to gain access to good jobs. Sure, it helped to have connections and to be able to network, but the same was true in what I'll call the underworld. Most of the guys I knew in prison didn't realize that the skills they possessed that allowed many of them to thrive in the criminal world would have benefitted them on the outs if they'd wanted to try that route. I was fortunate that I'd made the connection that my energies that had been directed toward doing harmful things could be channeled into a more positive pursuit. A lot of them didn't grasp that fact.

Many of them believed that their world and the rest of the world had no real connection to one another. It was a rigged game, the house always won if you played by its rules. So, the only alternative they thought they had was to operate outside the rules of legitimate life. Quite a few guys had no experience whatsoever with the existence that most of us take for granted as "normal." For them, it wasn't just a lack of vision or a clear understanding that hampered them. I saw it as fear, a natural and legitimate response to the unknown.

I had my own fears as well. So far, things had gone pretty smoothly for me. I was clean and sober, had resisted the temptation to buy any of the drugs that had been smuggled in, and didn't drink any of the prison hooch that was available. The only thing I was plagued by was self-doubt. What would it be like on the outs? Was I strong enough to resist those temptations? Had I cultivated enough good habits, allowed them enough time to mature, to thrive in a different environment outside of prison?

I was scared shitless that I would fuck up.

I was glad that the first time I went up for review on my rider and possibly earn early release from prison, I was told that I needed to serve more time. I agreed with that assessment. I felt I wasn't ready to get out. I needed more time to adjust to being this new self, to have that newly formed identity, that was still very malleable, harden into something that could resist the forces that would be out there and threatening to pull me and twist me into another shape. For the moment, I felt like I was right where I belonged. I deserved every minute of prison time I was going to do and probably even more. I felt like I was really changing and growing as a person, but I had been so junked out for so long that it was going to take a long time before I was ready for life on the outs.

Along with journaling, I began to write letters to my family, to my mom and dad in particular. This was the start of an ongoing process that allowed me to sort through some of what I was thinking and establish some connections with them. I poured my heart out to them, lavishing them with words of thanks and love.

It's clear to me that the pendulum had swung. I hadn't ever expressed those feelings of gratitude and love to my parents before. I was going overboard, as was my usual pattern, but it's just as important to understand what life was like for them and me when the pendulum was at the opposite end of this arc. I was still struggling to find that calm center, but this overly sentimental sap, was far better than what had come before.

FIVE

As much as I saw back then and see even more clearly now how much my issues with control played such a big part in my destruction and resurrection, another reality also plays a major role in my development. No matter how much I wanted out of prison before my sentence ended, that decision was essentially in the hands of other people. I was grateful that Judge Neville had seen something in me, or maybe even more generally in the possibility of human beings being able to change. The rider program he made sure I was eligible for offered me something that I hadn't had in quite a while—hope. That's not completely true. At various times, I'd hoped that I would die of an overdose, that whoever discovered my passed-out body would just pass it by and not take me to the emergency room where I could be revived and repeat the process.

I noticed another way in which I'd changed but was still stuck in place. I'd grown tired of being a parasite. While in prison, I was in a very real sense still sucking life out of another body—the money that taxpayers paid to house, feed, and clothe me—and that wasn't very much different from how I'd been living my life in those last few months prior to my suicide attempt. I'd lost my restaurant job for being caught on tape, drunk and completely out of control, defiling memorabilia at a sports-themed bar and restaurant, and supported myself and my very expensive drug habit by stealing. While being incarcerated and supported by the criminal justice system is a small step above petty larceny, it represented progress of a sort. But in prison I stewed about not being fully self-sufficient, and had to find a way to make sense of its necessity.

For a long time, I thought of myself as a loser, as a complete and utter failure of a human being. All of the reading I was doing, all of the journaling, all of the writing to my parents, and all of the workouts I was doing, were a way to build a framework around what had been for a long time an empty center, a void. Imagine scaffolding being erected without a building inside of it. That's what those months from January to March 2004 represented in my mind. I didn't know exactly what the finished building was going to look like, but I knew that in order to begin construction of it, I was going to have to have some tools at my disposal so that as that image grew, I'd be able to continue to reach higher and higher. Prison provided a kind of supporting superstructure for those efforts as well. If my building blocks weren't aligned properly, if the mortar I used to join them didn't set properly, the supporting framework of prison life, the regimentation of the hours, would keep me from collapsing completely. I needed that structure, something imposed on me from the outside and not something I built because for those first few months post-suicide, I couldn't rely on myself.

Simply put, I knew that I couldn't live on the outs without falling back into the same habits and destructive patterns. That didn't mean that I didn't want my freedom, quite the opposite, but I also knew what was best for me at that time—a rare case of me having that kind of insight for longer than just a few weeks or a few months. I settled into the life of a prisoner, understanding that a life in confinement was ultimately going to pay off for me and my freedom down the line. Paying back society would have to wait.

My workouts served multiple purposes. By July 2004, I'd shed a total of about forty pounds. The sense of accomplishment I felt in that achievement, those tangible pounds lost, weren't enough to completely push aside my feelings of shame and inadequacy, but they were giving me some much-needed momentum. They were the first evidence of me achieving something positive in my life since I had enrolled in college nearly ten years earlier.

I'd made solid progress in my physical rehabilitation, and I was sticking to my program. My aerobic workouts consisted at first of simply walking up the stairs in the unit. I can never forget that there were 22 of them, and at first, just getting up all of them was my task. I felt like my lungs were some kind of protomammalian creature trying to crawl their way out of my throat and onto dry land, but I kept pushing myself.

Eventually, I was able to do multiple sets of walking, and by the end of June I was running up and down them for a solid 45 minutes. I also varied the workout by bounding up them with a 5–6 step cadence per leg and using my arms and hands to give me better forward thrust. The only disadvantage that I saw was in prison I only had one set of clothes that I could wash just twice a week. I got used to the idea of being sweat-fouled, but I can't say that went over well with some of the other inmates, so I would wash them in the shower.

Running stairs inside the prison became a twice-daily activity that framed my life. I liked the idea of doing stairs, the climbing up and then the coming back down seemed an apt metaphor for what it was I was hoping to do with my life and a reminder that nothing was going to come easily. It would have been easy to just hang out in my rack reading or in the rec room watching television, but I wanted to do something constructive. Forcing myself to work out was a form of self-discipline that hadn't been part of my life in years.

Not all the corrections officers let me run the stairs, but enough did that my sessions got easier and longer as time went on. I'd log those steps and smile about the fact that just a few months earlier, I hadn't always been able to even walk up them a single time. I wish that I could say that I really reveled in my accomplishment, but I feel that I had to keep things in perspective. Just because I was now able to survive 60–90 minutes of doing stairs that was still a far cry from completing any kind of Ironman distance. That realization kept me working hard.

Those times when I was able to get outside in the rec yard—three to four sessions a week at most—supplemented my stair workouts. The yard was a 40 × 50 foot rectangle and I estimated that it took about 30 laps to equal a mile. Getting to 100 laps was a monumental marker in my evolution, especially since I was doing this in prison-issued Van's–like white slip on sneakers that had no support whatsoever in them. A few times the pain in my shins was torturous, but for the most part I just sucked it up and ran back and forth, like a predator in a cage exhibiting zoo behaviors. As I ran, I knew that I was only doing one of the three phases of the triathlon. I daydreamed about riding and swimming, and knew that if I had any hope at all of completing my mission, I was really going to have to get after it once I was released from prison.

With Pineapple, and sometimes with another inmate, I'd do bicep curls in four sets of 10–12 each. We'd alternate being on the top bunk doing the curls and sitting on the floor holding the sheet stretched taut. After that we'd do four sets of rows, and I can still picture how Pineapple's enormous feet dwarfed mine as we sat shoe-to-shoe facing one another. I was clearly the coxswain to Pineapple's prodigious rower.

At times I felt like he was going to snap my spine or rip my arms out of their sockets. From those first days of doing just a few push-ups, by the late summer and early fall I was able to do 200–300 push-ups a day depending upon how much other exercise I was getting. I continued to do my old school–type calisthenics as well.

In retrospect, I can see now that integrating my physical transformation with my intellectual and spiritual one was essential to my success. In prison, I didn't really have a way of accurately measuring and comparing my "performance" as a human being in the same way I did my growth as a wannabe athlete. I knew that I was staying off drugs, that I wasn't involved in any kind of criminal activity, but as far as an easily measurable metric to determine that I was getting better and not being a fuckup, that just doesn't exist. I couldn't step on any scale to see if the burden of my shame and my self-hatred was any lighter or if my worldview and attitude were truly progressing. It felt that way to me, but no unit of measurement exists to determine your asshole-to-good-guy ratio. I had to trust my perspective of myself, and that was important for me at the beginning. I believed I was a changed person, I saw some evidence of that in my physique, but the more important change, the one in attitude wasn't something I could ask others about in order to validate my impressions. That was just another form of self-reliance.

I did come to another realization. I can't say for sure that it was because I read a passage in a book or a magazine article, but prior to my first review in front of a parole board (where I was denied that initial opportunity) I had come to this conclusion: who I am was inseparable from my physical body that housed me. I had spent so many years denigrating my body and myself that as I began to get my body in shape, as I started to physically feel better and stronger, I realized that my outlook was improved. I'd hated myself enough to want to stop all of my biological processes from functioning, but my body had withstood that cord and all those substances I'd abused for so long. Something told me that maybe my body wasn't just an "organism," a collection of cells, tissues, and organs that mindlessly went about performing whatever functions they had evolved to do. Instead, it was a beautifully integrated unit that operated well when all systems were working toward something constructive.

I recognized that who I was as a person, as a sentient being who acted on and was acted upon, was inseparable from my body. Whatever I did to my body had an effect on every other aspect of my life. What I did to my body was going to influence the course and quality of the rest of my life. As a result of that idea dawning on me, my workouts took on a different tenor. It wasn't just about losing weight, shedding fat, and building muscle. The structure that housed my essence, what everyone referred to as Shane, had to be sound. What I did to improve that body also improved how I thought, how I felt, and how I responded to others. My body housed the energy system that was me. I came to believe that physical movement, getting from one place to another, represented a desire for improvement, for progress.

That last bit is important because it led to a kind of corollary thought. As humans we all share the common experience of living. We are all energetic beings, and whenever we interact with one another, we exchange energy. I had spent so much of my existence as a parasite. To every person I encountered, I was a sucking negative force. For a long time, I thought of myself as the life of the party, the guy who everyone wanted to be around, the crazy bastard who'd liven things up with his death-defying antics. In truth, I was just the opposite most of the time. I had good friends and I was loyal and for the most part trustworthy, but even in high school, when my parents were at their wits' end and kicked me out of the house, I stayed with the family of a friend for a bit, but I fucked that up by stealing from them. Eventually, everything I had going for me, I destroyed. My actions cast a shadow over every interaction I had with anyone and anything, and it was clear that I was a victim of my own thoughts and actions, but I had been unable to stop.

Exercise was the one area, the first area really, of my rehabilitation of self in which there was such a clear-cut and direct relationship between cause and effect. It was so clear that even someone with my diminished capacity to understand much of anything about reality could see the correlation. Effort produced results. If I did the workouts, I got stronger. I lost weight. I gained muscle mass. I could do X more sets of stairs, prisoner squats, etc. I also noticed that as I got better physically, as I became more consciously aware of how I treated other people, how my energy effected them, the more positive my interactions were. Simple stuff really but revelatory for someone whose focus for the last eight years of his life was centered on what he could stick in his arm and what he'd have to do to get that stuff. Without being on drugs or alcohol, it was like someone had taken a hood and halter off me. Not only could I see, but I could turn my head and look in a variety of other directions.

I'm not about to say that I was transformed overnight and that I emerged an enlightened being in those first six months in prison. That's not the case at all. I was just exiting, barely poking my eyeballs above the murk, so the light I saw appeared blinding after all those years in the darkness. They'd adjust after a bit, but it was going to take some time to get to the point where I could stand to be in the full glare of the daylight reality of being out of jail and back on the streets.

Shame is a powerful force, and I believe that if it wasn't for its presence in my life, I wouldn't have been able to so thoroughly transform myself. It worked like this: the more I remembered the shitty things I'd done, the worse I felt about myself, the harder I pushed myself in those workouts to smash up that shame. When I was doing my sets of stationary lunges, working on my sorry excuse for legs, it was almost like I was kneeling down in front of everyone asking them to forgive me for the shit I'd put them through. I didn't need dumbbells in my hands to increase the resistance and workload. I spent a lot of time thinking about all the things I'd done that led me to prison and all the previous attempts I'd made to reform my life before. I used the guilt and shame as a way to keep myself moving forward, to fuel my progress toward lasting change.

As I sat in the Ada County Jail waiting for my third hearing (got dinged at nine and twelve months by the parole panel who felt I needed more time and an anger-management class) to determine whether or not I'd be released upon successful completion of my rider, I was consumed with thoughts about how I'd do on the outs. Keeping clean in prison, after the initial shock of detoxing, had been relatively easy. What was it going to be like to never drink another drop of alcohol again? What was it going to be like to be in a grocery store, a minimart, walking past or in a bar or restaurant seeing those beaded bottles of beer, hearing the glacial chink of iced alcohol and mixers being poured in and out of glasses? Not to mention the siren's call of opiates that would echo along the Boise River corridor, where the smashed-up addicts and their shattered works were dashed along the rocks and the concrete abutments.

At least in Boise I knew my way around. One less adjustment to make; one less reason to cave when the pressure got too great. Besides, if I was going to do this clean and sober thing, then doing it where all the reminders would shout out at me, snatch me up by the collar and try to lure me back, was the challenge I needed to take on.

My guts were churning as I sat in the courtroom waiting for Judge Neville to enter and to render his decision. My mom, ever the devoted one, had flown out for the hearing. I smiled and nodded at her, trying to appear calm and confident. Judge Neville came in and looked at the sheaf of papers in front of him and then at me. I noticed he looked the same as before, his thinning hair in the same comb-over, his hooded eyes lost in the glare off his glasses. I was still grateful to him for the words he'd spoken at my sentencing. I hoped that he'd see the new "cleaner" and fitter me and understand that I'd taken seriously what he'd said about me being worthwhile.

He finally looked up, and I couldn't tell if there was a brief expression of confusion that crossed his face, if he'd truly been surprised by the appearance of the prisoner before him. The scene played out somewhat anticlimactically; he offered neither praise nor warning, he simply gave me my get-out-of-jail-not-so free card: ninety AA meetings in ninety days, seven years of parole, daily and then weekly and then monthly piss tests for an indeterminate amount of time.

When I heard Judge Neville pronounce that I was going to be released the following day, I felt that I-might-piss-myself sensation of cresting a hill at high speed. I turned to look at my mom. She smiled and I could see a nictitating membrane of her own fear and doubt pass across her face before receding. She held her interlocked fingers of both hands in front of her face, the old prayer position, and rested them underneath her chin and then extended them out to me. Still in chains, I couldn't return the gesture. I can't say that prayers were something I was capable of, but knowing that she was there, had always been, intertwined with me in ways that I was still trying to sort out, gave me strength. Just for a second, as I butt-scooted my way away from the table, I realized that my mother's and my entanglement had nearly snapped both our necks, added another victim to my list.

I was to be released the next day, and I spent the night before sleepless and pacing.

Okay, dude. You're getting what you wanted. You don't have a very good track record, but that was the other guy, the dead self. And lots of spiritual traditions talk about the necessity of that event transpiring in your life. Dying is easy. Life is hard. Life is better, too.

Each time I reached the end of my cell, it was like I'd shifted to a counterargument. Look, dude, nearly every day since you've been locked up for this stretch, you've gotten better at this. Look at your journal. Look at the numbers of sit-ups, push-ups, burpees, the steps climbed, the miles run, the books read. There's been visible progress. That fat fuck you used to be has melted away. Pounds gone.

Turnaround.

But what about the doc and what he told you about your liver function? Not good, dude. Not good at all.

Turnaround.

Tissue regenerates. That's what it does. Toxins out. Tissue restored. Fucking up out. Function resumed.

The obvious question that the court, my family, my friends, and I were all asking was this: which Shane was going to show up on the streets of Boise this time?

I could understand my parents being skeptical and questioning my choice about staying in Boise post-prison. If you looked at my transcript detailing all the ways that I'd fucked up, then somehow you'd have to notice that going out west had produced nothing but bad news. But after being expelled from high school the week of graduation, getting my GED, and then spending a couple of fruitless and fucked-up years going to junior college in Bloomington, I came to the conclusion that I needed to head out west and return to my roots in Colorado. I was fucked up completely on drugs when I came out to Colorado State University (CSU) in Fort Collins in the summer of 1997, but I decided that was the place for me. With my checkered academic career, I couldn't be too picky, but CSU accepted me and I accepted it.

I was determined to turn my life around. I was going to go out to Colorado and get a do over. I remember telling myself: I'm going to get out there, I'm going to quit drinking, give up the cigarettes, cut out the coke, find me a mountain girl, get my degree, move into the mountains someplace, breathe that good clean mountain air, and be a model citizen. No more than a few months later, I was on the lam. I'd incited a riot on campus, assaulted a peace officer, and rather than face the consequences, I'd lit out for Boise.

Fresh start part two.

Except my vision for what Boise was going to do for me turned out just as faulty as my Colorado dream. I applied to Boise State University, leaving off the part about enrolling at CSU and my criminal record, and was accepted there for the spring '98 semester.

I was as determined as ever to make a go of it. I even recruited a childhood buddy of mine, Tom Howie, with whom I'd spent those early years in Colorado, to help me get back to that place where I hadn't let alcohol and drugs take hold of me.

I'd contacted Tom when I first came back to Colorado. He'd just graduated from Regis University in Denver and was looking to get out of the area. He was back in Colorado looking for work, but he hated it there. He wanted to get back to the old days we had as kids, the Huck Finn shit, where we spent most of our time out hunting and fishing. Where we'd grown up, and even Fort Collins had changed so much, according to Tom. Too many people, too much bullshit.

Instead, Boise was the place where the new things I discovered were the adrenaline-rushing torrent of class V rapid running thrills injecting cocaine produced, and then later the all-consuming warmth and release of heroin. My guides into this foray were my new friends Isaac and Nancy, the poster children for retrograde hippiedom, the faux-hobo lifestyle that it entailed, the apotheosis of punk and grunge, and advocates of the mind-expanding possibilities of matter transformed alchemically from powder to injectable liquid or inhalable smoke, the purveyors and tutors introducing me to the wonders of chiva, the black tar heroin, the substance that abused me, transformed me, and nearly destroyed me.

No matter the high-faluting diction, the effort to make it all seem epic, I was living in my own self-constructed bleak house of self-destructive wrack and ruin.

Fortunately for me, my Boise experiences were truly my own tale of two cities; the first and second go-rounds in Boise were truly the worst of times, and only later, after my release from prison, was it the start of the best of times.

So, I loaded up the truck and moved to Boise. A few swimming pools. No real movie stars I knew about. No hillbillies to speak of; in these parts they preferred to be called rednecks. The home of Micron, baseball's Bill Buckner, George Kennedy (Dragline from one of my favorite flicks, *Cool Hand Luke*), Joe Albertson, the man and his grocery stores. And now me, Mom, and Dad.

And, oh, yeah.

Skinheads. Tweekers. Coke freaks. Heroin shooters. A few drunks whose consumption amazed me. Guatemalan and Honduran drug dealers who provided the little bit of ethnicity and a whole lot of potent pieces I'd buy for twenty to forty dollars, those one-eighth of a gram of heroin in the handy balloon packages, a prize in every one of them. Boise, a place where I could put my skills to work cooking and where I eventually spent my hardly earned dollars cooking in tea spoons, a lovely fusion of heroin, water, and cigarette butt cotton. Sure to satisfy and keep me coming back for more.

Eventually, I didn't want to live anymore, in Boise or anywhere else, but now I felt sure that with Judge Neville pronouncing me fit for life on outs, Boise was the place I had to answer those big questions looming in everybody's minds.

Was Shane finally going to really change? What was he going to do when the going got hard?

Life is difficult when all you have to your name, and not a particularly good or valuable name at that point I might add, is the $210 of your store you'd saved up from your prison job and family contributions. And unlike those movie scenes, nobody handed you the clothes you had on your back when you walked into prison. Instead, I had an XXL white T-shirt (which looked more like a pit-stained nightgown to me than an undergarment) handed to me, a lace-less pair of work boots, and a pair of jeans that I had to roll the hem of four times to avoid stepping on. I could do little about the oversized waistband, and had to walk with a fistful of denim in one hand to keep them from dropping to the ground. I had to stop for a second and wonder. Maybe this was my stuff.

I'd told my mom that I didn't want her coming to the jail to see me walk out of there. I didn't need that. She certainly didn't deserve to have that sight get imprinted in her memory bank. If this was going to be a new start, then we should meet up at the starting line. Along with those prior grandiose dreams with no clear process for how to make them manifest, there was another problem. I couldn't see past the drugs and the alcohol. I could not envision my life without them. They'd been a part of my every day existence for so long, that I really forgot what it was like to make it through a day clean or sober. Nature abhors a vacuum, and for so long my mind had been stuffed with thoughts about drugs that there was room for little else. Now my mind was filled with thoughts of becoming an athlete and a better and more complete person.

Essentially, I was biting off more than I could chew. I figured out in prison that it was important for me to snap things into smaller more digestible bits, chew them up, and then move on. What I had been calling a plan before really wasn't a plan at all. It's good to have an overarching goal, but without those incremental steps on how to get there, to experience some small successes along the way to let you know that you're making progress, it was way too easy for me to cave in when I encountered a setback. Also, I had nothing to lose. When you're down that low, everything is progress.

So, for that reason, because I knew the big scary was coming up, I had an immediate plan of action for myself, one that would help me mentally and emotionally as well as practically. I'd been driving illegally since Illinois. I wasn't going to do that anymore. Idaho wasn't going to issue me a driver's license given my past record of DUIs, and driving while suspended. Not a problem, I told myself. I was going to get myself a bike. If I was going to do a triathlon, then I'd need to ride a lot of miles in preparation for it, so commuting on two wheels would serve a dual purpose of getting me where I needed to go and providing a good workout.

Preprison days in Boise, I'd gone past Bob's Bicycles on Fairview Avenue, a fairly short walk from the Ada County Jail. Once I got out the doors of the jailhouse, I felt a huge sense of relief. Since I knew exactly where I wanted to go, I experienced none of the anxiety I might have otherwise. Walking north on Cole Road, I passed under a viaduct for Interstate 184, saw a few shopping carts, sleeping bags, boxes, and a couple of homeless men getting ready for the day. They were redemption men, guys who walked around the city picking up various recyclables, cans mostly, and their modest and motley caravan had just been a blurry background image to my days on the streets in Boise. I'd never done it myself, thinking it beneath me in a way, hating the idea that as I stood in line at one of the can redemption sites or in a grocery store, the stares and looks of antipathy or sympathy would be too much for me.

For a similar reason, I'd only worked a sign once (I made it less than twenty minutes), when things were really desperate. Somehow hanging out all day with a cardboard plea and a pleading look just didn't sit well with me. It was too passive of an activity, and I had little patience for it. I'd mumbled my thanks, but every expression of gratitude also reminded me of how far I'd fallen. So as soon as I had enough cash to buy a piece, it would be closing time for me. I knew that these guys were likely to be addicts or drunks like I was, and that any contribution I made would go toward their habit, but I wasn't going to be a dick about it. So, I took ten bucks out of my pocket, rolled it up and attached it to one of the carts with a binder clip that was already there.

I kept walking and behind me I heard the cart's wheels jittering over the cracked and glass-glittered sidewalk, grateful in another way. I only had a half mile or so to go, far fewer miles than those other men would have to trek that day and the next and the next. I wondered if maybe my gesture was more about me than them, but quickly dismissed the thought and kept moving until I was in the door at Bob's. I stood there for a few seconds, the scene in front of me so different from what I'd been exposed to for the last eighteen months. The bikes stood in rows and hung from a ceiling rack. It was as if I'd entered a cave with metal, rubber, and plastic stalagmites and stalactites, dripping and accreting.

I'd been reading cycling magazines in prison, drooling over the photos of racing bikes. I knew that I could probably find a bike at a police auction, one of the stolen, recovered, and unclaimed multitudes that a city the size of Boise churned up in a tidal flow of petty crime and indifference. I didn't want that. Mostly because I knew I wanted to race, but also because, I realize now, this was a fresh start for me and having something new, something without one person's history of loss, another's failed and flawed morality, was important.

After a few minutes of browsing, I found what I was looking for—a Giant TCR Composite 1 road bike, a full carbon fiber frame and fork model with Shimano Ultegra components. The price tag, one of those old-fashioned handwritten deals with the hole punch, the brown areola and the string, told the story—$1,800 for a leftover 2003 model. I knew that this was going to be a challenge, and the old Shane would have been figuring out a way to scam these guys. Test ride and dash? Grab and go? Instead, I prepared myself to do something I hadn't had much experience with for a good long while—telling someone the truth.

Eventually, I spoke with Dave and Vern, and I leveled with them. I was fresh out of jail and had my sights set on triathlon. The TCR Composite 1 was a great multipurpose road bike I could commute on and then convert into a time-trail bike, light and nimble and this leftover was my size. I couldn't pay for the whole thing right away, had a credit history that wasn't so much a history as a tragedy, but I could put some money down now and pay for the rest later? I need a bike to get around, and I'd even work around the place to do some sweat equity on the bike. What did they think?

If you don't know anything about the bike world, then this is necessary information. Most people who are into cycling, most small independent shops like the one Dave and Vern worked at, are owned and populated by people who don't vote Republican and don't take a hard line stance on law and order. So, when Dave looked at Vern, and then when Vern looked at Dave, and then when the two of them looked at me, and Dave asked, "You didn't kill anybody did you?" I was pretty sure he was joking. Just to be certain, I said, "No, sir. Drugs mostly."

They nodded and we worked something out. Who knows how things might have turned out if Bob's Bicycles hadn't helped me out immediately? Dave and Vern could have easily emasculated me and sent me tail tucked between my legs back out into the bright sunshine, squinting and grateful that the dazzling sunlight offered a plausible explanation for my tears. Instead, I walked out of there not only grateful but feeling like I was worthwhile, that somebody trusted me enough, was empathetic enough to give me a break. I didn't stop to question whether or not I deserved it, as I would most certainly have in the past, I just accepted what was offered and made good on the promises I made.

But mostly, I was so incredibly grateful. I could not have ever become what I've become without so many people lending a helping hand along the way. They sensed that I wasn't bullshitting them and they understood that they were giving me an opportunity to reclaim some essential part of me that I'd busted over time. And that bike was more than just a way to get around town. All those hours I would spend on it would give me the time I needed to really examine my past and to crystallize my future. You know what a catalyst is and how it sets in motion a reaction. That's what those guys did for me, and what dozens and dozens of people have done for me since.

I did not do this alone.

Truth was, I did feel like a kid with his first shiny new bicycle, and all those thoughts about how bad it was that I was a twenty-eight-year-old child-man, without a sign, essentially panhandling of a kind, had to be shunted aside. Pride goeth before the fall didn't mean a whole lot to me before, and as I wheeled that bike out of there, the ratchetlike clicking of its rear wheel keeping time with my heart, that sound echoed like the shopping cart beneath the overpass and those thoughts of who deserved what nearly overwhelmed me.

And it didn't help that when my mom swung by and picked me up, we headed immediately to the Boise Towne Plaza just across Cole Road from the Ada County Sheriff's Office and jail. She knew that I needed a job and that meant going into places where people might not be as accepting of my appearance as Dave and Vern had been. We shopped for clothes and then had lunch at the Cheesecake Factory. I hadn't eaten anything but prison food for so long, and to me the Cheesecake Factory was like dining at a Michelin Star–awarded haute cuisine establishment. I passed on the Beer Battered Fish and Chips, and inhaled Steak Diane and a salad, pausing only when my mom reached across the table and put her hand on my forearm, a gentle reminder that no one was going to take my food from me, I didn't have to finish and leave the dining room in some allotted time, and that the filet mignon was safe.

It was strange to be in a restaurant and not have to think about the check and how to get out of it. In Boise during my strung-out days, because I'd worked in so many restaurants and knew the drill, I'd perfected the art of the free meal. I'd call some place and make a bogus complaint about how I'd recently been in their Marie Callender's or wherever, and say that the meal was completely unsatisfactory. I'd listen to the manager's apology and if necessary press a bit more with veiled threats of complaints to higher-ups—this worked especially well with chains—until I got the golden ticket—a promise that a gift certificate of a free meal would be waiting for me the next time I came in. At its worst, my drug and alcohol habits were costing me as much as $400 a day, but my food costs were minimal. Whether I was scamming a restaurant or just walking out of a grocery store with a cart loaded with stuff, I knew how to not go hungry in America.

So, sitting there with my mom and talking to her about getting applications in all different kinds of places was a sketchy experience. I knew to avoid the places that I'd ripped off in the past, the thought of having to fess up about my criminal past was one thing, but knowing that I had, in addition to my drug arrests, a whole string of business burglary convictions as well, didn't bode well for me. I don't think my answer to the questions regarding my prior retail experience would be the one they were looking for. I might have been able to help them in loss prevention, since I'd done so much thieving from them in my previous life.

That's really not true. I wasn't the most sophisticated of criminals, working some computer inventory theft ring. Instead, as I walked through the mall with my mom, I recalled all the times I'd simply walked into some big box retailer and then just simply run out of there with merchandise. I was a big fan of CDs, DVDs, and especially video games. They were light enough that I wouldn't get slowed down too much by their heft, and they were easy enough to pass off to another smaller retailer who'd give me a few bucks per so that he could resell them. That meant quite a few shopping excursions per day for me, and it puzzles me now to think that I was so overweight given the highly aerobic nature of my "work" back then.

If the Cheesecake Factory lunch was deeply satisfying, then the first shower I'd taken in private in a year and a half was sublime decadence. For a long time, I stood under the soothing stream. It sounded like summer rain shower on a car roof. Eventually, I grew so tired, after the previous night's restlessness, that I sat down in the tub and only woke up when the water chilled. I woke up disoriented, wondering where I was, if someone had put me in that tub and turned on the cold water as an antidote for some heaviness I'd put on myself, a coke binge or having skated on the thin ice of a near heroin overdose like I had more than a few times in the past. The water turned cold and went from bracing to ball contracting, but still I sat there, letting my body remember what it was like to really feel, exposing those nerve endings to the full spectrum.

I knew my mother was next door in her room, likely wondering whether the hissing sound of the shower was supposed to be drowning out something more sinister. No drowning of any kind intended or needed. Spectral bits of that previous Shane would still haunt me, I'd catch him when I cast a quick sideward glance in a storefront window, and I was glad to see that he was a hazy outline, mostly opaque, fading. He'd left his mark all over that town and it shouldn't have ever surprised me when I bumped into him from time to time, but sometimes it did.

Looking for work over the course of the next few days, while my mom stuck around, had to be worked around a few other obligations. My days were full and that was good. I had AA meetings to attend— ninety of them in ninety days and at 8 miles per round-trip, I was going to rack up 720 miles, a daily check-in with my parole officer for the first two weeks at 18 miles round-trip that was another 252 miles to add to my cycling total.

My parole officer (PO) was a former army tank commander by the name of Tad Tadlock. (As a mark of my progress, I didn't even blink hard or give his name a second thought when he shared it with me.) I pissed in a cup each of those visits, noting that I had nothing to worry about, didn't have to consider buying the herbal golden seal as a masking agent for pot or any of the other inventive and inane ways that had once occupied my mind. I also had to attend a twice-weekly reintegration program for the first six weeks. Every Tuesday and Thursday night for that time, I had to sit through the program that the state of Idaho mandated for all newly released prisoners. I was grateful for the structure, though I didn't always like the group therapy nature of AA or the state program meetings.

It's worth mentioning that I made those reintegration meetings in cold, rain, and eventually snow as September turned into November. I rode on the highway, in the dark forty-five minutes in each direction. This is doing what it takes, whatever it takes to hang on to your freedom and toe the line, a reminder of all the hard work I'd failed to do in the past, I told myself as a means to keep going and get some warmth. During that time I heard every excuse from other parolees you can imagine for why they could not make it, or were late. You could always tell those who wanted a new life from those who were mired in the past.

I was glad that after only four days I could report to Mr. Tadlock, and don't even think of calling him Mr. Padlock I kept reminding myself, that I was gainfully employed. I had a few advantages to off-set my criminal history. I was white. I was college educated. I was the eagerest of beavers, and I was willing to do *any* kind of legitimate work to earn my keep. I'd hoped that my long history of working in the food business would pay off with a job waiting tables or cooking, but that didn't work out for me initially. I was able to get a job at the Boise Co-Op, a kind of Whole Foods grocery store. Having little or no money left, I jumped at the chance to swab their crockery while other more acceptable employees catered to the needs of the health-conscious and commerce-conscientious consumers. Seven dollars an hour wasn't bad coin compared to prison pay, but not nearly enough to pay back the money my mom and Bob's Bicycles had fronted me. A few days later, I made another major score, at least in this new life I was leading, when the owner at Smoky Mountain Pizzeria Grill offered me a similar gig at his place.

My mom had stuck around for those first few days, and I was really happy to have her there with me, but even more pleased when she left. I had no right to expect her support, especially since she vehemently disagreed with my decision to stick around Boise, and I fell all over myself thanking her. Not that that didn't grow old a bit, but I was more concerned about the need to wean myself off all the various forms of support and reintegration efforts I was receiving. I wasn't ready to quit cold turkey, but with the parole meetings, the state's shoehorning sessions, and my own fitness program, I felt ready to say good-bye to her.

We had been in contact sporadically since my days of exile from their home in Bloomington. During my ten years or so of wandering the desert of my increasing dependence on drugs and my criminality, that took me from living in Colorado, to Boise, to Hattiesburg, Mississippi, and then back to Boise, they'd often been there when I needed money for a lawyer, paying for a rehab program, or helping me out of some financial bind. During those seven years, from 1997 to 2004, Trent had graduated from high school, college, and was working in the computer software industry. He was someone else on whom I would come to rely in the coming years, with us flipping the older-brother-baby-brother script.

I wish I could say that the new version of me came out the box as a turnkey operation. That wasn't the case. I was able to say good-bye to Mom and really mean it when I told her that I was going to be okay because Brett Fox, one of my attorneys, allowed me to sleep on his couch for a while until I got enough cash saved up to rent a place of my own. Given that I was so busy, I wasn't around his place enough to really become a nuisance, but I know that it couldn't have been easy to have me there. This was another hand up when I needed it. Fox was always there for me. He took a big chance on letting me into his house given my history, but I rewarded him and myself by vowing not to stay there any longer than necessary, to not wear out my welcome as I'd done so frequently in the past.

I was in transition, making that critical move from con to ex-con to someone with convictions that he could point to and say of them, "These are the things I believe. These are the things that I've done. These are the things I'm going to do." As for the last of those, the one that was most prominent in my mind was to attempt to complete the Pacific Crest Half Ironman Distance Race in Sunriver, Oregon, on June 25, 2005, nine months after being released from prison. The irony of the connection between that time span and the average human gestation period wasn't lost on me. I was aware that a new Shane was developing, and in those early days it was a lot like I was in a protective womb. I wasn't prepared yet to expose myself to the full reality of life on the outs. That was going to take some time, but if I retained one trait, and there were others, from my previous self to my new self, it was my impatience. This time though I wasn't agonizing about how long it was going to take for that nearly instantaneous high to hit; instead, I was eager to make up for what I saw as the lost period of my late adolescence and my early adulthood. I was closing in on thirty, the time when most people are thinking about, or already have, settled down. I was just starting out and feeling very much the obvious reality that so many other people who would be competing in the Ironman races had a significant head start; they hadn't stumbled, fallen, and nearly taken themselves completely out of the running like I had.

always seemed to have trouble dealing with unstructured time. From the time I was a kid, to my days working various jobs in restaurants, even to my time as a student, I had far too much time on my hands. Some people are better about dealing with so-called free time than I was. I know people who've given up smoking and drinking, and they say that one of the toughest parts of that is not knowing what to do with their hands. They've spent so much time doing something related to smoking or drinking that without a physical object, a cigarette, a bottle or a glass, in their mitts, they feel like they've grown these new appendages and aren't sure how to operate them. I experienced that sensation all the time. Drugs were a way for me to feel like I was doing something and as a way to not do anything. Time loses meaning when you work irregular hours (or not at all) and are in an altered state most of the day and night.

I became keenly aware of all the time I'd wasted and spent wasted. If I was going to achieve my two goals—becoming a personal trainer and competing in the Ironman World Championship, I was going to have to work harder and occupy my time to a greater and better degree than I ever had before. I had lain awake many nights in prison worrying about what it was going to be like when I got out. I envisioned this vast void that I was going to have to fill in. Fortunately, the state of Idaho's Department of Corrections offered one solution in the form of requiring me to attend ninety Alcoholics Anonymous meetings in the first ninety days of my freedom. Also, for the first two weeks, I had to attend a reintegration class. While I had my doubts about the efficacy and necessity of the AA stuff for my situation, I at least had a safe place to go. The same was true with the class.

My twice weekly meetings with my parole officer held me accountable and made me keenly aware that negative consequences would result from a single failure of a urinalysis, an arrest, or even being spotted in the company of other felons, etc. I knew that I didn't want to go back to prison despite how contained that environment was and how much easier it would be to stay straight there. I appreciated my incarceration as an incubation period, but I didn't want to endure that again. I also knew the likelihood of me going back to jail was minimal. If I started drinking or using again, I was going to end up dead.

Those first three months were easier than I had anticipated. Between work and meetings, my days were fairly full. I also was doing my training on the road, pedaling my bike everywhere. That may sound like I was covering a whole lot of territory, but that's not really the case. It wasn't that I didn't want to have to ride or walk very far, but the less I spread out across Boise, the fewer reminders I'd have of people and places that I didn't need reminding of. Even working in the food and beverage industry again was fraught with potential danger, given the kinds of people that typically worked in that line. But the other option was to not be so busy, and no other job prospects were on the horizon. I was angling to get some work in the fitness world, but my earnestness and self-education weren't enough at that point to get people to buy into my vision for myself.

That said, my visits to Officer Tadlock were 18 miles round-trip. The AA meetings were an 8 miler, while commuting to work was a quick 2-mile or so jaunt. That didn't leave me a whole lot of time for other riding. In some ways the distances were irrelevant. I was sticking to a plan, and I was also enduring a lot. It's important to remember that I was released in September. Those first three months on the outs spanned the end of the year and the start of winter. Like a lot of mountainous regions, Boise and its weather are known for its variability and its winds. What I remember of those first few months, and on into the start of the year until the spring and summer of 2004, was that it seemed as if no matter which direction I was headed, I was going into the wind. Sometimes that wind was accompanied by various forms of semifrozen and frozen precipitation. I know the old line about the Eskimos and their many words for various forms of snow, but I learned a new one in the English language for a particularly torturous form of frozen moisture—*graupel*. Graupel is also known as "soft hail," but "soft" is a relative term. When you combine its weight with its falling velocity, the force of the wind, and the speed at which you're riding, soft hail can feel like being pelted with BBs.

The funny thing is, as much as those rides were painful in one sense, I took great joy in them. After being confined for as long as I had been, I was so damn lucky to be out in the world and moving freely. Not only that, I was lucky to be alive and I was loving life. I also took some pride in being out there on days when I knew that other athletes, hell, any sane person, might have opted for a bus or bumming a ride. I liked the idea that I was propelling myself on foot or in the saddle into my own future I was creating. Along with being grateful for the people who'd reached out and helped me, I was pleased that I was doing things on my own.

As much as I enjoyed riding around, I knew that I had to continue the strength and conditioning work I'd started in prison. There I'd dreamed about joining a gym and using all the equipment. The day after I was released from jail, I rode over to the Gold's Gym in the Park Center section of Boise. I'd heard good things about the place and its general manager. Andy Slagel was a great guy. He had been a lineman for the University of Washington football team. He was this mammoth bald-headed guy, really gregarious and I had to stare up at him as I gave him my post-prison spiel. He gave me a two-month membership there and later exchanged me doing clean up work around the place for use of the facilities. His giving me a leg up when I was broke and trying to claw my way into some stability and routine was enormous. He didn't have to and I could have found other places to work out, but with my desire to stay localized, having a gym nearby to work out in was critical.

Also, the facility was state of the art. It was by far the nicest place of its kind I'd ever seen. I thought that by associating myself with a place and a clientele of such a level, I'd be lifting myself up in turn. If I could get a job there, that would be saying something about me. For years I'd taken shit jobs and not really cared about the work, the facility, or much else for that matter. Aligning my interests and abilities with a positive location was an important part in my gaining some self-esteem, my sense that despite all I'd done in the past, the future was full of possibility.

Besides avoiding places in Boise that held bad memories for me, I also wanted to condense work and home geographically so I could optimize my time and effort this way. There are only 168 hours in a week: 56 are out the window after sleep—working two jobs cuts another 60–70 hours—and from there all my time went toward training. I needed to optimize my available time if I was going to make a go at this Ironman thing.

My strength training evolved a bit because no gym I know of has a 300-pound Samoan to do sheet pulls with. Instead, I used a combination of free weights and machines to do my workouts. I wasn't into segmenting my training into upper body one day and legs another. All of me needed the work, so I did a variety of exercises—bench press, lat pulldowns, leg presses, knee raises, and biceps curls. I also incorporated walking lunges, reveling in the fact that doing eight steps in one direction didn't have me bumping up against any walls.

The other reason that I'd wanted to work out at Gold's Gym was because it had a pool. It was a tiny 22.5 yarder that could induce vertigo in someone doing the kinds of mileage I would have to work up to with all those flip turns. Of course, at that stage, my only real frame of reference for a flip turn was that it was something you did if you got arrested and needed to turn state's evidence on someone else to save your own ass.

After getting those two months of free passes, I swam twice a week. Thrashed the water is probably a more appropriate description for what I was doing. I could only make one 22.5-meter length at a time before being completely gassed, so a flip turn wasn't even something I needed. I'd hang out there at the end of the pool for a few seconds, very definitely proving that I was a land mammal through and through, accustomed to easy access to oxygen. By the time October ended, I'd worked my way up to about 25 lengths in those first few months, consuming the same number of minutes in alternating thrashing and resting. I'd spend some of those rest moments clinging to tile horrified by the prospect of eventually having to swim much farther in open water if I wanted to complete my first Ironman. How the hell was I ever going to get there?

I stuck with it, and my endurance improved. I was able to silence my inner mammal, the one that was used to having constant access to an unlimited supply of oxygen. With my breathing getting easier, I was calmer in the water but I can't say that I was really getting fast. I had the goal of reaching 1,000 meters by the time November ended, and just after Thanksgiving, I did it. The gym was mostly empty, with people sleeping off their Thanksgiving overeating or out doing the Black Friday thing. I was the only one in the pool, and I remember how hard it was to keep track of the count of the number of lengths I had to do. I was working so hard, I couldn't remember if I was supposed to do 45 lengths to get to the magic 1,000-yard mark.

I continued to plough through the water, and did 46 lengths just to be safe. When I finally came to a stop and clung to the wall, my pulse was beating a drum solo in my ears. I took in great gasping breaths and the taste and smell of chlorine was sweet. As my breathing steadied and the riot in my ears subsided, I heard the gentle slapping of the water against the pool's sides and watched the lane lines bobbing a steadier EKG line. I clambered out of the pool and walked unsteadily toward the showers, a crazed smile of accomplishment splitting my face. Only later, while paddling a pizza out of the oven at work did I think about how I was only one quarter of the way there, that the full Ironman swimming distance was nearly 4,000 meters and my 1,000-meter journey had taken a woefully slow 30 minutes.

Still, I'd done what I'd set out to do.

I was excited about my progress, but I kept a lot of my emotions and my progress to myself. Partly, because my goal seemed a little ambitious, and I wanted to be sure I could do it. Also, I was sensitive and didn't want to expose myself to ridicule or doubt; I had enough of that.

internally. I did mention it to my parents who were supportive, but I sensed that (in the beginning) they thought it was probably just a phase that would pass. Other than my family (who eventually came to my first races), I didn't tell anyone unless they asked, and even then, I was short and measured in my responses. I was still very uncertain of myself at this time in my life.

From Gold's Gym, it was a quick few blocks to my early running grounds, a dirt path that ran along the Boise River. Generally, I headed south first to avoid the Boise State campus before heading east and the Greenbelt path that ran along the river. During those first early runs when I was fresh out of prison, I hadn't learned that while cotton was king, I didn't know that the full expression was that cotton was the king of chafing. Only when I'd get home, would the sting of hot water on abraded skin in very sensitive areas bring that point home. As my selection of proper running and cycling gear improved, so did the amount of time and distance I was able to cover. I was sneaking in three 35–45-minute runs per week. As I did when I was riding, I was ecstatic to just be out there and not running in the prison yard.

In hindsight, maybe I should have paid better attention to how I was running. I realize now that in those early days, my running form was either a mess or nonexistent. I was one of those runners who seem bent on bending the laws of physics and propulsion. I leaned backward, slightly leading with my hips. I scrunched my shoulders up around my neck. My stride was way too long. (Picture that cartoon "Keep on Truckin'" guy.) That, combined with my habit of coming down hard on my heels with a slam, was like me applying the brakes with each stride. Not only wasn't I biomechanically efficient, I was putting enormous stresses on joints and muscles.

Early on, I'd bought a copy of *Swim, Bike, Run* by Wes Hobson, Clark Campbell, and Mike Vickers, a triumvirate of triathlon experts.

Surprise, surprise, but I still lacked the impulse control to not dive headfirst into the training regimen they recommended, despite being twenty-nine, only just beginning to resemble anything near fit, possessing an only recently ex-smoker lung capacity, and a limping liver. Soon other parts of me had me limping along with shin splints, iliotibial band syndrome, and sacroiliac joint pain. The origins of which could be explained by one thing: maniacal overuse. As a result of my feeling that I had to hurry up and catch up, and my generally obsessive nature, I was *way* overdoing it with my running, swimming, and biking workouts, as well as any of the strength, plyometric, and other exercises I was doing. I did pay attention enough to the book's information to know that I couldn't do all three disciplines in one day, but I was tempted to when I wasn't enjoying my newfound habit—ice and Advil.

Still, as painful as my workouts were, they were a reminder that I was alive. Today I can clearly see that I was exceeding my physiological boundaries and that I had no coherent system for progressing my training loads. I was definitely in the "gut it out mode"—never taking the time to figure out how rest and recovery figured into things. Because I'd been abusing my body for so long, I had an unusually high tolerance for pain and as a result really overloaded my body.

In some ways, I wish that I could return to those early days when every time I went out for a run, the possibility of a fresh achievement was there for the taking. My pace wasn't as quick then as it is today. I was able to amble along at around 10 or 11 minutes a mile, but each time I went farther than I had ever gone before, I felt an amazing sense of self-satisfaction. Also, in a way that I hadn't since my first days in Boise back in October 1998, I appreciated the beauty of the place. Running along that river, heading out toward Lucky Peak State Park Reservoir, I did indeed feel very fortunate. I can't say that I loved every minute of those runs, in fact, they were frequently very, very painful, but when I thought about some of the things that I had done while there both the first and second time around, I really couldn't feel any other way. I was lucky to be alive, and at times the difference I felt between the thens and the now nearly overwhelmed me. The first time I came to Boise, I was hopeful that I could turn things around; the second I was certain that I was returning to a somewhat familiar place to die, like an elephant returning to some area of land to breathe its last. The third time is the charm according to the expression, and I was more determined than I'd ever been to finally end the cycle of addiction that had plagued me for so long.

In prison, staying clean—once I was through the detox phase—was relatively easy. Part of the reason why I wanted to live, work, and train in a relatively circumscribed area of town was to reduce the temptation level. I knew that I could walk into just about any convenience store, grocery store, neighborhood bar, and buy or order up a drink. I couldn't avoid those places completely. I also knew that I could walk or ride my bike to the places where all the rest of the junkies and I used to hang out and score whatever substance I wanted. I couldn't say for sure that the same dealers would be around, but I was pretty sure that most of them had come through unscathed—especially in comparison to their customers. The drug trade, like any business, is all about supply and demand. There was an endless supply of users in Boise. That fact surprised me back then, especially since I'd done my share of acquiring drugs in places like Chicago and New Orleans, and the community of abusers in Boise seemed more hard-core than anywhere else.

I know that in AA and other programs like Narcotics Anonymous, you keep track of the last time you used and mark that anniversary. I didn't fully buy into what AA had to say about the nature of addiction.

Sure, when I had to do that 90/90, I went along with the program and said, "Hi, my name is Shane and I'm an alcoholic." That didn't mean that talking about myself that way was the limit of who I was and what I wanted to become. My sense was that prefacing all my statements with, "Hi, my name is Shane and I am an alcoholic" in a meeting was a statement of worldview. Those were not the glasses I wanted to see the world through. I wanted and needed my identity to be something other than that of a diseased alcoholic or addict. I wanted to become more than an addict, so I didn't refer to myself as one. In my estimation, to do so would anchor me and limit my expansion as a human being. I didn't want to be weighted down with that label.

That's not to say that I was in denial. I knew what I'd done and how I'd behaved. I might just as easily have said, "Hi, my name is Shane, and I'm a suicide survivor." I didn't identify myself that way either, and I never really talked about the attempt with anyone to any great degree, but I did remember that date.

My previous experiences in Boise were nightmarish to the extreme. After my release I was living in a kind of dreamworld. A lot of the things that I'd hoped would come to pass were actually happening. I was employed. I was on the verge of getting an apartment. I was getting healthier, stronger, and was certainly more focused and disciplined than I'd ever been. As I ran along the Boise River on that day in October, I did something that I hadn't done yet. I stopped and took another route. Going another way hadn't been easy for me before; I didn't understand that it was simply a matter of choosing.

I had to learn that in case the street I pedaled down or pounded along was part of the interstitial tissue that connected where I was to where I had been. So what if my route along Ustick Road ran parallel to Victory Road and that the two never intersected? All I had to do was make the turn. I also knew it was important to never forget that once, just prior to my final arrest, at the cross streets of Swift and Westland, I'd held an unloaded gun to the head of a lazy-eyed Honduran named Chewie. I'd called him to get my piece for the day, knowing full well that I didn't have the cash to pay for it. So, when he showed up, I demanded all the money and all the drugs he and his partner had with them in their Jeep Cherokee. And when they handed me the cash and the bag of red, blue, and yellow heroin-filled balloons, I took off running faster than I'd done in any of those early training miles. The squeal of their vehicle's tires and the roar of its engine motivated me to pick up the pace. But the machine was faster than the man, and when my eyes locked on Chewie's just before his front fender clipped me and flipped me, we each had an instant to contemplate just how it was that our lives came to intersect in that moment when flesh and metal were about to collide.

What had each of us intended? I knew that I was so in need of drugs and money that I risked my liberty and my life by committing armed robbery. I was dead serious in my intent to end my troubled life in the same way that my troubles had begun.

For his part, Chewie let me know that he was willing to play a part in my death wish, ending my life for me in a way I hadn't really expected. He jammed the car in reverse, the piercing sound of its squealing tires like a starter's horn signaling the racers into action.

At the time I thought I was lucky to have tumbled into a blind alley, that by scrabbling to my feet and continuing my run until the fenced dead end turned my race into a leap of faith, I was somehow crossing the finish line victorious. I got away with the drugs and the cash that day. And a few days later, I walked into Grace's house with those groceries for her and her kids, feeling like somehow the worm had turned, that every dog has its day, and I was one happy little mutt.

Little did I know.

Little did I know.

And little did I know about what it might take for me to complete the June 2005 Pacific Crest Half Ironman one week more than two years removed from my suicide attempt. Fresh out of prison, with a few months to prepare, I had so much on my mind, I was only beginning to understand the importance of both looking ahead and looking behind. In racing, experts tell you that when you look back, you lose forward momentum and you send a signal to your opponents that you're weakening. Well, I think its human nature to see how much distance you've put between you and those behind you. It gives you perspective and it can either break your heart or give you courage. Sometimes, it's only when your heart is broken that you can find within you what you need to go on.

I knew that I couldn't avoid every spot in Boise where I'd had some bad experience—there were just too many of them. I also knew that I couldn't just run away from those memories and those difficult post–high school years prior to my final arrest and my final decision. I had to account for them, accept that as much as I wanted to believe that this new me was newly created, he was a product of that past. Many times when I trained, and often when I slept and dreamed, I did something that I didn't do when those events I was putting through this mental review process first took place. I took stock of them and thought about the process that had me spiraling downward. If I was going to climb out of the pit I'd dug when I finally nosedived into the ground, I absolutely had to examine carefully what had led to that leap in the Ada County Jail.

When I first started attending Boise State in 1998, I'd cut down on my drug consumption, but I'd been exposed to new ways to do them. Since high school, I'd been either snorting or smoking coke regularly. In Boise, I discovered the perverse pleasures of banging coke. As best as I can describe a coke high, it is like getting a major shot of adrenaline into your system. You become almost hyper aware as your senses sharpen, and injecting it brings those sensations on nearly instantaneously and much more intensely. The first time I injected the drug, I heard the *whoop, whoop, whoop* sound of a helicopter's rotors starting and that was a bit scary. So was the intensity of my sensory perceptions, and that's what coke does. It is an edgy high, and most of the time I was drinking alcohol, so the depressive effects of that took some of the edge off the coke.

The one and only time I banged cocaine without having alcohol or heroin in my system was in that bathroom at Boise State, in the nursing building. I was immediately hit with that blast of adrenaline and the sensory overload—imagine the intensity of the feeling you experience when someone startles you—only instead of that feeling lasting a few seconds, it just goes on and on. Well, in this case, I had overestimated the amount of coke I could handle, and I wobbled out of the stall, the rig still in my arm, the belt still around my biceps. When I woke up, I was in the hallway, a group of nursing students looking down at me, wondering, I imagine now, if I was part of some surprise practicum they needed to complete for their degree.

I think you can see why when I ran along the river, I avoided the campus area.

Boise also was where I met Isaac. Like me, he was a cook at Louie's Pizza. He was a punk rocker and along with his girlfriend, Nancy, they'd been all around the country, following their favorite band, Snot, until they'd settled in Boise for a while. They'd work signs and do other things to save up some cash and then just move on. It was during one of those periods, in 1998, when I first got to know them. Nancy and Isaac didn't turn me onto heroin. I'd snorted it several times going all the way back to my time in Bloomington, but they were the ones who introduced me to the joys of banging heroin. I knew, even back in Bloomington, that heroin had captivated me above all the other temptresses I had sampled. It just tripped a wire with me—I fell in love with its depth and warmth. From those earliest days—it was always in the back of my mind. Somehow I knew it would be my undoing years before it was.

Just as my first drinks of alcohol initiated a love affair with the warm sensation it produced, so did my first experience injecting heroin. Isaac had encouraged me, saying that if I was going to do heroin at all, the *only* way to do it was through a needle. One of the reasons why I hadn't done much injecting back in Illinois, along with my violated vow to not cross that line, was the availability of needles. Back there, you needed, in a sense, a prescription proving that you were a diabetic who needed to use hypodermic needles. In Idaho, that wasn't the case. As a result, the key part of your works was readily available.

Isaac's urging to just try it at least once, produced such an immediate, long-lasting, and pleasant high that lasted nearly forty-eight hours, I went back to his place as soon as the effects began to wane and told him I wanted another. He was willing to oblige. From that point forward, with a brief intermission in Mississippi when prescription drugs like Vikes and OxyContin, which produced a similar kind of high and gave my collapsed veins a rest, heroin dominated me.

Injecting heroin had a kind of capillary action effect on me. My mind and will were powerless to prevent its flow into me. It was also as if those molecules that comprised heroin had the power to transform me. Over time, I felt far less empathetic than I had before, particularly when I was "ill," when I needed to get well and had to steal in order to get the money I needed to buy that marvelous feeling of false well-being that heroin produced.

If injecting cocaine made me feel hyper aware and paranoid, then heroin made me feel hyper well, an opioid euphoria unmatched by anything I had ever tried before. Isaac schooled me well, cooked for me the first few times, and then turned me loose while the drug turned me inside out and upside down. I knew that no matter how shitty I felt, whether because I was hung over, depressed, stressed, anxious, angry, or any combination thereof, relief was just a phone call away.

In the spring of 1999, staff at Boise State had contacted my parents, on top of that, random bills for ambulance services when I'd overdosed a couple of times in Boise and had refused to pay the charges had bounced to Bloomington. I was given another one of those this-is-your-last-chance kind of speeches over the phone. I must have not sounded the right note of contrition or conscious awareness, because my parents organized a surprise intervention with John Southworth. They picked me up under the guise of "taking me to breakfast." I was extremely high, as I had just done the first dose of the day around 9:00 a.m. I went to the intervention and refused the help. I was fine, and I was not ready, I told them. I was in college and this was just what people did.

Truth was, I was well beyond any acceptable form of partying. The line is drawn at inhalation of substances. My arms were pincushions. They were black and blue. They usually hurt. Once you start using needles, the game changes. Once you wake up to a drink, the game changes. It was a black time in my life. Had I not gone to Mississippi shortly after an initial refusal, I wouldn't have lasted long.

And just so you understand, Boise may seem to be the most benign of places, but the peek behind the blue-sky mountain valley scrim revealed a place as sinister as anything I'd seen. I'd hung out on the South Side of Chicago, copped dope in New Orleans' 9th Ward, and they had nothing on that town. Just like the paper mills that bear its name, this was a place that could cut you down, strip you of your bark, and grind you into pulp.

I had been so right to tell myself to not ever cross the line to use needles. I had been so wrong to make that move. I don't know if I can adequately convey the evil and true-to-form nature of using needles. I injected cocaine and heroin daily. My abscesses oozed. I overdosed and cursed the doctors who brought me back, the friends and strangers who phoned me in.

There is no such thing as recreational injection. It is the end of the line—and it is not something that normal "well-adjusted" people find themselves doing. I was in a very dark place, an underworld, a place that few ever ascend from.

The act of injecting yourself with a needle is an act of violence, of penetration, of literally and figuratively fucking yourself with a substance so vile and so beguiling, so seductive and so destructive.

The intervention failed. I made them see a light that even I couldn't make out.

However, within about three months after this refusal I called my parents from jail to take them up on their offer.

I was so strung out on cocaine and heroin, and I had warrants out for my arrest for grand theft and driving on a suspended license. I was accused of stealing firearms (antiques) from the guys I had rented a room with. This was probably the only crime I was ever accused of that I truly did not commit. I knew it had to be one of the junkies that I had associated with at the time—most of whom are dead now by the way.

I began hallucinating from all the cocaine I had been injecting, so, I checked into a Boise rehab to seek refuge from the law. Instead, the police pulled me out and took me into custody. From there I called my parents and asked if I could still do the rehab they wanted me to do. Playing the I-want-to-go-to-rehab card, along with my parents' assurance that I was going to leave the state, got me out of jail. In early May 1999, Dad came to Boise and dragged me out of there. I was so addicted to heroin, that I packed up knowing that I was heading to rehab in Hattiesburg, Mississippi, and would need to make this easier on myself. I grabbed a bunch of needles and what was left of my stash. On the way to rehab, I used rest stops as a chance to shoot up in the stalls of gas stations. And when I ran out of the drug, I pounded the old cotton balls I'd previously used in cooking, rehydrating them and injecting the dirty water they excreted hoping they retained some trace of my beloved heroin in them. Imagine being so hooked on food that you washed a plate that once held a hamburger with a sponge, squeezed the liquid out of that sponge into a glass and hoping that beverage would fill the void in your gut, give up some infinitely small taste of that beef patty and fixings.

I knew on one level that no drug was going to enter into my system, but I had become so needle-phyllic, so habituated to piercing my skin and veins, that I had to inject something, anything, hoping that somehow that act of penetration would be enough.

That's how desperate I became as the miles rolled underneath us and I sat in the car knowing that Hattiesburg may as well have been Hades.

As it turned out, the time I spent in Pine Grove from May 1999 to early July 1999 was a kind of blessing in disguise. I went through the first part of the detox program and was well into the second phase, appropriately enough called, the Next Step program, when I did what I'd always done. In Next Step, we lived in dorms and could, more or less, leave the facility at our discretion. Somehow, I wound up in a Ford Explorer with four other guys in the program; our intention was to break out of the routine of eating the rehab center's food. A Chinese restaurant beckoned. A bad meal morphed into a night of drinking, and when, because the others were such lightweights, I had to do the driving home, proud of the fact that I still had the skills to consume mightily and show fewer ill effects than my rehabbers even after an eight-week layoff, kind of like being able to hit a home run in your first spring training at bat, I also experienced that familiar, this-isn't-going-to-end-well feeling that had become a near constant in my life. We were caught, one of the four midvomiting, and were booted out of the program.

I don't know exactly what happened that night that made me decide to drink again. Maybe it was the fact that the other four were, maybe it was that to me my alcohol consumption had always been so benign in comparison to my drug intake (compare running around with an ashtray up your ass to robbing various retail outlets) or that I was fearful of what it would mean for me to be clean and sober and have to resume my life with nothing I could think of to fill the void that abstinence would create, but I caved in. The consequences weren't particularly severe at first.

My parents were disgusted, so asking them for money wasn't possible, but I did manage to find a job, again at a restaurant, this time one called Chesterfield's, and I did enroll at the University of Southern Mississippi (USM). My parents and John the Interventionist had chosen Pine Grove because of its location—it was in Southern Mississippi, far away from old friends and places where my habits had grown so worse.

And for the first six months after being bounced from Pine Grove, I didn't relapse. Not completely of course. I did drink, but I found a new crowd to associate with, undergraduates like me, years younger than my twenty-three going on twenty-four. That first semester I was at USM, I served as a kind of novelty cautionary tale for my new friends. Having been in rehab earned me a weird kind of cachet with them. I was worldly, a man who'd been there and done things they had never even dreamed of. They were amazed by how much I could drink, sometimes appalled, and I became very good friends with some of them. I was back to that likable guy, the one who if he would only just apply himself, would turn out okay. As I said, Hattiesburg was my introduction to the world of prescription pharmaceuticals, which inexorably led to me being introduced to people who also happened to be friends with two substances with whom I had a somewhat ambivalent relationship—cocaine and crack.

Primarily, I look at that time as my prescription phase, and inevitably, in the spring of 2002, I was arrested for altering/forging prescriptions for OxyContin, got the felony reduced to a misdemeanor known in those parts as "false pretense." I had by that time, managed to graduate from USM, with a degree in history, but was still waiting tables in a restaurant. New Orleans was a short drive away, and there I met a crack dealer named Donny who became a "friend" to the tune of me basically turning over my paychecks to him to keep me supplied.

Supply side economics the Niemeyer way resulted in me then

having to start altering customers' credit card slips, adding a few bucks here and there to my tips. It was a zero-sum game if there ever was one, until I got evicted from my apartment for nonpayment of rent, lived in a buddy's VW van, freezing my ass off in the cold nights in the Deep South that no one had ever told me about. My manager at Chesterfield's, a self-identified coon-ass Louisianan named William Littlejohn had to fire me when he caught on, and the whole thing just kept spiraling down the drain, and just before the last belch-suck sound signaling that I was for sure sewer bound, I reached out to a buddy back in Boise, and he said, "Come on up, I got a place you can crash for as long as you need it."

And the pattern had once again repeated itself, and the remorseless entropy of the data and the messages I'd been receiving for the past ten or so years, took hold and I escaped one near lack of heat death down south, only to dabble in another kind of death up north, the polar extremes of my debased life, the leaking energy of my systematic self-debasement pointing toward one thing.

In 2002, strung out and broke, I decided to return to Boise.

I wasn't so much going to Boise to be back home but to die. How long that would take depended on a variety of factors, but I knew I was bound to do it. The numbers didn't lie.

I sat on that plane trying to recall all the names of those I'd known, among them a few I'd loved like brothers, who'd lost their lives to drugs and alcohol. I wondered, when roll call was made, who'd answer for me, who'd raise a hand and in the grandest cosmic irony of it all, say for me, "Here."

Loveland? There.

Mission Viejo? There.

Bloomington? There.

Fort Collins? There.

Boise? There.

Hattiesburg? There. *There* were all the places I'd tried and failed, quit or caved in.

That was the roll call that mattered to me when I first slogged through those training miles on foot and on my bike, when I thrashed through the chlorinated waters of the pool. I couldn't outswim or outrun those days and those places. I had to account for them though. If carrying those memories around with me was a kind of baggage, then so be it. I'd never be able to think of those shitty days as emblems of honor, as scars earned in war, but to forget them completely would be to deny who I am. I didn't dwell on those moments for long, but I did, ironically enough, become a user again. Those memories helped build me up along the way. Sometimes we motivate ourselves by thinking of what we want to become. Sometimes we motivate ourselves by thinking about who we don't ever want to be again. Everything we do is part of who we are. How we chose to use those memories, to motivate or to submit is entirely up to us. It's both as simple and as complicated as making a choice.

With the Pacific Crest triathlon in front of me and all those lost years behind me, I knew that there was no going back, no turning around, no stopping halfway. Go all the way had been my modus operandi for a long time. Trying to kill myself was just one form of that. Some force had helped me turn around from that dark and bleak moment. I was back in control, grateful for the nudge the other way.

SEVEN

When I look back on those early days just out of prison and my training for the Pacific Crest, I'm amazed that I even made it to the starting line let alone the finish line. Old habits are hard to break, and though I'd broken the addiction cycle, I still was battling with being my own worst enemy. Like most people, I faced obstacles in order to achieve my goals. Like most people, many of those obstacles were ones that I put in front of myself. Part of my drug use was a means to numb myself from the pain and self-loathing that I felt. Just because I stopped using and got released from jail didn't mean that I was instantly in love with myself. Yes, I was grateful, and yes, I loved my freedom, but I sure as hell didn't like myself very much.

Even as the miles of swimming, running, and cycling added up, I still hated myself for the abuse I'd heaped on my family and essentially all of society. In the early days, I used that inner-directed anger as a means to propel myself through my training. It became the tool

I used to process those very dark emotions. In prison, my workouts served a similar purpose. I was still a very angry young man, and if it weren't for my workouts, I'm sure that I would have turned my anger on my fellow inmates—people who I tolerated but whose behaviors and lack of vision for themselves made me think of most of them as idiots. I knew that this was definitely the pot calling the kettle black, but I didn't have my shit together in enough ways to really manage the proper perspective. I wasn't the just recently sober individual preaching to others; I was seething internally rather than outwardly.

As much as I'd read Krishnamurti and others who'd helped me shape a different worldview and establish goals for myself, I was still very much a work in progress. I was always a very impatient person, so when it came to my training, I had some idea of how to go about it, but my lack of impulse control nearly did me in. For example, five weeks out of prison, I entered a local running race called the Table Rock Challenge.

A table rock is a name frequently given to a geological formation that rises up and then has a large flat section at its top. In Boise, the Table Rock is easily accessible because it's located near downtown and is a favorite "easy" hike. The Table Rock Challenge is an out-and-back race of 9 miles. By that point in my training, in early September 2004, I hadn't come anywhere near achieving that distance. I had no business trying to run 9 miles—especially since the first 4.5 were all uphill and the second were all downhill. To be honest, the downhill was the most painful part for me. I thought of stopping a bunch of times, but I gutted it out.

I felt a real sense of accomplishment when I crossed the finish line, but I paid the price for the next week or so. I hobbled around, but I didn't skip a single workout. I was so fearful that if I skipped a day,

I'd fall farther behind and risk sliding down that slippery slope to giving up entirely. I'd experienced so much failure in my life that I didn't really know what to do with any kind of success.

The thing about living in the Mountain West is that there are few places that you can train that are flat. That means lots of ups and downs. Some gradual. Some severe. It seems appropriate then that it was in that area of the country where I began my training and racing. To be honest, I didn't really have a choice. I didn't have a car. I didn't have a driver's license. As part of my parole, I wasn't allowed to leave the state without going through a paper trail of permission seeking. As a result I stuck to races in and near Boise. I'd heard people at the gym talking about the Race to Robie Creek, a half marathon whose slogan is "The Toughest Race in the Northwest." Of course, I had to enter it. I figured that it was only 4-plus miles longer than the Table Rock gig, and I'd survived that, and I would be another six months further along in my training by the time the race was held.

I registered in February and kicked up my training. The race started at an elevation of 2,725 feet. The summit, about 8.5 miles from the start, topped out at 4,797 feet. For each mile, the racers gained 244 feet in elevation. To put that in perspective, that's approximately 20–24 stories. Imagine climbing that many sets of stairs.

Those first 8.5 miles were a killer, and I really struggled along. I had no notion of what it meant to taper before a race, so I'd been doing my usual workload and I began the race on tired legs. By the time I got to the top, well behind almost the entire field, my legs were shredded. I mistakenly thought that the worst part was over, but the final 5 miles was all downhill and pretty severely so. That was even tougher on my legs as I tried to keep gravity from doing its thing and hurtling me down the road and trail. Worse still, I was so far behind that the aid stations were out of water or already closed by the time I got to them. I didn't think to carry fluids with me, so I was dehydrated as well as exhausted. I had long since stopped running, and was walking along with my thumb out hoping to hitch a ride to the finish. I was thoroughly demoralized.

I was a newbie to the world of endurance sports, but I was an eager student. I read a lot about what top-flight athletes did in their training and figured that was what I should do. I wasn't systematic about it all. I didn't so much look at training as a progression, but as a full-on charge to the top. No pacing for me. If I read (as I did) that the average training volume for athletes prepping for Kona and the Iron-man World Championship was 280 miles per week on the bike, 50 miles running, and seven days per week in the pool swimming, then goddamnit, that's what I was going to do.

I set out to ride 300 miles (more is better) and run that 50-mile total. I'd reach those goals, but I was so overtraining and breaking down my muscles, not allowing them the time to recover, that I was going so slow, shuffling more than running, and always in pain. I didn't understand that those numbers were part of those athlete's training cycle—they didn't do that kind of mileage and that kind of intensity all year long. Also, they were professionals in the sport, had spent years training themselves to attain that peak level of fitness—I was nowhere near their ability level. My body broke down a lot in those early years of training, but my mind and my spirit grew strong.

I look back on those days now and shake my head at my ignorance, but for me, I had to learn things the hard way. I had to figure out what my limitations were. I had this kind of romanticized ideal about my training, the whole no pain/no gain mentality. Despite how badly things went for me at the Race to Robie Creek and how much pain I was in, I was receiving mixed signals. The pain seemed to be doing me some good. I did my first 40-mile bike ride on a cold and gray late November afternoon. Snow began to fall and sting my eyes—I couldn't afford glasses—but I kept going. Most other athletes would have said it was time to put the bike up on the trainer and do the training indoors. I didn't have a trainer, so I had no choice. I could barely dismount the bike when I got back home, and the pinprick pain of my thawing feet is something that I can still feel today. After that 40 miler, I was so chilled that it took two hot showers (I had to let the hot water heater refill after the first one) and a nap smothered beneath every towel, blanket, and bit of clothing I had, to finally thaw myself.

I was learning something not just about self-discipline but also about delayed gratification. In early June of 2005, I did a training ride with a few local cyclists. Jeff Gasser, Tad Hamilton, and Justin Rose were among the best of Boise. It was hot as hell and a dry high desert wind kicked up. We were supposed to go 80 miles that day, farther by 10 than I'd ever gone before. It was tough, but I kept pace with them for most of the ride. I took my turns riding at the front of the pace line, though we weren't formally organized in any way to do that. I put myself in the hurt locker for much of the ride, and before I knew it, we were at 55 miles, headed back toward Boise, and I was feeling pretty good. At that point in the ride, we were faced with a 3–4-mile climb up of Garden Valley. I'd been sitting in for much of the ride, and as we began that climb, I went to the front and by the end of that uphill stretch, I'd gapped them a bit.

I didn't know if I'd burned up too much energy and they were conserving it for the remaining 15 or so miles, but just looking at them, I could tell that they were gassed. I also realized that if I was hurting and they were hurting, then it was just a question of who was willing to pay the price and gut it out. Even though these guys were much more fit than I was, that didn't mean that they were invulnerable to pain, that this was ever going to get to the point where it was easy and pain free.

And I did pay a price for that all-out effort on the climb. Once we summitted and began the descent, I was overwhelmed by thirst and hunger. My legs began to cramp horribly. I'd look down at my quadriceps and see them twitching, not from the road's vibration but my own stupidity about hydration and nutrition. Fortunately, we had an 8–10-mile downhill stretch to look forward to. At the bottom of that, I knew there was a Chevron gas station mini-mart. It was the proverbial oasis in the desert for me, and as the thermal heat waves rising from the pavement urged me toward it, I felt a kind of preconsumption euphoria setting in. I was barely able to click out of my pedals, and did my impression of a drunken woman in high heels as I skittered into the mini-mart. Eighteen dollars poorer, I came out with a two-liter bottle of Coke, a box of donuts, and assorted candy bars.

I knew better than to sit down, so I stood there gorging myself and guzzling. I did have the good sense to buy water as well. Today, I know that all those high glycemic inflammatory foods were not what I should have been consuming, but back then I didn't really care about nutrition very much. I'd given up the greatest pleasures in my life—drugs and alcohol—and I wasn't about to do without the foods I wanted. It was the only thing I could consume guilt free and with the only concern being how much enjoyment I got out of it. I ate to celebrate my achievements—I ran 10 miles, then I deserved a cheeseburger and fries. I swam a mile, so eating an entire family-sized pizza the size of a life preserver was well earned. I ate when I was bored. I ate when I was bummed out. Food was the last vestige of my old life, a crutch I used to prop myself up.

Like most people, I ate to fuel my emotions and not my body. My

P.F. Chang's phase is a good example of that. I ate there repeatedly not because its balance of low-fat protein, vegetables, and rice was good for me, but because they offered the Great Wall of Chocolate as a dessert.

I hadn't really studied nutrition at all to that point so I didn't realize what I was putting into my body was only intensifying the negative effects of overtraining. With overuse of my muscles and tendons, I was creating inflammation. The foods I was eating, high in saturated fats and various simple sugars, also caused systemic inflammation. I was putting additional stress on my already assaulted immune, endocrine, and neuromuscular systems. It was no wonder that I was always in pain or on the verge of being ill.

It took a long time for me to get that component of my training under control. I used to assuage my guilty conscience by telling myself that the Clif Bar that I ate for breakfast every morning for nearly three years straight was good nutritionally. The holy triumvirate of peanut butter, oatmeal raisin, and chocolate chip, weren't going to save my soul or my body, but those flavors were the mainstay of my Clif addiction.

Even when I was training and racing, hydration and nutrition remained the weakest parts of my game. I never took in enough fluids or foods to perform optimally. Maybe that was my subconscious reaction to having spent the first nearly three decades of my life overdoing my intake of bad things. All I know is that I bonked on more than one training ride or run and in a bunch of races.

One particularly bad experience had me thinking of my days of homelessness. I was doing a 40 miler on the bike out to a town called Emmett. Again, it was a very warm day, and I was on the side of the road, after having weaved unsteadily along for a few miles, light-headed and on the verge of puking. Of course, I didn't have any money with me, but I was desperate. In the old days, I would have gone in and dashed out with a twelver of PBR or whatever beer I wanted. Instead, this time I talked the manager into letting me have a gallon of water and three Snickers bars on the come. He agreed and I made it home. The next time through, I paid him off.

That may not sound like a milestone in someone's personal development, but for me it was. In the past, I had talked people into giving me all kinds of things, had stolen even more, without any real remorse and certainly no intention to ever pay anyone back for what I'd begged, borrowed, or stolen. I felt as good about myself for returning to that gas station and paying the guy back as I did about some of my achievements on the road and in the pool.

As the Pacific Crest Half Ironman loomed, I continued my maniacal training regimen. When I went out for a run, I always had in the back of my mind that I had to do those 6 miles faster than the previous time I'd run. I had no concept of periodization and the importance of rest. Even on my long run on weekends, I still approached it as if every time out had to be faster than the previous one. The same was true in the pool. I was making some real advances, and I'd also moved on to a different Gold's Gym in downtown Boise that had a 25-meter pool. The gym was on the fifth floor of the Bank of America building, and the view from the pool area was spectacular, looking out to the mountains and over the town.

I did a lot of observing of the good swimmers and saw that they frequently trained with aides—Styrofoam buoys that they used to float their legs while they propelled themselves solely with their arms. They also often used flippers on their feet and paddles on their hands. At first I wondered why the hell they would do that, but I imitated them. It felt like cheating at first—the paddles made it easier to grab larger volumes of water and therefore go faster.

Eventually I talked with a couple of the better swimmers, in particular a guy a few years older than me. Jeff had swum competitively in college and he was fine with informally coaching me. He helped refine my form, in particular letting me know how important the hips were to good propulsion, and with his help I progressed.

I could now regularly do 45–60-minute sessions. A popular test of your swimming proficiency is to do 1,000 meters for time. I did that regularly and kept track of every second it took. Prior to that June race I'd targeted, I'd managed to get my time down to 21 minutes in March. By May, I'd whittled another 2 minutes from that—still slow, still in a pool and not in open water, but atleast it was measurable progress. I was also able to get my 50-meter reps down to about 50 seconds, and my 100-meter time down to 1:45 on my best days. I swam alone, and that's always hard because you don't have anyone else to motivate you, but I still was pleased with how I was advancing. Swimming is a very complex and technique-driven activity and progress is always slow. I was learning, and that was the important thing.

I was smart enough to know that I had to do some open-water swimming.

By this time I'd become friends with Kenny McDaniel. Kenny was a good runner who'd competed in high school in cross-country. We worked together at Gold's and we got along well. He'd run for a year at Boise State—one of the hotbeds of collegiate cross-country and track and a place that attracted a lot of runners from foreign countries—so he was considerably faster than me. He ran with me on his "easy" days—a concept that he explained to me and I took a while to put into practice—and I credit him with really improving my running. I started to slow down and lengthen my runs.

He was good company, and having someone to run with kept me going and kept my mind from wandering too much into I-want-to-stop land. Also, Kenny told me that if I couldn't talk and run at the same time on those training runs, I was putting out too much effort and should slow down.

At the time he was just running, but I think I piqued his interest in triathlon. Over time he saw me training in the pool and riding in and out of the gym all the time. He was a much faster runner than I so I tagged along with him a few times per week. Mostly I tried to stick with him and used his form as a model that I tried to integrate into my own form. He ran so smoothly, like a deer it seemed, he was so light on his feet.

From what I'd read, and what I could imagine based on my experience boarding the Pacific, open-water swimming was another animal entirely. I couldn't do anything to prepare myself for what it was going to be like swimming with a bunch of other people who were competing for the same buoy line at the same time. I knew that was going to be outright scary, but at least I could get into open water. Kenny and I used to go to the Clocktower pond in Boise and spent even more time in the Lucky Peak Reservoir in the foothills east of the city.

Lucky Peak was a beautiful spot to swim, but in April and May that water was very cold. I'd worn a wet suit before, but never to just swim. The first time I put one on to swim was in early May at Lucky Peak. I felt like I had no range of motion, that I was back in that security blanket post-suicide. I started to panic, thinking that I'd get in the water and not be able to move freely enough to stay afloat. Add to that the frigid water, and I stood on the bank of the reservoir shivering and straining against that neoprene wondering just what in the hell I'd gotten myself into. I tentatively stepped into the water a few times, felt the slime-slick rocks beneath my feet and the cold of the water and retreated.

Kenny was of the all-at-once-is-best school, so when I gathered up enough courage, I jumped in. The shock of the water paralyzed me. Some primitive lizard brain physiological response kicked in and I couldn't breathe. I remember thinking about what that response was originally designed to do—how it must have been a way to save us humans when put in a foreign and threatening environment. How the hell then was I ever going to get comfortable in the water? Another physiological response helped. Once our entire bodies were in the water, including our heads and faces, all our flesh went numb. I didn't feel the cold. I didn't feel anything. In time, I'd get accustomed to that sensation. I was learning how to deal with all levels and varieties of pain. Often we fear pain because it is a kind of unknown, unfamiliar sensation. I'd experienced so many varieties of it in so many different environments, that I could apply the lessons I'd learned as a drug addict to help me through.

I wish I could say the same about the attention I paid to what I put in my body. Nearly fainting during that ride to Emmett wasn't the only time I bonked that badly. I can still remember how my vision swam and my head spun on a 40-mile ride up toward the Bogus Basin. I had the good sense to get off the bike before I wandered into traffic and got flattened. I lay there on the side of the road alongside my bike, the whine and drone of the semitrailers preceding the gusts of wind that spun my pedals and cooled me. I looked at my watch and it was 1:24 in the afternoon. The next time I opened my eyes it was 1:47 p.m. I'd passed out for that long. I managed to ride back down toward town, found another gas station, and once again crammed in as many calories as I could. I had a rudimentary understanding of what a blood sugar level was, but never applied that to my training. I lived with the fear of running out of gas, but I didn't, for a long time, do what was necessary to prevent that fear from being realized.

I don't know if I understood this at the time, but maybe I was so accustomed to being fearful after I was released from prison that that was my normal state. Maybe I didn't want to get too comfortable. Comfort might have led me back to those days when I was in constant danger but was so addicted to drugs that I'd risk anything to get them. In my addict days, I was a curious mixture of hypervigilant and apathetic. I wasn't so much afraid of dying or arrest as I was feeling the effects of withdrawal and being sober.

Coming out of prison, I was terrified of failure, of going back to abusing drugs. In the beginning, even in prison, when other inmates were using and I refused, I did feel awkward. It was like I was rejecting them and putting myself on the outside. I was always a very social person, and being an outcast in a group that's already been ostracized by the larger society, and not having that bond of being a part of the band of brothers who do drugs made me feel rootless. A few times other inmates gave me shit and called me a pussy for not using, but for the most part I was left alone. I remember one occasion sitting in the cellblock playing spades for hours with several of my fellow inmates while they got shitfaced on some hooch they'd made from fermented fruit. I firmly declined their offer.

When I was first out of prison, I knew that my newly constructed will wasn't firmly enough set to withstand too much temptation. In some ways, working at the Boise Co-Op and at Smoky Mountain Pizzeria wasn't the best idea. However, since I'd had a long string of food-service–related jobs, they were about the best that I could do. Both places served booze, and both had employees who I would learn were stoners and drinkers. I was never a very confident person, and that was especially true after my release. I knew that if I started to hang around with the people who did drugs and drank, I was likely to cave. For that reason, I did my work and went home. In prison, I was plagued by dreams of needles and spoons and beers and liquor. I'd woken up sweating and disoriented, cursing myself for having used again. Those dreams intensified the closer I got to release, but as my physical fitness level increased, those dreams lessened in frequency.

Eventually, I was able to loosen up a bit, get to know some of my coworkers and even go out to bars or to restaurants with them. I still suffered from those hunger pangs and the what the fuck do I do with my-hands-and-mouth fits. I took to asking for straws. As the night progressed, I'd have a pile of straws near me, tied up in knots, and I'd down an endless stream of cola and water. I'd always thought that I had to impress women by showing them how much I could consume and how crazy I could get. Again, that lack of confidence in myself led me to do stupid things. Fortunately, as I accomplished more in my training and felt better about myself as a person for staying out of trouble and not drinking and using, I realized these women didn't need to be impressed with that whacked-out version of me. I was okay as I was. People liked me when I was sober, and that was a revelation.

I have to admit that in this sense, I was a VERY late bloomer. I was finally starting to mature a bit and not still living in that high school daze when you think that being able to pound the most beers and all the rest of that stupidity was a way to earn accolades and get laid. I also cultivated an air of mystery that didn't hurt my chances with women. I was a bit older than most of the people I worked with and socialized with. I didn't tell anyone about my past other than a few facts about places I'd lived and worked. I wasn't about to lay it all out for anyone, both because I thought that might lower their view of me, and because I didn't want the sympathy vote from anybody. I wanted them to know, like, and accept the current version of me.

Also, because I was now spending a lot of my time at the gym, I was meeting people who were really into competitive running, cycling, and other sports. These people took care of their bodies and while they had an occasional drink, none of them took drugs. Limiting my exposure to people who could negatively influence me was crucial to my success at maintaining my sobriety. All of these fit people helped inspire me and also instructed me to one degree or another.

At Gold's I met and befriended Lynne and Gary Stott, a husband and wife, who were among the better athletes in Boise. Lynne had competed in the Seoul Olympic games in the summer of 1988 in the 10-kilometer race (she'd also run a very impressive time of 2:30 in the marathon) but had turned to cycling. I rode with them 2–3 times a week. They took me on my first mountain bike ride, which was a revelation since I'd been riding exclusively on the roads, and with them, I did my first 50 miler.

Gary was a realtor and Lynne worked at home designing and administrating Web sites. They were in their midforties, totally laid back and accepting. They took me in like family and I came and went through their house as I pleased. This was significant—they trusted me. In those early days I always felt awkward when someone trusted me. Gary and Lynne provided me with lots of insight into the necessity of ingesting calories, and the importance of rest. Lynne was an Olympian. I used to talk to her all the time to glean any insight I could into the requisites for success as an athlete. At the time, I was lifting intensely four days a week and she told me that I couldn't do it all full tilt or the lifts would eat into my endurance training. I would need to change their structure and intensity.

She also told me about how she wished she had rested more as an athlete, and since she didn't, she never raced to her potential (took me a long time to learn that lesson). I rode more with Lynne, because Gary had to work and was training for a 100-mile run at the time. Lynne could get away during the day.

We were an odd pairing because I was an ex-con and they were grounded, older, and had their shit together, but they were awesome people who took me under their wing treating me like family. They even taught me how to clean and do simple repairs to my bike. Lynne was a pro mountain biker, the two of them taught me how to ride a mountain bike FAST downhill—how to corner and look down the trail. Eventually we would rip downhill and the mountain bike was an awesome way to train in the foothills. I came to LOVE riding the mountain bike and it was welcome relief from road monotony. They taught me to hold back in my training and some days ride easier. They told me not to be such a "hammerhead"—someone who goes hard all the time.

For what seemed like the first time in my life, I was coming into contact with people who were concerned about what they did with and put into their bodies in a way that was radically different from my addict acquaintances. In time, I was able to save up enough money to move into an apartment with a woman I met through some of my coworkers. I also began dating a woman I met at Smoky Mountain, and she was one of the first people I had to explain a bit about my past to. Kim was understanding, and though she wasn't competing in races, was a good athlete and kept very fit. That was one thing I found about Boise. As much as I previously thought that Boise was the center of drug culture in the Mountain West, there were also a lot of incredibly active people.

One of the reasons why I had to tell Kim a little bit about my past was I needed her to drive me to Sunriver, Oregon, for the first Half Ironman I was going to do on June 25, 2005. I also had to ask permission to leave the state and deal with all the rest of those logistical issues. I wanted to be honest with her, but not overwhelm her, so I didn't mention the suicide attempt, just the stuff about being imprisoned.

Fortunately for me, she'd only seen the new Shane and I'd given her little indication of what the other one was really like. Words versus actions finally worked in my favor. Telling her about my past seemed to round off some of the sharp edges of what I'd experienced. I didn't intentionally downplay that part of my life, but I don't think I was able to translate into vivid images all of the shit I'd seen and done. I was grateful for her companionship and her support, and as race day neared, I was even more excited to put this new self to the test out on the course.

The race was part of a much larger sports festival that ran from Friday through Sunday. The total number of participants had to be in the thousands, and the competitors ranged in age from young kids, some toddlers doing mini-events, to adults in age groups ranging from twenty to eighty. I'd been to a bunch of concerts and the same kind of festive atmosphere, minus the pot smoke lent the atmosphere a festive tone. I was that combination of nervous and excited that made me act the way that I had probably acted as a kid. I did a bit of oversharing, telling the volunteers what was probably pretty obvious just from my eagerness—this was my first race, couldn't wait, hope the weather held, what's the water temperature going to be, how are you doing, pal?, and thanks for being here and helping out, much appreciated.

I was happy to be there, but I also felt like a man on a mission. Because of how the course was set up, the first transition zone from the swim to the cycling was out at Wickiup Reservoir. I had to get my bike out there, and I didn't want to have to do that the next morning and deal with crowds, closed roads, and all the rest. I could have paid to have my bike caravanned out there by a local bike shop and its crew, but those few bucks they charged were too precious to allocate for something I could do myself. We loaded my gear in the backseat of Kim's car, after I extracted my bike from there. No money in the budget at that point for a rack. I got the front tire back on and Kim followed along as I pedaled out to the T-1 zone to drop off my bike.

I'd forgotten to hang my number from the bike's top tube, but the volunteers were cool about it, joking with me that it was still early in the season. Just how early it was for me they had no way of knowing. With that task out of the way, I took advantage of the opportunity to go for a practice swim in the lake. The course was already set up, so it was good to get in the water. If you've never swum in open water, then what I'm about to say may not make a whole lot of sense. Swimming laps in a pool is a lot like hitting golf balls at a driving range or swinging at baseballs in a batting cage. It's sort of the real thing but not really. Sure, if you're going to race in a pool it *is* the same thing, but being turned loose in a large body of water and having to swim from point to point (and sometimes to other points) without lane lines beside you and a big black stripe on the bottom that you can follow is a whole other ball game. I knew that there'd be a bunch of other swimmers in the water with me, but even so, the swim was probably the biggest concern that I had going into the first race.

I was used to being in the water, and in fact felt very comfortable in that environment, but I'd mostly just paddled by board out and ridden back in when I lived in California. I wasn't afraid of the swim, just worried that I might take the most zig-zaggy route and end up being in the water far longer than necessary and time spent was energy stores depleted. Also, hauling my still somewhat fat ass out of the water at the tail end of my wave would be an added burden, knowing that I had so much ground to make up on the rest.

That night, I didn't sleep. It was almost as if I was back into my junkie's routine of staying up until all hours of the night, wound up from the coke I'd done before work to get me through a shift after having had done heroin to quiet the hangover riot that was going in my head and body from having had to drink all that alcohol to take the edge off the coke that I'd done to escape the nod that the heroin had put on me. Almost like that but not like that at all. I had a sub-stance flowing through my body, but it was organic in nature and not manufactured somewhere in South America but in my own little adre-nal glands. Instead of vodka, I was guzzling water, and my body was not yet accustomed to such a foreign substance being forced upon it in such large quantities. Water was for bongs. Water was for diluting dope. Water was not meant to be taken in whole. Every time I lay back down after peeing, I immediately felt the urge again. My cells weren't having it, and it seemed that for every ounce I consumed, my kidneys produced twice as much. I imagined my urinary tract like the Big Thompson River during the flood, minus the cars.

I tried but failed to not think of some of the things that had gone down when I was in Boise. I knew that I was facing a good 5-plus hours the next day of intense effort and little mental stimulation. I was hoping that I could store those memories for use later, but like the water that flowed out of me, so did all those thoughts and recol-lections. Mostly, I just lay there and watched them stream by. Me standing in a Best Buy, the displays of DVDs and CDs in racks that rose up like church pews, too wide and heavy to get out the door in their entirety. The skeletal framework of the roofs of the vans I lived out of in Hattiesburg and Boise, were the first thing I'd see when the midmorning light roused me to the smell of my own funk. Grace and her kids, their little pipe-cleaner arms swallowed up by shirts too big and tattered. Almost inevitably that led to me thinking about be-ing in jail, and in a half-sleep daze, I could hear one of the COs taking attendance, only he wasn't using numbers but names. Craig Sweeney, Roger Hubbel. Jamie Boring. Joe Obrien. Brian Krull, Ryan Smith, Julio Barquero, Jeff Hammer. . . .

All of them dead, and me still here. Except here I was in Sunriver about to do a triathlon putting a hurt on my body in a way that didn't involve injecting drugs into my system. I didn't know if I could do it. I wondered if I'd panic during the swim.

I've never been inside a blender, but that is what I imagined the swim portion of the race was like. That little bit of practice I'd done in no way prepared me for the mayhem of thrashing limbs and kicking feet that churned up the water and threatened to drown me before I'd even gotten the first 10 yards. The good thing was, all those bodies turned us into a school of fish and I just clung as tight as I could to my line and followed the rest of them from point A to point B and finally, after a little more than a mile, point C, the end of the swim. The swim course had been a triangle, but I couldn't really have guessed that except for looking at the course map ahead of time. All I really saw was all those other bodies and the split screen water and sky views on my breathing strokes. What really surprised me was the volume of sound we produced. Normally, swimming in a pool where maybe one other person was in at the same time, swims were a quiet, contemplative span. This was like being on meth or some other substance that tuned me up, a surreal and somewhat unnerving aural and visual overload of foam and bubbles, splashes and clicks and grunts, and glimpses of bright lights and shadows.

Some 35 minutes after I'd entered the water, I came up into the transition area, feeling like the first aquatic species trying to draw breath on dry land. My heart was thudding like a running shoe in a clothes dryer, my breaths tore at my throat, and through my sodden vision, I tried to navigate my way to the transition area on inarticulate legs. Once I got to my rack, I sat down on the ground and struggled with the zipper of my wet suit, my fingers blunt and stupid things that failed me. I tried to tell myself to calm down, and was only half-aware of the dozens of other bodies around me in various phases of dressing and undressing. Finally, I managed to get out of my suit and into my cycling gear, cursing at my helmet's clasp when it pincered the flesh of my index finger. Half trotting, half tottering on the cleats of my bike shoes, I Charlie Chaplined my way out of the transition area, sensing that I was well behind on time. The clock didn't lie. I spent 3 minutes and 45 seconds in the transition area, a lifetime among elite competitors, and even among the top finishers that day who got in and out in less than 2 minutes.

I wouldn't know this until later, but I exited the water in 128th place out of 565 starters. Not bad for a first go, but in my head, and without that knowledge, all I could think of was the serpentine column of back wheels and asses that trailed ahead of me. I had 56 miles ahead of me as well, and they posed far more danger in my mind than any of those 127 people.

My legs felt distended, a blood gorged hard on of meaty muscle. I had to remind myself to make circles, to pull up as much as I pushed down on the pedals, but that was difficult. My quadriceps seemed to be in a battle for dominance with my hamstrings, and they were clearly the superior force, wanting to do the bulk of the work, refusing to strike a balance. For 2 hours and 42 minutes, those two opposing groups of muscles duked it out, and I ended up finishing the bike portion in 29th place, moving up considerably into 37th overall. I averaged a respectable 20.73 miles an hour.

I would pay for that "good" bike portion by struggling through the 13.1 miles of the half marathon that concluded the race in 1:45, an 8-minute-per-mile pace. That sounds pretty good for a first timer with no history, and to be fair to myself, it was. That said, the rest of the field was much faster than me, and it was hard to have so many people blow past me. Once again, the lack of time and attention I paid to nutrition and hydration doomed me. By mile 8 of the run, I was wondering just what in the fuck was I doing thinking I could finish this race, let alone one twice those distances in just another two months. The 90-degree temperatures didn't help, and consuming only about 40 ounces of water during that entire 5 hours and 8 minutes of racing, instead of what I understand now should be about that amount per hour, really had me hurting.

I ended up 96th on the run and finished 50th overall. Those last few miles of the run were agonizing. I'd had to stop several times along the course, which dispirited me in a way that is difficult to describe, but as we approached the town of Sunriver and the finish line, the crowds grew larger. I have an ego like anybody else, and I didn't want to stop in front of those people, but the truth was, I was a half-ironman as I limped it home—my right leg was cramping so badly that with each step my arms involuntarily spasmed to reach back and clutch it.

I can't say that the pain and anger overruled the elation I was feeling at having finished. I wanted to cry. I had known so much anguish and pain for so long before taking up this sport. I had hated myself for so long, saw myself as being so weak and nothing but a complete failure. I was so miserable I'd wanted to die and done something about that desire. It had been so long since I'd been proud of myself for accomplishing something good, that when that sense of satisfaction hit me as I crossed the line, at first I didn't know what that sensation was. I was shocked that I felt good about myself. It was almost as if I'd just discovered, after years and years of living in silence, that I possessed the power of speech, that from that point forward, my life was going to be very, very different as a result.

When I came across the timing mat, I wanted to sink down to the ground a few paces beyond it and kiss the ground. I felt the deepest sense of satisfaction I can ever remember. I finished the hardest thing I had ever attempted. I didn't quit. Somehow through the suffering, wanting to stop many times and *not* giving in to the impulse, I had become a better person. I had grown and learned something about myself. Times prior to the race more than a few "haters" had been discouraging and for me the finish line allowed me to rise above.

I was becoming tougher, fitter, looking better, and feeling better. It felt good—and in a different way than getting fucked up. I was actually achieving something real by having to work for it. Sacrificing comfort for discomfort—to achieve something that required Consistency, Discipline, Devotion, things I had no prior concept.

I wanted to be able to get right back up and proceed to the finisher's area to enjoy some post-race food and fluids. I didn't get there for a while. A volunteer wrapped me in a Mylar cape, an endurance athlete's version of a congratulatory balloon, I guess. I lowered myself to the ground in an area just past where the finisher medals had been draped around my neck. Immediately, I was seized by cramps. They started in my legs, forcing my body into a stretched-out position like an electrocuted cartoon character. It was as if every one of my limbs wanted to get away from that twisted brain that had told them to do this horrific thing to themselves. Every time I moved to try to massage my cramped leg, another part of my body would react to being asked to move by cramping. I knew that the cramps meant that I needed to hydrate, but when I tried to twist the top off the bottle, the hands in my muscles cramped, my fingers splaying like bamboo rake tines. Raising the bottle so that I could use my teeth as a vice to hold the top while I twisted the bottle produced another set of cramps in my biceps, my neck, and jaw.

I wanted to shout for help, but I was afraid of what would happen to my lips and tongue, and I imagined myself lurching around in the finisher's area like some horror movie creature named Cramp Face. Eventually my twitching and thrashing attracted the attention of another cashed in competitor who must have thought I was having some kind of grand mal seizure. Someone from the medical staff came over and helped me into a tented area where the rest of the casualties were being administered to. Fortunately, I didn't need to get an IV drip (as you know I have a history with needles and who knows what that might have done to me) but with the judicious administration of fluids, I was eventually able to limp out of there. I'd felt for a while like an animal at a children's zoo, being fed by bottle by various volunteers who looked on me pitiably.

Truth was, I really didn't care how badly I looked at that point. Better to be a bit of human wreckage sprawled across the gravel parking lot than a strung-out junkie in the back of a van. With Kim's help, I managed to walk to the car, probably the best thing for me was to get as much of the lactic acid flushed out my muscles that felt as hard, compact, and unyielding as golf balls. We celebrated that evening with a healthy dose of pasta and protein at a local Italian place where a bug-eyed waitress finally gave up trying to keep the lone breadbasket and water glasses filled and just brought us pitchers and loaves. The water wouldn't stay in me very long of course, so I had to hobble to the bathroom. The great thing about events like the Pacific Crest or any other is that the towns get inundated with athletes, so no one really stared at me as I stiff-hipped and locked-kneed my way back and forth from the table to the bathroom.

I had to laugh at myself when I tried to sit down. I thought of those old tape rules that carpenters used—not the metal ones that spooled into a kind of case—but the wooden ones that pivoted and whose segments stacked up on one another like pieces of lumber. My dad used those, and not surprisingly, thinking of him and rules and my family and everything else that had gone on got my eyes all teared up. I was exhausted and elated, up and down, and as much as I wanted to take something to knock the edge off, I knew that I couldn't. I fucking hurt like hell at that moment, and for days afterward, but I wanted to feel every bit of it. The physical pain was the evidence, the proof of the work put in and the growth that would occur through that discomfort.

Later, on the drive back to Boise, I sat uncomfortably contorted in the passenger seat. I tried to stretch my aching muscles as best as I could, but I was ice-bagged like a halibut in a ship's hold. I thought of a poem that I read in high school. Robert Frost's "To Earthward" is about a man looking down from some celestial place and recalling his experiences on earth. He thinks about all the things he misses, all the simple things of a fragrant rural life. What I remembered best and what I understood least when I first read it are the lines about him recalling the pain of leaning hard on his hand and the pain grass and sand left when he took his hand away. He said that now that he was dead, that pain wasn't enough and he wanted to feel that not just in his hands but also along the entire length of his body. I sat in the car watching the high desert scrub flash past, the tires' noise a soothing monotonous symphony, and I had to agree with the old white-haired Mr. Frost who in every photo I saw of him seemed like a prickly old bastard. Yes, I was glad that I was still around to be able to feel pain. Yes, the absence of pain, of all sensation, was death. But in a way that was far different from what he meant, the hurt was not enough. I wanted my body to stop hurting. I wanted to stop hurting other people. But each is a necessary component of life. Even if the nature of my hurting was being altered, that didn't mean that was enough. I had some other kinds of healing to do as well, with myself and with the relationships I had threatened.

I'd crossed one finish line and knew that there were going to be many more ahead of me. They say that you have to learn to walk before you can run. I've never done things the easy way, taken the safe route, and I'd hit the ground running in my rehabilitation of self. I had another event, a full Ironman, already booked for two months in the future. I knew that I would have to do some serious limping along for the next few days, but they also say there's no rest for the wicked.

EIGHT

I probably should have been more pleased with the results of my first triathlon. I don't know if it was my inexperience or just an innately competitive nature (that used to take pride in being able to outdrink and out snort my peers) but all I could think about was the 49 people who had finished ahead of me, the other 3 in my age group who crossed the line before I did, and not the more than 500 who finished behind me. I can see now that for someone doing this for the first time, I had a hint of natural ability, or maybe it was my willingness to push harder and endure more pain, but at my core, I had some facility for competing. I had only just cracked the top 10 percent at my first race and I knew I would have to be much more competitive if I was ever going to qualify for the Ironman World Championship in Kona.

To qualify for Kona the field would be much larger and the race twice as long. Most Ironman qualifiers have between 2,200 and 2,500 athletes competing for only 50 Kona slots that are allotted based on the number of participants per age group. This meant that in order to qualify I would need to be in or near the top 35 overall (top 2 percent). I was also still obsessed by the idea that several other very real clocks were counting down. I had a full Ironman to prepare for in less than three months. That would mean I was going to have to nearly double the distances I'd just managed: 2.4 miles of swimming, 112 miles of cycling, and 26.2 miles of running. Also, I was coming up on my thirtieth birthday, which meant I would advance to a more competitive age group category.

While the professionals competed against one another regardless of what age they were, the rest of us, the vast majority of us who actually were amateurs, were also placed in age groups so that we'd get a better sense of how we did against our peers. Those categories sometimes include those within five years of age of another—for example the 20–25 group, 26–30, etc. In some events, the groups span ten years. Also, competitors are placed in two groups based on gender. Your final time would determine where you placed overall, in your age group, and within your gender. But even early on, I was more focused on my overall finish than any of the other categories. Despite my focus on overall placement, I was never able to get over the fact that I was getting a late start in the sport, that in many ways, when the gun went off on race day, I was already incurring a time penalty. Knowing that I was starting at such an advanced age made me insecure and reinforced my tendency of trying to cram everything in all the time overcompensating for my past.

To be honest, I had something else of more immediate concern on my mind the day after I returned to Boise. How was I going to get out of bed? After that, a series of other challenges faced me: walking to the bathroom, the kitchen, and how was I going to ever be able to bend over far enough to put on and tie my shoes? I was in a world of hurt, and even the little bit of satisfaction I felt in having completed my first triathlon was struggling to keep up with the pace of that soreness. Among several other accidents over the years, I had been hit by cars, run over by a jeep, rammed a car into a utility pole, flipped a car at relatively high speed, purposely cut and burned myself, yet I hadn't experienced the kind of post-event trauma that this triathlon produced.

I could not believe how painful that experience had been. In the adrenaline rush that crossing the finish line had produced, I'd severely underestimated how much damage I'd done to my body. Everything between my toenails and my neck and shoulders was either painfully sore, swollen, or stiff. I couldn't believe that I could feel so bad, after doing just a single race that was half the distance of the goal I'd set for myself. Even I, as new to the sport as I was, sensed that there wasn't an equivalency of hurt that existed between the half and the full Ironman distance. Just because the distances were twice as long, the pain, I suspected was going to be exponentially greater.

Still, I was committed. I mounted my bike, feeling very much like I had been mounted by my bike that weekend, and pedaled sore assed to Gold's Gym and later to Smoky Mountain. I was doing my version of the postal carrier's duty to let neither shattered shins, knotted knees, and hammered hamstrings keep my from my appointed rounds.

I didn't just ride to work, but I resumed my training almost immediately. I wasn't going to take a few days off and let my fitness erode. That's laughable to me now, knowing how important rest is, but back then it was full speed ahead all the time, despite the good advice I was getting from a number of people.

After those first few months of working out on free passes, I negotiated a kind of barter arrangement where I'd do cleanup work and whatever else was needed around the gym. Part of my vision of becoming a better person and rebuilding my life was the need to enrich and contribute to the lives of other people somehow. It occurred to me in prison that I could help fundamentally influence the lives of other people by becoming a trainer. This would immerse me in an environment where I would be surrounded by people who wanted something better for themselves and were always in pursuit of personal growth. All I needed was the chance and some guidance to fulfill that part of my plan. Again, someone reached out to me and offered me an opportunity that he didn't have to. In this case, it was Matt Brundage. He became my mentor in the fitness industry.

Matt was the director of personal training programs for a group that owned five other clubs in the Treasure Valley. He was also the director of education. In what I thought was a very forward-thinking move, he required that all newly hired trainers at the gym had to attend a bi-weekly class he conducted for the first eight weeks of employment. Matt said that I could attend the class, but he wouldn't hire me. He did say that he would see how I performed and how he felt about my capabilities before he could make the move to employ me. It was clear given my history that he wanted to hold my feet to the fire and determine if I would see it through.

I was thrilled to have the opportunity to take the class. I was highly motivated and naturally interested in the anatomy and physiology elements of the class, but what I really enjoyed was his incorporation of the behavioral component to the curriculum.

I began taking classes in February 2005 and finished them up in the end of March. I learned a whole lot, from the basics of cellular structure and function to more advanced topics like the relationship between agonists and antagonists. We also studied nutrition extensively. You would think then that based on what I'd learned in that classroom, I would have applied that to my own training. Obviously,

I didn't, and that's where the behavioral component came in. Matt stressed to his pupils that it wasn't enough to understand the science behind the physical conditioning we would lead our clients through. He told us that more or less the science essentially stayed the same but the emotional/behavioral component varied greatly. As a result we had to understand the mind-set of the person doing the workouts. Without that understanding of the human motives all the science could be rendered useless.

Clearly, my situation was a case of the doctor who treats himself has a fool for a patient. I had the knowledge but I just wasn't applying it to my situation and myself. The lack of rest was especially problematic because I had injured my foot in my suicide attempt and it had never fully healed. I have the worst bunion I have ever seen, which completely deforms my left foot. It causes an extreme lateral protrusion (bony prominence) that juts out sharply where my big toe should be. My big toe, in turn, is completely cocked to the side (internally toward the second toe). In biomechanics the 1st ball/metatarsal is called the 1st MTP or first ray. It is the principle stabilizing force of the foot and makes first contact in running. Mine is so jacked that it used to cause bleeding through the shoe and would eat holes in the side of the shoe. To this day, it still affects movement, but rarely bleeds because the skin is so tough.

In order to prepare for the full Ironman, I knew that I had to increase my training volume. I was feeling discouraged at that point, and didn't want to think about the distances that I would have to travel, so I kept track of the time spent training as opposed to distances covered. Prior to that late July race, I managed to ride for 5.5 hours and run for 2 hours and 20 minutes. I hoped that I could complete the 112 miles of the bike within that time, but knew that a 2:20 marathon was completely out of reach (the greatest runners in the sport have never run faster than 2:38 off the bike). I just didn't know how much longer than that I would have to pound the pavement. Swimming wasn't so much of an issue for me. I knew that I wasn't particularly fast in the water, but that was okay. The swim training was easier because it was low impact and didn't put as much strain on the joints that were really troubling me. In addition, swimming makes up the smallest percentage of time and distance in any race.

At that point, I was a mess physically. In addition to that painful foot, I had shin splints, and my hips had me limping like a dysplastic dog. I'd already tried to put myself down, so I had no fear of that, but I was really, really doubtful about my ability to finish the full Ironman.

Whatever confidence I had after finishing the Pacific Crest had evaporated in the hot high desert winds, and on the day I did my longest training run, I was completely crushed. I didn't carry enough water with me, and the last 6 miles were the equivalent of a French Legionnaire wandering lost and hallucinatory in a sandstorm. Worse, I beat myself mentally most of that run, a negative feedback loop of alternating statements of "I'm not ready," "I'm not an athlete," and "What the fuck are you doing this for?" ran at a pace much faster than my rickety stride could carry me.

If I was all giddy and excited at the Pacific Crest, I was bundle of neurotic anxiety as I stood on the banks of the Russian River ready to begin the Vineman in August 2005. The Vineman touts itself as the oldest independent (not a part of the "official" Ironman organization) triathlon in the continental United States. The unique feature of the race for me was that the swim portion was held in that river. I hoped that the whole swim would take us downstream and that the current would carry me faster. As it turned out though, for meteorological, logistical, and hydrological reasons, that wasn't the case. First, the area got very little rainfall; second, the swim course was two loops of downriver and upriver components; and third, the Russian River was dammed in several areas upriver of where we would start. All that meant that there wasn't much current at all, and whatever advantage you gained going with the current was more than offset by having to swim against it.

At least the river was narrow in comparison to a lake or reservoir, which made it harder to wander off course and end up swimming a longer distance than necessary. By the end of the 1 hour and 10 minutes it took me to complete the swim portion, my shoulders were on fire. I kept telling myself to be grateful for the fact that the rest of the race I'd be relying on my legs. It took a long time to get comfortable on the bike, and for a while my back, neck, and arms were very, very tight, but eventually they loosened up. The 112-mile bike course was one of the most beautiful rides I'd ever been on. Instead of the bare scrub of high desert scenery, we began in a redwood forest and then spent most of the time in the vineyards. It could have become monotonous, but compared to what I was used to, this was lush and jungle-like scenery.

With only 150 or so competitors in the entire field, I rode alone for almost the entire ride. I remember thinking (most of the time) about prison and my old life; I used those impressions and memories and the feelings that accompanied them, to motivate me across the terrain. I tried to use my self-doubt as fuel to force myself on when I had difficult patches. I went to the race with NO expectations—just a strong desire to finish. At the time I was very inexperienced in every way. The only thing I had to go on was Doug LaMott's best IM time at this very race (11:24), and it seemed to me that he had more experience, so I just wanted to finish, and walk as little as possible on the run course.

I wasn't doing a tour; so despite the pleasant surroundings, the 6 hours on the bike weren't a pleasure cruise. I was within shouting distance (okay, a very loud shout) of my training time and finished the 112 miles in 5:53. That translated to 3 minutes and 8 seconds per mile or 19 miles per hour. Not horrible, but certainly not Kona-worthy.

For the run, even though I was alone for the bike, I hooked up with another runner, Jeff Sneed who really helped me get through the marathon. He was a stout competitor who'd come to win that day but had struggled, so he hung back with me for a while. The run was a blur. The run course was three loops and Jeff was on his last loop while I was beginning my first. He was good about reminding me to stop at every aid station to drink, and he told me that my stride was way too long. I was running more like a sprinter than a distance runner, and he informed me about cadence—the number of steps you take per minute. Since my stride was so long, I was taking fewer steps per minute than I should have been. My long-loping stride kept me in the air longer when I should have been turning my feet over like a wheel's propelling me forward. This time I spent in the air added up and the force of each foot strike was greater. As a result, I was literally pounding myself to pieces and braking with every step.

I'd eventually learn that elite distance runners have a cadence higher than 200. They also kept that cadence consistent throughout a race. For someone like me, a 160 cadence would be better than what I was doing, but still not as efficient if I was in the 180 range. Jeff's advice helped get me through the race, but it would be years before I was able to integrate the mechanics necessary to make my running form work for me instead of against me.

What was mostly working against me in the last portion of the Vineman was my head. Wisely, it was telling me that I was doing real damage to myself. I imagined my brain as I was plodding along as kind of an emergency control center. It sat there at a command post with a set of headphones on and all kinds of dials and monitors. It was receiving reports from all different parts of my body over those headphones as well as an avalanche of data. A huge monitor was flashing the word STOP, and a klaxon was sounding, and eventually so much negative data was coming in that the dials started to go up in smoke. The word on the big screen switched from STOP to QUIT, but I didn't. I finished in a woeful and painful 4:04 for a total of 11:14.

Despite how painful the experience was, as I counted down the last miles and then saw the finish line come into view, I felt like instead of an emergency control center, my brain had become a kind of airport tower. The plane was damaged, but the pilot had managed to get the bird near to landing. I felt light-headed, both from the effort and the elation. In fact, I felt light of spirit and body as well. It was as if those aches and pains had been shed like any excess fuel the aircraft no longer needed and posed a danger. Instead of being a passenger with his head between his legs hoping to God this thing didn't crash and burn, I was at the controls bringing this baby home safely. I crossed the line, and just stood there for a moment soaking it all in. In my whole life, I'd never felt such a deep sense of satisfaction. I'd loved the buzz that came from drinking and the sense of warmth and well-being that came from injecting heroin, but this was better than those by far. I was ten months out of prison and just finishing that race was a huge accomplishment for me. As I crossed the finish line the dam broke and a flood of memories from my old life came rushing back and overwhelmed me with the deepest sense of satisfaction and self-worth I had ever known.

It wasn't like I was a bright and shiny and relatively new aircraft that had developed some issues, I was an old and abused and war-torn air beast that had been ravaged by time and my own stupidity. Somehow, using spit and grit, I'd gotten the thing airborne again and now safely back on the ground. Coming so close to the temptation to quit, on myself, on life, on the race, made the finishing feel even better than if I had breezed through it. I knew that I was going to continue on this path. I wasn't afraid of flying as a result of my near disaster. Instead I was going to really take control, really master this thing called my will and myself.

I paid a price for that race. I had to walk downstairs backward for two weeks after it. I couldn't really sit, and I had to become a master bombardier in order to drop my load into the toilet from a quarter-squatting position. I gave myself a break and managed to go seven days without working out before hitting the road again. I understood that the stakes had been raised in a lot of ways. To that point, I'd not missed a day of training since I started. I was proud of that achievement, but just as it was with my sobriety, with each day that I put between myself and drinking or using or with my fitness regimen, I had more to lose if I failed to meet my commitments.

So many times in the past, I'd fallen victim to the "fuck it syndrome." All those stints in rehab, all those other times when I'd tried on my own to quit, the sense of futility and loss of self-efficacy that I experienced was a figurative noose around my neck. Add to that, the cognitive dissonance—my rock-solid belief that we are responsible for our situation in life mixed with my utter inability to stop or limit my usage—confounded me on the most profound level, eroded any confidence I had left, and made me wonder if I was determined to have no self-determination whatsoever. I was out of control, and now that I was gaining more control over myself, the physical hurt replaced some of the angst that had become such a natural state of my being.

I can do this thing, I told myself. It's going to take some time, but

I'll get there. Because I was so aware of the time deficits from which I was working, I fought a battle with my brain and my body on my return to Boise. My head told me that based on what I'd read, I needed some rest and recovery time.

My body told me another story, "Listen, dude, we've done pretty good so far, but we've got to stick with the program." I'd always been a "more is better" kind of guy, so I went with that approach. Besides, by this time my workouts had become a critical part of my day. I noticed that if I made my workouts a priority my days went more smoothly, and I was more levelheaded. I felt as though I operated at a higher level with exercise and when I didn't work out I felt flat and uninspired. I can't say that what I did was wise physiologically, in fact it was very unwise, but getting those workouts in when I should have been in more of a recovery phase was sure better than the possible option that loomed.

As some of my other obligations (AA meetings, the reintegration program mandated by the state) slipped away, I took on other projects to keep me occupied. In this case, though, I was interested in more than just filling up time to avoid being tempted by drugs and alcohol. For a long while, I'd been interested in psychology, both as a means of understanding my own behavior and also as a possible way to help other people. Given that I was nearing thirty, was still weighed down by student loans, the thought of getting a graduate degree didn't hold much appeal. I already felt like I'd spent so much time outside the mainstream of what most people construe as normal, so delaying my entry into that even further by enrolling in a program to get an advanced degree would just put me further behind.

Instead, I saw a way of converting my intellectual needs and interest in fitness into something that could benefit me financially as well as physically and emotionally. I'd already passed the class that Matt Brundage at Gold's Gym had required me to take, but I needed additional education and training in the field. That meant enrolling in classes that would prepare me to take my first certification exams through the National Academy of Sports Medicine (NASM) out of Tampa, Florida. I started out with what they called their Certified Personal Trainer (CPT) program that focused on, among other things muscle physiology, metabolism, exercise physiology training principles, strength training and aerobic conditioning, systematic progression, body composition analysis, nutrition, psychology, motivation, ethics, and success. In addition it also gave you a primer on the business of fitness.

I don't mean to come off as too critical of an industry that has allowed me to support myself for nearly a decade, but as is probably true with most jobs, the emphasis on being a personal trainer, from a management point of view, is less on how much you know about training people and more about producing revenue. I really got into and studied the material about physiology and exercise. I went above and beyond the call of duty on that one, and read extensively outside of the textbooks the NASM provided along with various instructional DVDs. I felt the need to truly become an expert in the field. Also, because I knew it would benefit me to have an understanding of more advanced concepts, I got to the point much further down the line, when I could keep up with anyone regarding subjects related to nutrition, biomechanical movement models, physiology, strength, and conditioning in general.

To be honest, I didn't earn a couple of Trainer of the Year accolades at Gold's because of my technical knowledge. The NASM certification materials and tests were right to include something about psychology and motivation and the business side of things. The reason I won those awards was because I was top earner, and spent part of my days doing the orientation sessions for prospective members, sticking to our sales pitch. Ironically, given my own state of mind, I felt uncomfortable with the notion that our primary driver was fear. As part of our spiel, we would take people interested in joining out onto the floor and have them perform three relatively simple movement patterns as a kind of assessment: a seated row, an overhead squat, and a yoga plank. I didn't always stick to the script completely and sometimes substituted other movements, but I did do what I was told to do. Look for postural distortion or any other areas of weakness and point them out.

In a way, it was like what happens at some auto repair shops. You bring your car in and then they tell you that x, y, and z are not looking too good. You can go ahead and keep driving it that way, but eventually something's going to fail and it's going to cost you a lot of money down the line. Do it now, as preventative maintenance, and you'll come out ahead. And that's what we did with people. It may not be hurting you much now, but if you let it go, it's going to get worse. There was a lot of truth to those statements, but I felt it was too coercive and focused on the negative. We didn't talk about the benefits of exercise so much as we talked about the detriments of failing to exercise. Over time I stopped going with their program and developed my own system with a more positive tone, and as I got healthier myself, I could see how my own transition from fearing not working out to wanting to work out because it made me feel better produced good results. My motives were beginning to shift from avoidance of failure toward the pursuit of success. I wanted my clients and anyone who joined the gym to do so for reasons other than fear of injury.

Just as I won't listen to someone lecturing me or telling me what I need to do, people need to be brought down that path through some directive inquiry. They need to talk about how exercise would make their life better and richer than it is currently without exercise. They need to explore the things that brought them through the door of the gym in the first place. This way they are autonomous and self-directed. Also, it can generate strong and lasting positive associations instead of temporary motivation through fear or negative focus on the things not wanted instead of the things desired for change or achievement.

I have to admit that being a goal-oriented person, I wanted to outperform the other trainers. That was at least one way that we could keep score, determine who was good at the job, and who wasn't so good. I was trying to outdistance my past history, prove to myself that I wasn't the *worst* at everything, I could be successful. I wanted to make good on the promises I made to Matt Brundage and Andy Slagel and prove to everyone (mostly myself) that people can change. We also used the same technique to get already enrolled members (and new ones) to buy training sessions. That is how I began to build up a client base. Getting people to buy those packages was really the main way I earned the money I needed for entry fees, travel, and equipment. The split was 65/35 with the gym for those blocks of personal training time.

I knew that I wasn't ever going to get rich doing what I was doing, but that was okay. Maybe because I had always spent most of my money on drugs and alcohol, I came out of prison a far less materialistic person than most of my peers. Riding my bike everywhere started as a necessity but soon became a passion. It simply made sense to do it on a lot of levels. Seeing people I knew driving a quarter of a mile to get somewhere instead of walking blew my mind. I don't mean to imply that I became a green crusader, a "freegan" who dumpster dove in order to feed, clothe, and equip myself. It's just that I had different priorities. I had done the math on all the money I could save on a car payment, insurance, and gas. I decided I would be better off without a vehicle.

Besides, I had been reading a great deal about greenhouse gases and I didn't need to add my emissions when I could easily ride everywhere I needed to go. Additionally, I wanted to place my emphasis on *living* and *feeling alive* through experience. I had pissed away most of my life to that point, barely existing and not really living at all. It was as if I was finally awakening to the experience of a meaningful life for the first time as an adult. I was acutely aware of the fragile and transient nature of our existence. We come through this way *one time* and I wanted to hold each moment close.

Since movement and exercise were a key to my recovery and my new way of life, I wanted to become an expert in everything fitness related. I was obsessed with learning as much as I could about the latest exercise modalities—I used them myself and applied them to the work I was doing with clients. From core strength to plyometrics, from interval training to elastic recoil, I read the studies in the *American College of Sports Medicine* journal and tried to stay on the cutting edge as best I could.

I really enjoyed the one-on-one nature of my interactions with my clients. Through 2006 and 2007 I was well regarded by my employers for my sales work, but planning and helping my clients execute a fitness program was what I really loved. Because of the nature of the work that I did, I got to know my clients very well. Having someone bare their soul, tell you about how they really feel about their bodies and their abilities to meet goals and to stay motivated, creates an emotionally intimate relationship. My job was to push and to challenge people, holding them accountable for their thoughts and behaviors that were creating their reality. Many of them had body image issues or were dealing with rough patches in their personal or professional lives. Success required a level of involvement that extended well beyond the walls of the gym. It was a mutually beneficial arrangement; by allowing me to help them change their lives, they were improving the quality of my own and giving me a sense of purpose.

At first, I was hesitant to share my past with them. I remember two clients I had who were women, and both were by all standard measurements obese, when they came to me and wanted me to help them get a grip on their lives. They were both emotional eaters with what they considered to be tough lives. At first, I just hinted about the fact that their excuses for their past behaviors and their present failures to really commit to the work that needed to be done were pretty lame. I also hinted that I could tell them stories about the difficulty of breaking old habits and the incredible fear that making lasting changes can put into a person. Little by little, I let them know about what I'd experienced. I didn't do it so that I could trumpet my success but to let them know that I wasn't full of shit, I had been there and worse. So, when I finally did that and saw that my telling people where I started from in my fitness life actually gave them hope, I did so with greater frequency, when it was warranted.

They responded to my not being all rainbows and sunshine or someone who'd devoted his whole life to purity and the path of healthy physicality. I was real. I had known dark times and let them know about it. My relationships with my clients became deep and lasting. I got to know everything about them and their lives, their hopes, and their difficulties. I came to think of them as close friends, almost like family.

I don't know if I could have done that if the relationship wasn't as reciprocal as it was. Hearing about some of the circumstances that people were dealing with, from divorce to deaths of loved ones, helped me keep a better perspective on my life. Also, most of my clients were very successful, unlike everyone I had associated with for so long on the streets or in prison. It was refreshing and many of them unwittingly provided me with a model of conduct that I could emulate.

I really did feel like, as clichéd as it sounds, that the people I met through Gold's became like family to me. For whatever reason, many of my clients were health professionals. There's a kind of law of attraction that exists between people heavily involved in the drug culture—the negative connecting with the negative. Well, as things started to really turn for the better for me in Boise, I was attracting much more positive influences in my life. I can't say it was coincidental or divine intervention, but mostly I think it was a case of making the right choices that put me in the right situations at the right time. Most of the personal successes and growth I experienced was with the help and guidance of others. People like Terry Keller. He was an anesthesiologist in town. We seemed to hit it off pretty well, and eventually he introduced me to a number of other partners in his practice. More important, he got his wife to agree to have me be her trainer. Pretty quickly, I couldn't call Karen by her first name anymore—she became Mom or Ma.

Ma Keller really took me under her wing and helped me in so many ways. She knew that I was living apart from my family, and there was something about her warm and engaging maternal side that made it easy for me to connect with her and tell her about what I'd done and where I'd been. She sensed that even though I was making progress and that I had built up a kind of momentum with my training and my sobriety and my career, that a big component was still missing from my life—family. At first she didn't press too hard on the notion that I really needed to connect with and to sort out some issues with my family.

In fact, she was pretty satisfied to allow me to be a part of hers. I spent Christmas Day 2006 with the Kellers after Karen learned that

I wasn't going to be spending time with my family. Their son, John, was my age, an advanced-degree Tulane graduate, while their daughter, Becca, became the kid sister I never had. I enjoyed seeing how much pleasure they all (including their other son, Ryan) took in one another's company. On some level she knew I needed a mature and adult influence. These people helped me to smooth the transition to a "normal" and healthy life, from the twisted and dysfunctional. I was still really rough around the edges. I could be overly profane and at times more crude than I should have been.

For so long, the Christmas holidays had been spent in rehab or with me strung out instead of stringing lights, and the few times I'd tried to spend the post-suicide holidays with my family I'd wound up feeling far worse for the wear. On the surface we were all pleasant with one another, but the underlying tension still existed. I couldn't blame them, because their wariness was perfectly understandable. They were still expecting the old Shane to emerge, just as he had every time he'd gone to rehab. The old Shane would seem to be getting shit together, and then flame out in some spectacular fashion. They didn't see me very often, so they had little to base their assessment of me on besides what I told them.

Add to that the fact that I had lied to them so often in the past about how things were really going okay—the little-boy-who-cried-wolf phenomenon was a part of our every interaction. I had decimated the trust between us so completely that it was going to take time, lots of time, as Ma Keller reminded me, to rebuild that. And, honestly, I wasn't sure I wanted to invest that much of myself in doing that. I had this new life, and I was moving forward on several fronts, and it was like seeing them was a reminder that while I had this bright and shiny new house I was living in, I still had a bunch of shit stored back at their place. My new place was uncluttered (this is of course metaphorically speaking since not even Ma Keller my mother, and all the mothers in the world united could have gotten me to literally clean up the home-neatness part of my act) and I didn't want to have to bring all of that junk out of storage and deal with it.

Along with that came the reminder of all my past failures spending time with them inevitably brought to mind. None of this was their fault, I knew. I think it's natural that my family could fix me at a point in time, and they couldn't but help bring the past into our interactions (though they never did overtly) and sometimes, somehow it felt limiting or constricting. But most of this was on me. I knew that they had seen me through my worst, they had been there by my side walking through the shit, and seeing them and hearing from them reminded me too strongly of who I was back then. I'd broken away from the junkie crowd I'd known in Boise and was now with a more fitness-oriented group, but there was no way that I could break completely from my family. I both didn't want to and couldn't, and they were incredibly supportive.

But it was as if my vision was altered somehow. I saw them and saw how well they were treating me, but I also saw a kind of shadow, a penumbra, that reflected some of my guilt and anxiety. Seeing them was a reminder that I couldn't pretend that *that* Shane and *those* times were something that I could wipe away completely. I wanted to move through that and past all the pain I'd caused, but like a kid with a loose tooth, I kept poking and probing that sore spot.

Oddly, phone calls with my mom and dad were mostly okay. My mom stayed on my ass about finances and the future, reminding me that as a legitimate wage earner there were these things called income tax returns that I had to file. She also was very supportive of my competing. She didn't understand why on earth I wanted to put myself through all that, but she was glad that my plan seemed to be working.

As I reported on my results in training and eventually my racing, she certainly recognized that my undertakings were a very good outlet to channel my intensity and energy.

My brother, Trent, was really there for me in ways that I often felt I didn't deserve. Even though he was my little brother, I counted on him a lot, from simple things like how to burn a DVD or CD on my computer to more complex things like how to handle delicate matters in dealing with management at work, I needed his advice. We talked about women, his impending to Carrie, and I was amazed by how insightful he was, how mature, and how much more grounded in the reality of everyday life than I had been at his age and was even now as I was knocking on the door of thirty. Sure, he gave me some shit every now and then about how I needed to make a giant leap into the new century and its technological offerings and stop being such a dumbass, but it was all good natured and true. I enjoyed the hell out of my brother becoming my best friend.

My friend Ann Sabala also had an enormous influence on me. Though she was in her fifties (she hated discussing her age) and had kids older than me, she became an unlikely confidant and sounding board. She was one of the hippest most well-read people I've ever known, and very open-minded. We talked all the time and she helped me navigate some more difficult and stressful times. Best of all she never hesitated to call me out on my bullshit, and always walked me through the rough patches in romances, career, and finances. She was a tremendous influence on my worldview post-prison and helped me to reframe many of the crooked thought processes that I had carried with me into this new life.

Even though age thirty was on the horizon, I was still very much a kid in a learning phase. I had that permanent record/transcript that detailed all the times I'd been expelled, transferred, and the rest. I was living in one place and working at a fulfilling job, things that should not have been remarkable for someone my age. I was very, very aware of how far behind I was in my triathlon career, but the lessons I was learning there were finally starting to transfer to the other parts of my life.

NINE

When I was in the maelstrom of my descent from pot smoker/drinker to full-blown heroin addict/criminal, I never had the sense that time was moving slowly. Even in retrospect, it seemed like one day I was sitting on the roof of my parent's home in Bloomington, Illinois, with my high school buddy Brian drinking Boone's Farm, and the next I was lying in the emergency room in St. Luke's Medical Center in Boise. Brian and I were bitching about how much we hated life in Bloomington. In Boise, I was yelling at the doctors and cursing whichever of my junkie friends it was that had called 911 instead of just letting me die of an overdose. That's progress of a sort, and I suppose that when you're descending, the gravitational pull of drugs, addiction, and criminality eases the effort in some sense. Life certainly wasn't anything like easy back then. I had to hustle my ass all over to steal what I needed to feed my addiction, and living out of a van in a harsh winter isn't exactly cozy.

When I had a roof over my head, a few creature comforts, a steady job that I really liked and took great satisfaction in, there was, of course, going to have to be the other side of that. Yes, life in the legitimate world of adulthood was in some senses easier, but the effort it was taking to reach my goal of qualifying for Kona was enormous at times. I don't know what I really expected when I sat in that security blanket in the Ada County Jail and first hatched my plan. I don't think I had any idea if it would take me a year, a decade, or millennia to accomplish what I'd set out to do.

The first year or so out of prison, everything was fresh and new and life had its ups and downs, but my trajectory was definitely trending upward. It's easy to stay motivated when your performance keeps getting better and you see marked improvement in every area of your life. So far, my life had been a bunch of peaks and valleys—I spent very little time in the flats.

After that first year of competing and into the next phases of really getting more serious and more fit, I tried to stay focused on the present, the proverbial live-in-the-moment kind of thing, but that was hard for me. I had a goal in mind, and I couldn't help but wonder how much time it was going to take to get there, or if I would get there at all. I was gaining confidence that I had what it took to stay committed to being clean, becoming a better person, and becoming a more competitive athlete, but I did wonder how I'd respond when life became routine, when, or if, the novelty of this new and healthier life would wear off. I couldn't imagine that life in Boise or in the city I really wanted to be in, Boulder, would ever get like it had in Bloomington. Still, that bit of fear of stagnation and boredom motivated me to keep finding new ways to keep my too-active brain occupied. Also, my too-active brain produced a large quantity of self-doubt. I truly wondered nearly every day if I had what it took to qualify for Kona.

But I was seeing steady if not spectacular improvement in my performances. My progress was incremental, but that was good. In fact, that was better than good. Who knows what might have happened if I'd suddenly gotten to the top of my game too soon. I was enjoying the dedication and effort required to perform. I'd spent so many years cutting corners, looking for the angles and edges that would get me what I wanted with the least amount of sweat and tears possible, that the painful and painstaking steps I was taking were their own reward. That's not to say that I wasn't frustrated and impatient as well. I wouldn't be me if that weren't the case. Still, when I look back on that period, I think of it as a period of maturation and refinement. I was no longer a true newbie struggling to figure out how this whole thing worked. I also certainly didn't know a whole lot and didn't presume to know it all by any means.

In retrospect, my decision to embrace triathlon proved far wiser than I could have imagined back in that jailhouse in Boise. Having three separate disciplines to master as well as the complexities of racing, becoming increasingly proficient in the transition zones, fine-tuning my nutrition and workloads, all kept my mind occupied. I sometimes wonder what might have happened to me had I chosen a less complicated pursuit. Even if I'd chosen to focus on any one of the three activities of the triathlon—let's say running a marathon, swimming the English Channel, or doing the cross-continental Ride Across America—I'm not sure I wouldn't have hit some kind of plateau and probably would have become bored.

The few times when I went off drugs and alcohol, I eventually gave in and drank or used. Instead of just chalking that up to a little mistake, I applied the "fuck it all" principle and immediately went into a steep dive. And it wasn't as if I resumed my intake of substances after a period of abstinence because of some catastrophic or life-altering incident. Frequently, I just got to a point where things were relatively calm in my life, and that didn't seem good enough. I had to stir the shit in some way, make things a bit more exciting for myself. A kind of tinkerer who couldn't let well enough alone, and triathlon gave me a warehouse full of elements to tinker with. Whether it was the fit on my bike, my running stride, my swim stroke, or my gear and equipment as well as what I put in my body, there were enough permutations and combinations of those aspects of training and competing that kept my mind engaged.

To be sure, I had a lot of ups and downs in that first year, but I didn't give up when things got tough. Having reached the point of suicide gave me a different perspective on life and effort. Not only did I use the "you've experienced more pain before" rationale as a whip to keep going, my struggles helped me to understand that surrendering is more painful than anything else. I've talked with a lot of endurance athletes, and few of them can say with any honesty that they gave of themselves completely in a competition, that they burned every reserve that they had. I don't know that I can say the same either, but at least I understood what it was like to have done it once, to have been so broken that you choose not to retreat in order to fight another day but to choose to not ever fight ever again.

After the Vineman recovery period, I went back at it in the gym pretty hard. Strength training was something I really enjoyed, though I didn't go about it in the best way for an endurance athlete. I knew that when I felt stronger, especially in a way that was easy to measure—amount of weight, number of repetitions, and sets—mentally I was able to put up with the pain of longer and longer workouts in the pool and on the road. I still have my logs from those days, and even in looking back at them, I take a lot of pride and get a lot of pleasure from remembering how I felt in the middle of a set of squats or heavy lunges, how great it felt to feel my legs overcoming the forces exerted by the loads I piled on the rack that bore down on me. Something about pushing weights around and taking control over them fed my desire to improve and achieve.

Along with that, I was becoming increasingly aware that I needed to develop a physical component of a psychological trait I'd already had in spades—explosiveness. The first time I'd gone up for review for parole I'd been denied and assigned an anger-management class instead. I still struggled with my temper, and though I didn't often let it get to the point that I reacted violently, I was still easily frustrated. Anyone who has ever ridden a bike, especially if you've commuted on one, will know that you fight a never-ending battle to be recognized as a legitimate possessor of road space. That's a very fancy way of saying that you engage in daily battles with asshole drivers.

I'm very aware of my fragility when I ride, and I try as best as I can to obey all the rules of the road while asserting my presence as a vehicle in traffic. I realize that there's enough blame to go around and that cyclists can sometimes be their own worst enemies, but when someone on an approximately 20-pound bicycle with 160 pounds of self engages with at least a ton and more of metal and plastic, there's a legitimate chip on the cyclist's shoulder. One time, the driver of a Chevy Suburban ran me onto a soft shoulder while honking his horn. I flipped him off and threw whatever stones I could find, all the while screaming obscenities at him at the top of my lungs. I fumed for the rest of the ride, cursed at every car that I felt had passed too closely to me, and kicked my legs at them—not the wisest choice and definitely not the most mature response to one asshole's aggressiveness, but there I was in all my pretransformation glory. I'd been warned time and time again that my temper would some day get the best of me, and that failure to control it was certainly the worst part of me, and the part of my old self that hung on the longest.

I don't know why it was, and even the anger-management classes that I'd been forced to take didn't really help me understand it, but at times, I just went from zero to one hundred on the anger scale. Imagine a thermometer and the steady rise of the mercury as the temperature increases. That wasn't me. There wasn't anything slow or gradual about my responses when I lost control. I exhibited the proverbial flipped switch—lights off/lights on, and not just a middling 60-watt bulb, but also a white-hot theater spotlight. After every incident like this and others, I'd be enormously remorseful, berate myself for allowing something to flare up to such a degree.

What was worse, if that something did escalate into a physical confrontation, I was the one out on parole. Any kind of assault charge could have landed my ass back in prison and all the good work I'd done could be obliterated in that instant of lost self-control. Not good, I'd tell myself, not good at all.

The quality of explosiveness in muscles isn't something you normally think about when you consider endurance sports. After all, as the very words themselves imply (*explosive* and *endurance*) one is brief and the other long lasting. That said, my research and study of muscle physiology had me begin to dabble in explosiveness training. Another term for this type of workload being placed on your muscles is plyometrics. Essentially, as it was commonly used in the field in the first decade of the twenty-first century, plyometric protocols could be applied to almost any kind of exercise. However, what I learned and employed can probably be better labeled jump training. The reason for that is simple. What I incorporated into my training was jumping. I'd do four sets of 20 repetitions onto and off of a 36–48-inch-high box often holding 15–20 pound dumbbells in each hand.

As I later came to know, the trainers who developed exercises to promote explosiveness, in particular Dr. Yuri Verkhoshansky who is considered the father of plyometrics would disagree with categorizing box jumps as a plyometric exercise. In fact, he rejected the term "plyo-metrics" and preferred to use the term "shock method" or depending upon how the Russian words were translated you could substitute the word *impact* or *hit*. As my career as a trainer advanced and I studied more, I realized that just jumping onto a box, while its still a good exercise, isn't strictly speaking plyometric. The difference is that un-less the actions are being done very, very quickly—for example the transition from landing to taking off—within say .1–.2 seconds, then you aren't doing plyometrics as the old Soviet Bloc athletes were.

The neurophysiologic explanation for the intent behind this kind of training was that the exercises were designed so that the hit or im-pact (landing on the box or the floor) produced a strong involuntary eccentric contraction of the muscles. (An eccentric contraction is one in which the muscle contracts in response to some resistant force—the decelerating phase or slowing down of a body part.) The jumping part of the exercise produced a concentric contraction (positive force to propel or accelerate a body part). In the first, a muscle is lengthened; in the second, it is shortened.

Both are necessary, and I didn't think about it then, but much of what I was learning about muscles and exercise was another way to think about life generally. Muscles can have an agonistic/antagonis-tic relationship. They are most efficient when they complement one another. As one group produces a force the other effectively reduces it and the result is smooth, integrated movement, establishing a balance and synergy between them.

What I was trying to do in my training and in my life was to get into better balance, to become more efficient, to, in a very real sense, stop working against myself in order to succeed. In those early days, I was taking a scattershot approach to this, and one of the reasons why I was frequently so sore and so often injured wasn't just the abuse that

I heaped on myself but the fact that my muscles were out of balance and my mechanics and timing were frequently poor. I was doing as much tearing down as I was building up and those oppositions/polarities were often as much mental as they were physical.

My training journals from back then reflect this. At the 2006 Oceanside Ironman 70.3 held in March near Camp Pendleton in Southern California, I finally broke the 5-hour barrier for that distance. This was a significant milestone for me, but I walked away from it feeling like I had fallen short by not making it into the top 50. I was only two years into my training at that point, but still I was focused on how far back in the field I was. I thought more about the people who finished ahead of me, in this case about 100, than I did about those who finished behind me—nearly 1,900. I know that you can never succeed at anything by not aiming for the absolute top, but this tension within me was both an asset and a liability. I was particularly upset with my swim. On the one hand, I felt better about it because I'd made considerable gains over the previous year, but I knew that I still had such a long way to go. I was so inefficient in the water that I was coming out of it far more fatigued than I should have been, which negatively impacted my performance on the bike and run legs of the race.

In hindsight I can see that my recognizing cause and effect was important—as much as it was for me as a person as it was for me as an athlete. In the past, I lived as though I existed in a bubble, and that only my needs and desires mattered. As an athlete, I was seeing how effort and results were interrelated.

The Wildflower Half Ironman near Lake San Antonio in Central California proved to be another test, a bit of a failure, and a lesson learned. The course is very hilly, portions of it is conducted on dirt, and something about the whole event brought out the worst in me and another competitor that day. I suppose that it's safe to say that triathlons and other endurance sports attract a certain kind of overachieving, intense, type A sort of person. You have to be driven in order to compete, but rarely do those competitive traits bring two athletes into direct conflict. Toward the end of the bike portion, I was coming up behind another rider. The rules of triathlon are clear; you can't sit on anyone's rear wheel. In other words, you can't draft or sit in the slipstream of another rider thereby benefitting from the person ahead of you cutting through the wind.

As I came up on the rider ahead of me, I saw that I couldn't go around him. An official race vehicle was coming from the other direction, and I couldn't pull into that lane until the car passed us. I dropped back to what I thought was a "safe" (in the sense of the no-drafting rule) distance. As soon as the lane was clear, I moved out to overtake the rider. As I was passing him, I heard him yelling something about drafting, and then he took a drink from his water bottle and spit at me—not just once but twice. I couldn't believe this douche bag was actually spitting at me. All of a sudden, the "new" Shane who read books by the Buddhist priest Thich Nhat Hanh was replaced by the old Shane from the street and prison who understood that backing down from any challenge had dire consequences. Over the years I had been indoctrinated with the idea that people had to show me respect, and spitting at someone is one of the highest forms of disrespect. I lost it.

Instead of letting it go and passing him, I rode right alongside the guy and just ripped into him, "You fucking pussy. You're a coward. Just because I passed you, you have to spit on me?"

He started to give it right back to me, and that just got me even more fired up. As we continued our verbal battle for the next few minutes, I kept challenging him to get off his bike, stop being such a chickenshit, and even though he was bigger than me, he should prepare for me to crush his skull.

Eventually, I rode away from him and finished the race, but was still so pissed off that I wandered the finisher area, looking for his number so that I could—I wasn't sure. I was still feeling so heated that I might have done what I'd threatened. I'd like to think I would have told him that this was all a misunderstanding, but I doubt that's what would have gone down. I realized that I needed to keep my other self under wraps. The incident was a stark reminder that I needed to work on my temper before it set me back somehow.

I also had to work my way through a mixed message that incident signaled. I finished in the top 50 in that race, 43rd overall, in the top 3 percent. There were 1,656 participants, including approximately 30 professionals, so I was in pretty good company at the finish, and couldn't help but wonder how many positions I had lost during my meltdown with the spitter.

Maybe getting angry helped fuel me through that race. I was still dealing with a lot of guilt and shame, and my work-out regimen was still a way of dealing with those feelings. So maybe when racing I needed to bring those emotions to the surface. I also wondered if maybe it was a case of me being so accustomed to using anger as a motivator—consciously or subconsciously—that rage was my normal state of being. I knew that I couldn't keep going like that; eventually, that fuel was like the junk food that I consumed to get my system right after I'd bonked on some training outing. It was a fix, but a stopgap solution. I sensed that over time my anger would eat me up. In the long run, I'd be better served by figuring out a better way to deal with my emotions.

The mixed messages continued. In September, I raced the full Ironman distance in Madison, Wisconsin. As we entered the water, the sun was shining, but clouds were on the horizon. About 20 minutes into the swim, Lake Monona, one of four lakes right near downtown

Madison, got churned up by a cold front, with four-foot swells forcing race officials to fish many panicked athletes out of the water.

This was one of the most chaotic scenes I'd experienced in racing. As bad as the wind was on the water, it was even more of a problem on the bike. The cold front had the wind blowing a cold rain sideways, and just keeping the bike upright when it came in from the side or making forward progress when it was a headwind, wreaked havoc on everyone. At mile 80, on the way back to the transition zone, the wind was into my face so hard that there were periods I was riding as hard as I could and only going between 8 and 12 miles an hour. I was soaked to the bone, and freezing, but I drew on what I'd experienced that first winter in Boise and then later. I'd gone out into shittier conditions, often early in the morning and was underdressed, but managed to tough it out.

In Madison, I knew I could gut it out, that I'd presuffered enough times before this to make this race doable. I'd kicked my own ass out on those cold and lonely roads when my only reward was the sense of satisfaction that came from being able to think to myself that everyone else was snug and safe in their gym or at home on their trainer while I was out there pedaling in the shit storm.

I also drew on an experience I'd had in prison. Two of the COs who I never got along with laughed at me when I told them that I was one day going to race an Ironman when I got out. I clung to that memory, the sound of their derisive laughter, and I felt a bit warmer. I also reminded myself that I'd been a hell of a lot colder some nights in Boise, when the thin steel walls of my van, the cracked and leaky windows, put up little defense against a remorseless enemy.

My body also sent out some mixed messages to add to the confusion and chaos. During the run, I was so cold I had chicken skin the entire time. My receptors were so busy sending signals to my brain that I was freezing that they outshouted the organs of my digestive tract that were standing around with nothing to do. I hadn't eaten a thing 13 miles into the race when I just crumbled. My starving muscles could eventually be heard above the storm clamor and my brain suddenly got the message—I was as hungry as I'd ever been.

I wobbled into the aid station at mile 13 and for about 10 minutes I ate and drank whatever I could get my hands on. Coke. Cookies. Pretzels. I crammed as much into me as I could. I didn't think that it was possible for me to be so thirsty since as I ran, the wind-whipped rain felt like it was being forced into me through my mouth and skin. It was like running with an all body IV drip, but still I guzzled down as much Gatorade and water as I could. You might imagine that stopping in those conditions would have made me colder since my muscles weren't as active, but with all the grabbing and chewing I was doing, that wasn't the case at all.

I was energized by the fact that I'd seen the carnage out on the course in all three phases of the race. The attrition rate was incredibly high, and on the run, I saw a bunch of people doing the walk of shame. (I'd eventually learn that dropping out was more like the walk of the sane.) I knew what it was like to feel completely helpless and hopeless, and a little wind and a little rain and the feel of a sodden pair of socks squishing and abrading against a shoe's liner was nothing in comparison to some of the things I'd experienced.

I was also motivated by the presence of my family who were there watching me race. I'd heard their voices several times along the course and each time it helped me move forward, but when I crossed the finish line and then found them in the reunion area, I was overwhelmed. Trent, Carrie, his wife, and my mom and dad had all traveled to see me. They were all hooded and dripping, but gleeful. My dad was beaming; his ear-to-ear grin warmed me. When he told me how proud he was of me, I felt all the agony of the day being wrung out of me like the chamois cloth he insisted I use to dry his car back in the day.

I'm not too proud to admit that even at the age of thirty, I still sought my dad's approval. He'd seen firsthand that I had the fortitude that he did, that willingness to gut it out and pay the price. Mostly, he'd seen me at my worst, the quitter, the loser, the one who was powerless to overcome himself and the substances he ingested.

I can't say that he saw me at my best, that I'd qualified that day, but I'd shown him a far different side of me than he'd ever witnessed. I'd been keeping them apprised of my progress in our phone conversations, but seeing is not just believing, it's inspiring, life affirming, and maybe the best cure for uncertainty in existence. His praise warmed my body and soul, and as we all gathered together in a tight cluster, trying to keep the rain off us, I allowed myself for those few moments to really let go of the past and revel in the present.

When I got back to Boise, I knew that my second race season was over, and though I wasn't yet able to walk straight, after two days of rest, I climbed onto an elliptical trainer, knowing that while I was still spinning, maybe not a perfect circle, I was making progress. Despite all the mixed signals, the rising and the falling of my body as I worked those tender and torn muscles on that stationary machine, the trend was still forward.

My depleted immune system sent me another message. The flu wiped me out and I spent several days in bed, a miserable snot-producing, fevered runner who lay there smiling, grateful that all this resulted from my body's inability to fight off a virus and not me being dope-sick. You can measure success in lots of ways, and that was one way. The other was that I was learning, though it would still take me more time to truly grasp it and apply it: anatomical and physiological boundaries exist, and if you cross them, you will pay a heavy toll.

TEN

I probably always knew on some level that the human body is an amazing machine. When I was abusing substances so heavily, I didn't appreciate its capabilities and tenacity; in truth, I sometimes raged against its ability to take whatever I was dishing out and keep going about its business of synthesizing the harmful chemicals I was putting into it. When I first started training and competing, I don't think I marveled at the fact that all the miles and laps I logged caused so much cellular decay and damage. All I knew is that the soreness and the pain was a sign that I was doing a good thing. Eventually I figured out that I was wreaking havoc on several of the body's systems, and the "no pain, no gain" ethos was not the right philosophy to follow so literally.

Still, despite the abuse I heaped upon my body, it kept bouncing back. Once, I came across an old magazine lying around in the gym. When I leafed through it, I saw a Nike ad. The copy read: "The heart is the most resilient muscle. It is also the stupidest." I had to laugh—truth in advertising. My response was a mix of appreciation and guilt.

I understood what the words meant about the heart's senseless efforts to keep on beating no matter what we did to the body. We could never voluntarily mentally stop our own hearts from beating—that function was a part of the autonomic nervous system. Doing so would require more drastic action than just thinking about it.

In much the same way, I seemingly couldn't prevent my family from loving me. Just as I'd beat the shit out of my body for most of my life, I'd done the same thing to the people with whom I had the closest relationship in this world. Still, they kept coming back for me. I'd heard it said that inside every endurance athlete beats the heart of a masochist. In some ways that's true, just as it was within lots of families. That sounds harsh and reduces the complexity of those relationships to some kind of psychological problem, but there were times when I had to wonder. After all, I was having a difficult time accepting and loving myself because of all the things I'd done to others and to me. How could my mom and dad and brother see anything worthwhile in me given all that I'd done to damage their lives?

That my family showed up to support me in Madison in 2006 and everywhere else along the line is more of a miracle than me turning my life around and managing to finish all those races and eventually qualify for Kona. I don't know how much effort it took on their part, if they had to develop work-out routines and stick to plans of action as carefully as I did, but I don't think so. I believe that's what the Nike ad was suggesting in calling the heart the stupidest muscle. It just knows what it's supposed to do and does it, unthinkingly, unquestioningly, but with definite purpose.

Shortly after I got out of prison in 2004, my family gathered for the first time in quite a while to share a Christmas meal. For most of my adult life Christmas hadn't meant more than just another reason to get drunk or high.

As I made my way to Colorado to be with my family, I remembered that eleven years before, I'd spent the holidays in rehab back in Bloomington. 1995 was a tough year. I was at Heartland Junior College, making myself believe that I was on the right track. I'd long since been kicked out of the house, but my mom had agreed to cosign on an apartment lease. I lived there with my buddy Chad Overton. We were both going to school and working, me at a place called Jim's Steakhouse. My place was one of the gathering spots for the group of friends, many of them abusers and drunks, I'd gathered since coming to the great state of Illinois. Among them was Roger, Chad's best friend since high school.

In October, Chad and I were at the apartment when the phone rang. When he picked up and just sat there staring and not speaking for what seemed minutes, I knew the news wasn't good. And it wasn't. Roger had died. He was taking a shower at his house and when the water kept running and running, his mother walked in to see what was up and found him collapsed in the stall. Eventually his cause of death was identified as kidney failure. I didn't know that when Chad told me. Chad was fucking gutted, and so was I. We'd just been drinking the night before with Roger, when he'd had us all rolling on the floor with his usual drunken antics.

Now Roger was dead, and I remember thinking immediately that none of this made sense. At the time, I was scared shitless. My mind raced, starting with maybe he'd overdosed on coke and that he wouldn't have OD'd if I hadn't had given him that first taste, and, fucking shit, I had just scored a bag for him, and what would happen if they did an autopsy, and what a goddamn senseless waste and a sucking cunthole life was if the coolest dude we knew was the first one to go, a guy who was the kindest and gentlest among us ends up fucking dead while a dirtbag like me just keeps catching all the breaks, and what was the point of even giving a single grunted shit about anything if it can all just be yanked out from under you in a second? And maybe that live hard, die young, and leave a good-looking corpse isn't just a bunch of some meaningless bullshit, maybe you *should* just grab what you can when you can, and holy fuck, his poor mom having to find him, and we have to do something to honor our boy the way that he would have wanted us to, and why couldn't I be the kind of mellow cat he was, and what the fuck am I doing using past tense about some guy who not more than twenty-four hours ago had crashed on our couch and we were ripping him a new one because he had pissed himself and our couch when he was too lazy to just get up, and did that have anything to do with his kidneys because that wasn't the first time he'd done that, and what can you do to fill the gaping hole in your soul you're feeling right now?

As much as I'd overdo it and abuse my body all the time, I did the same thing with my brain most of the time.

I didn't go to the funeral. Couldn't do it. That was too much for me, sad to say, and as much as I wanted to man up and go, I couldn't see Roger like that. Instead, I just sat in the apartment drinking vodka, honoring him the weakest and only way I was capable of. And instead of sitting there thinking that maybe it is true that life is short and I better get my ass in gear and do something productive with the time I was given, I was thinking fuck it all and it just doesn't matter what you do because the whole thing is just a randomized joke at our expense, and the only rational response to irrationality is another act of irrationality.

For a long time, maybe the whole time I was in Bloomington, I'd been edging toward the abyss of nihilism. Roger's death just pushed me over the edge.

And then, a few months later when another good buddy Jamie,

wrapped himself and his motorcycle around a tree, he became the second killed in action in our little war against ourselves. Same thing. Couldn't go to the funeral. Couldn't see that the logical thing to do was to get clean and sober.

Chad took losing his childhood buddy Roger really, really hard. I'd come home from work or school, and for a while he'd be there on the couch drinking at all times of the day. Meanwhile, our mutual friend Woody and I also started really hitting it hard. We were constantly drinking, freebasing coke, doing bong rips or one-hitters, and eventually the whole pharmacopeia of so-called recreational drugs, including acid, shrooms, ecstasy, and eventually heroin—doing nods (unlike myself, Woody knew better than to mess with the heroin), snorting it in its powdered form, but never injecting it. I'd drawn a line in the powder back then—no needles. No needles. No needles. No needles. In hindsight, I'd eventually wish that I had been more like Chad who never did anything but drink.

Needless to say, I'd eventually cross that no-needles line, but not then. We'd sit around our place, having cooked up steaks I'd stolen from Jim's Steakhouse, America's future all gathered in that cosigned-for-by-my-mother apartment, feeling like we were the shit. We'd have our fun for a bit and then get down to business. We weren't going to end up like Tony and Felicia and the rest of the old people at Jim's. Could you imagine being in your late twenties or early thirties or even older than that and still working some shit job like that? Not us. We were in control. We had a plan.

From time to time, I'd realize that my plan for college and beyond maybe required me to straighten up. I was in a dark, dark place, I knew, and at one point, I went to my psychology professor, a woman who taught a class that I really liked and who seemed to have her shit together. I told her that I was losing control, that I was fearful that I wasn't ever going to be able to pull up on the stick and keep myself from spiraling into the ground. At her urging, I went to Parkland Recovery Center in Belville, Illinois, and did a stint at rehab over Christmas of '95.

Funny that I spent more than one of those holidays in rehab or locked up over the years. Maybe that was my way of going home, my own snowy version of "I'll Be Home for Christmas." Each one of those instances etched a dark spot in my memory and had me feeling different about the holidays than other people I knew.

Woody was the only one who came to visit me, to wish me a merry Christmas with a gift of a box of chocolates. "And do try those peanut butter ones, Shane. You're really going to like them," he'd say. And I did. They seemed to have some added ingredient that lifted my spirits. Woody picked me up when my two-week rehab stint was over. I hopped in the car, and he pointed at the passenger side footwell. A case of Budweiser for the ride home and a way to ease back into my normal life. I didn't hesitate for a second, just popped the top and gulped it down. Welcome back my old friend we said to one another.

Even as I kept pounding down the beers, proud of myself for not caving into the desire to smoke some foils with Woody, I kept thinking that this quitting thing seemed impossible. A guy we knew on the fringes of our group showed up at our place, whipped his jacket open to reveal a T-shirt that said, REHAB IS FOR QUITTERS. I laughed along with everybody else, but a thought that I'd been carrying around in my head for a good long while choked it off. I knew I couldn't keep going in the same direction I'd been traveling. I was losing my grip and I knew it, but I put on my party hat and hoped no one could sense my fear. If I could just get out of Bloomington, a place I'd once despised and now had converted into my own little personal fiefdom of failure and fucking up, this quitting thing wouldn't be so hard.

I had set my sights on Colorado. You know, going back to the place of origin, the source of it all. Things would be better there. I was sure of it. Surer than I had been of anything else in my life to that point.

Now, here I was eleven years later making the trek south to be with family again, those memories of all the havoc I wreaked stuffed into the duffel bag in the overhead rack of the Greyhound bus making the twelve-hour trip from Boise to the Boulder area. For so long, the Christmas holidays had been spent in rehab or with me strung out, so along with those memories and my clothes in that duffel bag, I came bearing a gift of anxiety.

As a family, the Niemeyers were edging closer to a healthy relationship. I was grateful for that. The good thing was, despite my propensity for overdoing it and causing damage, at least as far as my family was concerned, I'd ended that habit. My letters from prison had been overly dramatic, a kind of make-up-for-it-all-at-once outpouring of Hallmark-rejectable sappy sentimentalism. Relations between us were normalizing, to borrow an expression from the geopolitical world, and that was a good thing.

Using work as a reason for not attending the holiday gathering in 2006 isn't as weak as it may seem; or maybe more so depending on your perspective. In the fall of 2006, my dad had essentially been handed a death sentence by an oncologist. He was diagnosed with pancreatic cancer and it was in its advanced stages. A pancreatic carcinoma is a sinister bastard, often growing without the patient experiencing any symptoms to warn him or her that anything is amiss. Ralph Niemeyer was always the toughest man I had known and despite all the rough going that he and my mom had endured, they really had each other's back. When he was first told that at best he could expect to live for three months, they didn't pack it in; instead, they packed their bags and went to Rochester, Minnesota, and the Mayo Clinic.

The doctors at Mayo were more optimistic. They could treat him and extend what my dad wanted—more days where his quality of life wouldn't be compromised. Not wanting to extend existence at the cost of good and solid time, he dealt with his illness head-on. Since prison I had developed a strong sense of urgency, and learning of my father's illness intensified that sense. I had let so many years get behind us and had taken for granted that we would have time to mend fences between us. The news of his illness made me feel desperate. I was evermore thinking of time and the finite nature of it.

My dad had to endure his own version of an Ironman (but far worse), enduring intensive chemotherapy and then being splayed out on an operating room table for more than ten hours undergoing what is called a Whipple Operation. Basically, the head of his pancreas was removed along with a part of his duodenum and then he was sewn back together.

Doctors told my mom and dad that the survival rate five years out was 20 percent. So while I was keeping track of my time in the Half Ironman and the Ironman, we were all keeping track of my dad's time in the ultimate race. I can't say how many times I looked at what I was doing, trying to become a top-tier endurance athlete, and thought that it was a selfish pursuit, a ridiculous attempt to push my body and my spirit beyond its limits to no good end other than maybe gratifying my ego. What my dad was enduring made me feel even more like my pursuit of Ironman verged on the pointless. Also, as I studied more and more about human anatomy and physiology, I learned that for most cancers, the genetic predisposition to eventually develop one was something like 2 percent. That meant that 98 percent of the time, some other factor, environmental and nutritional ones mostly, were responsible. I also knew that stress played a huge role in determining who gets cancer and who doesn't. I understood that I wasn't the only cause of stress in my dad's life, that he had grown up on a steady diet of it given how execrably his stepfather and others had treated him, but I was certainly a huge contributor to it.

I was the talker in the family, the lone one among us with a gift for using words. I don't know whose idea it was to not talk about my suicide attempt and overdoses, but we all tacitly agreed that such things were best not spoken of. I can't say that I wanted to go into any kind of detail with them or share the stories of the degradation and despair that led me to it. But what about that underlying tension I mentioned? I think that my dad's condition and the role I played in it, my decision to not circle the wagons and rejoin them in Illinois, was a part of what made us all edgy around one another. That said, as soon as a plan evolved for them to move to Colorado, I was immediately with it. Then when he was diagnosed, I made an immediate plan to move closer to them.

We were good at doing the solid Midwestern thing, soldiering on and making sure that we didn't do anything to step on one another's toes, though the tango we had to perform in order to avoid doing so was a taxing and sometimes flamboyant dance. You try to make it look effortless and natural, but in truth it exhausts you mentally and physically. My mom kept me apprised of my dad's condition, and for the most part, post-surgery he seemed in good shape. Funny that my old man wanted to return to Colorado, just as I had. My mom, ever the devoted one, took early retirement to be with him and spend as much time as she could before—. The sentence always ended there, the dash that stood for dashed hopes and dreams.

It seemed to me that things were coming full circle. My dad's desire to die with a view of the Rockies, in the place where he had started our family, was reminiscent of my own get-back plans. And, at times he was doing so well we forgot that he was ill, and we were lulled into the thought that perhaps he would escape the clutches of what would turn out to be a most wicked fate for him. Other times I was snapped back to the reality of his illness, and that made me even more aware of the nature of time and a body's fragility and decline.

In the past, if there was something that I wanted to do, I did it immediately and with little planning. As much as I felt the urgency to get back to Colorado as soon as possible, I couldn't. I had been sentenced to an intensive seven-year probation by the state of Idaho. Essentially, they still owned my ass and dictated where I could set it down. My mom had never stopped hinting for me to move back home, and with the knowledge I had about survivability rates and all the rest, she didn't have to press very hard to get me into action. I tried to be sensible but that old Shane, the impatient, pleasure-seeking, gotta-have-it-now Shane emerged.

Neuroscientists would probably tell you that I have a highly active amygdala. That means that the emotional centers in my brain tend to overpower the more rational parts. Hearing my mother say those words to me, at a time when I was feeling fairly vulnerable myself, was gas on an already blazing fire. I decided I had to go as soon as possible.

Having spent much of my adolescence and early adulthood stealing most things that I wanted but couldn't afford, I was constantly stunned by how much it cost to keep myself solvent. I knew that if I was going to move to Colorado, I was going to have to petition the state of Idaho for permission. That meant getting a lawyer to file the necessary papers and plead my case for me. Lawyers meant money. Money that I didn't really have. Panicky about my dad, I did something I regret to this day. I asked some of my clients to pay me directly. I wasn't going to give the gym their cut of the proceeds. I knew the rules. I knew that I was breaking them, and whether or not the percentage take the gym demanded was equitable or not was beside the point. I was violating the terms of my contract with them and I knew it.

I thought that was the quickest way to get the cash I would need to do this thing. I also have to admit that I was eager to move to Colorado, and more specifically to Boulder, because it was the Mecca for endurance athletes. I had become a bit of a big fish in a relatively small pond in Boise. Just like a performer dreams of making it big in Hollywood or in New York, that's what Boulder represented to me and to thousands of other athletes.

For a few months my plan worked. I was a nervous wreck the whole time, fearful that I was going to get caught, and I was. A review of the books revealed the discrepancy between the hours I was logging with clients and the gym's take of the proceeds. I was suspended for the violation and was later threatened with legal action. My previous response would have been to get out of Dodge immediately, but I worked with the management and eventually paid them what I considered to be a fair and accurate amount to settle the account. I was glad that I had my brother, Trent, to help talk me through possible settlement scenarios. I was very disappointed that I was leaving Boise with a reputation that had suffered a black eye.

Hearing the chief financial officer throw around words like *embezzlement* and *theft* scared the shit out of me. The possibility of going back to jail, the possibility of feeling guilt, regret, and self-condemnation for taking a shortcut stressed me out and twisted me up. This was a major setback for me, and I felt like a failure on so many levels. My best friend, Ann Sabala, and a few others were instrumental in keeping me from spinning out of control and destroying everything I'd worked so hard for. Sitting in those offices, listening to my accusers, I felt like I was back in the day, feeling those same desires to deny, deflect, and damn myself.

My clients weren't upset with me; they viewed the arrangement between trainers and the gym as unfair. Regardless, I knew the rules and I'd violated them. I was glad that things turned out as they did. I don't know exactly how management's pursuit of a legal proceeding would have impacted my desire to be granted permission to move to Colorado. I can't imagine it would have been in any way positive. My deciding to try to take a shortcut had nearly cost me.

Boulder is a unique place. Its altitude (5,430 feet above sea level), abundant sunshine, and relatively mild winters make year-round outdoor training possible and attract the top endurance athletes in the world. I had wanted to move there ever since I read that article in prison. I felt like I'd accomplished what I needed to in Boise. I had become one of the top athletes in the area, and more important, I'd learned an incredible amount about myself, my capabilities, and most important, what kind of person I wanted to be. I had made a stand and turned things around in the very place where my life had crumbled. I felt, for the most part, I had faced and conquered my demons and could move forward.

Along with Ma Keller, I'd had a few other clients who showed me what it was like to be an adult, to have a purpose in life beyond what I was doing as an athlete. I'm particularly grateful to Ian Davey, a radiologist and a native of South Africa. He was someone who I wanted to emulate, because of his nearly unshakable calm, and when his calm was replaced with passion and fire, it was always warranted. It wasn't that he was a completely laid-back chill kind of guy, but he was unflappable. I'd see him dealing with his kids and his wife and even when things were somewhat chaotic, as they're going to be when you have young children demanding your attention, he always seemed to be so reasonable with everyone, including me. Ian and I had a few talks about an issue that troubled me for a long time after I'd been released from prison.

Ian was real. He was a radiologist and had a successful business. He could be slightly foulmouthed and very funny. He told me what he thought and how he felt without the trappings of correctness or posturing that permeate many interactions. His worldview was unique and insightful for me. Not only was Ian a mentor of sorts, but he always gave me medical advice (I didn't have insurance at the time). In being an excellent radiologist, he knew a lot about everything. Several times he gave me a quick examination to ensure me that nothing was broken. One time, I had a growth appear on my testicles out of nowhere. The sudden emergence of a third nut scared the hell out of me, but Ian drove me to his office to take images and cleared it as a benign calcified fatty deposit that would likely resolve itself (as it did). That was the kind of guy he was. I had all these great people looking after me at this time in my life, and I was so grateful for it when all I had known in the not-so-distant past were the people lurking in the shadows, other addicts and crooks who would always choose their own ass over mine.

People talk about criminals owing a debt to society, and I had no problem acknowledging that I was a criminal and that I certainly did owe society and individuals something. In time, I struggled with the question of when does that debt go in the books as being paid? It was like I wanted some kind of karmic bank account to let me know when I'd put enough on one side of the ledger that would tell me, okay, you've done enough, or not okay, you need to do more. It wasn't as if once I arrived at the point where I felt like I'd done enough to make up for all the shitty things I'd done I would resort to my old ways. It was more like for how long should I go on carrying that load of my past around with me? I didn't ever want to just forget about it or pretend that it had never happened, but how long was I going to let that part of my life define the new life I was leading? I suppose that's why the incident with payment and the gym was so unsettling to me. That was the first real strong evidence that remnants of that old Shane were still there.

Ann and Ian both told me that I couldn't go around carrying the cross of my past forever. They also reminded me that I'd done so well in the years since, and that was where my thoughts should be focused. Along with those words of encouragement, they also shared their own experiences and their own reading, providing me additional input and information, which helped to shape and enrich my life in those formative years.

I guess I had mixed emotions and mixed motives about moving to Colorado to be closer to my family. Was I doing it for them or for me? Did that really matter? Did I want to be the prodigal son or was the reformation of myself more important and something that I should do independent of them?

I should also say that, despite my initial feelings of urgency, it wasn't like we were on a deathwatch with my dad at that point. Because his pancreas was compromised, he developed diabetes, but he was, for the most part still doing well after that Whipple procedure. So, I guess what I'm saying is that I struggled with the idea of want and need. I didn't want to go to Boulder only because I felt I owed my father something. I knew that I could never repay him for everything he'd done for me anyway. He deserved better than to have me come crawling back out of a sense of duty alone. I had to want to do these things because they were the right things to do.

Eventually, because it was the right thing to do for all of us, and because I was fortunate that my dad's oncologist intervened with a letter on my behalf, I did make the choice to go to Boulder. Looking back on that stretch of time, I can see that I was maturing. Initially my wanting to get to Boulder ASAP had been impulsive, and I'd acted rashly by violating the club's rules. After that, I was able to step back and make a choice, not a half-baked reaction, but a reasoned and reasonable decision.

When I did move to Boulder in late August 2007, my dad and I didn't take long walks holding hands hashing things out between us. That just wasn't how we did things in my family. We started with just being father and son again. He wanted to help with the unloading of the moving van. He wanted to check out a car I was interested in buying. Later, he wanted to repair and maintain that same vehicle. He wanted to do the typical things that a father does for a son, even when that son had previously never shown him the kind of gratitude that he ought to have. We were taking tentative steps, walking before we could run, both us knowing that we were recovering from a trial that had tested our endurance in ways that could never be measured with a clock.

Even though we both knew that time was finite, as it is for all of us, we weren't going to take on anything too strenuous, anything that might aggravate old injuries, rush into anything. We were going to take some time to heal up properly.

In retrospect, I wish that some of those lessons that Shane the person was learning translated to Shane the athlete. I was still hitting it too hard, still intensely feeling that time deficit, and still trying to cram too much into my routine. Weight training still occupied a lot of my training time, especially on leg and core days—the hours devoted to my lower body. I was doing regular squats in sets with weight varying from 185–375 pounds, the leg press (180–900 pounds), dead lifts (135–145 pounds), and walking lunges with 20–40-pound dumb-bells. I'd also learned some things about the importance of adding single-leg and dynamic movements into the mix.

I liked doing box jumps and added dumbbell weights (15–20 pounds per hand) to make the work even more difficult. I'd arrange four boxes of various sizes (from 2–4 feet high) in a circle. I'd place a Bosu half ball in the middle. That device was a cushioned, inflated semicircle affixed to a firm and flat platform. Jumping onto the ball reduced the amount of force, impact on the landing, but because the surface wasn't completely firm, I'd have to use smaller intrinsic mus-cles to stabilize myself. I'd do a circuit of that ball and those boxes and be crushed by the intensity of that protocol. I also incorporated a ball into my squat routine by standing on a big Swissball. I got to the point where I could jump from the ground onto a ball, land, do a squat, and then jump to another ball and repeat the process. I wasn't always successful, and the ball sometimes won by ejecting me. A cracked rib and a couple of sprained wrists were the price I paid for looking cool. Looking back I was foolish to train like that, the intensity and risk associated with those exercises was far too great for an endurance ath-lete preparing for longer events. The only utility they really had would be for a Cirque du Soleil performer.

I was still running with Kenny McDaniel up until the day I left for Boulder, and I loved to see how fluid his mechanics were, but I was often so sore that I had to devote most of my mental energy to simply keeping myself moving. I couldn't really concentrate on the efficiency and economy of movement the way I should have. Kenny's dog, a German Shorthaired Pointer named Bailey, frequently joined us. Talk about an efficient runner. I may be making it sound like I was torturing myself, and in certain ways I was, but those runs were great stress reducers. Just Kenny, Bailey, and me, out in the woods or running along the river was incredibly therapeutic. I found great solace in the solitude of running in the trail system north of Boise. I sometimes rode my mountain bike out there, stashed it in the weeds, then took to the single track system, enjoying getting lost, and taking satisfaction in finding my way back to the starting point.

I continued to use exercise and movement as a way to process the inner turmoil I was dealing with. It wasn't just my past I was negotiating, but present difficulties like my decision to move to Boulder, my dad's health, various issues with women I was dating, finances, and all the things that make up living the life of an adult. I could say that I was using exercise in the same way I once used drugs and alcohol, but clearly that was a better alternative.

I returned to Oceanside in 2007 and covered the 70.3 miles in 4:36. I set a PR for the Half Ironman that day, but I barely cracked the top 100 athletes (80th out of 1,890 athletes). I was getting faster, but so was the competition. In June, shortly before I moved to Boulder, I did the Coeur d'Alene full Ironman. I finished in 10:12:28. I had set another preliminary goal for myself at the beginning of the racing season. I wanted to crack the 10-hour barrier. Mother Nature wasn't going to cooperate with my plan, and she threw a 90-plus-degree day at us, nice if you're picnicking in Idaho in June, but really damn hot if you're racing. I'm not making excuses for my failure to meet my goal but once again my failure to hydrate properly caught up with me. My hamstrings completely cramped up at mile 90 on the bike, and one of the main sources of cramping is loss of electrolytes and poor hydration.

By the middle of the bike leg I had ridden toward the front of the race, but when I started cramping I fell off and began getting passed by several other riders. As each one went past me, I became more and more angry with myself, and thought more and more about how shitty I was doing. That mind-set is not the best to carry with you into a 26.2-mile run in that kind of heat. A 3:45 marathon is respectable for a recreational runner but not for someone who was aiming to be a top age-group triathlete. Still, anything under 4 hours is decent, at least in terms of effort, and I knocked more than an hour off of my first full Ironman time. When I got back to Boise and my friends and clients asked how I did, all I could talk about is how I should have done better. That made it hard for people to be happy for me. I had a hard time keeping that glass half full, and was never good at giving myself credit. I was, as I always had been, my own worst critic.

I can see now that my life was out of balance. Most days I woke up at 5:30 a.m., trained clients at the gym in the morning, got in my work, then was back at the gym from 4:00 until 7:00 p.m. with more clients, and then did more of my training. I'd get home after 9:00 p.m., eat, study, or read before bed, and then I was up and at it again. It was a complete grind that revolved almost completely around triathlon training and competing. I still had to have every hour accounted for, and I told myself that I liked the grind. I told myself that whatever pain I felt, that was the weakness leaching out my body. Everything I did was part of the process of becoming someone different, someone better, someone faster. I felt an overwhelming urge to prove to myself and others that I could succeed. I'd eventually realize that there was more to life than this, but in those moments, when I compared who I was then to who I had been in the past, believing that I wasn't good enough was much better than believing that it was better to just die already.

I couldn't have realized it then, but despite all my doubts and frequent negativity, I was on the verge of some major breakthrough performances as an athlete *and* as a person.

ELEVEN

In many sports, athletes sometimes struggle through what is called their "sophomore slump." They experience a lot of success their first year competing at a certain level, but then, whether because the novelty wears off a bit, they rest on their laurels, or the competition catches up to them and exposes some weakness in their game, they struggle to attain that same level in their second go around. Fortunately for me, I started at an age and level of experience and in the truest sense, ignorance, that I didn't have any expectations other than just finishing the races my rookie year. I knew what I wanted to achieve, and as I made it through my first and second year, I established a set of subgoals to attain that big picture I had in mind—qualifying for the Ironman World Championship in Kona, Hawaii.

With any activity, you're going to experience both a learning curve and a performance curve. As I entered my third season of competition at the beginning of 2008, those curves were both sharply upward. I was fortunate that my move to Boulder also exposed me to a higher caliber of athletes. With my experience at Gold's Gym, and those Trainer of the Year awards, my education, and my own success competing, I was able to get a job immediately.

That wasn't as easy as I thought it was going to be. I wanted to work at the Flatiron Athletic Club (FAC)—named after a range of sandstone formations that dominate the views in and around Boulder. Initially they denied me employment because I didn't have a client base established yet. I was determined to meet their standards, both so that I could work there and benefit from training there. The FAC was the source—the fountainhead—of triathlon, the place where Dave Scott, Simon Lessing, and Wolfgang Dietrich coached many other top pros and amateurs.

In hindsight, I should have just sucked it up, done what I could to cut expenses elsewhere and paid one of these three legends to coach me. I didn't. I was hoping to figure it out on my own and with the free advice and goodwill of the community. That worked, but I might have been able to speed up the process and avoid some of the pain had I gone the other way.

I found work at the Rallysport Athletic Club instead. Many of the trainers there were smarter and more highly educated than anybody I'd come across in Boise. I'd definitely taken a step up compared to the old home base, but I still had my sights set on working at the FAC. It took me eighteen months of busting my ass to attract enough clients to get into FAC, but I wasn't discouraged at all in the beginning. Just like at that point I knew I'd eventually get to Kona, I was sure I'd do whatever it took to work at FAC.

I used to tell people that in Boulder, you could be walking down nearly any street, randomly throw a penny, and you could hit somebody who'd once competed in a world championship or an Olympics. In time I'd meet Craig Alexander who would win the World Championship that year, then again in 2009—becoming only the fourth man to win it back-to-back, joining the ranks of the legends Dave Scott, Mark Allen, and Tim DeBoom. I also got a chance to meet Chrissie Wellington, a Brit who won the world championship three consecutive years (2007–2009) before capturing the title again in 2011 before announcing her retirement. I sometimes felt like I was some googly-eyed groupie who had been reading about these people for years and was now seeing them in the flesh. Tim O'Donnell, Julie Dibens, Michael Lovato, and Matt Reed were also among that elite group. They were all gracious and answered my questions about how they organized their training. Craig Alexander, multiple world champ and a hero of mine whose career I had been watching since my days in prison was especially helpful. He always let me stop him to pick his brain.

I was most fortunate that Joanna Zeiger, an Olympian and an Ironman Champion was willing to share her expertise and training philosophy with me. Joanna is an amazing woman, an Ivy League educated world-class swimmer turned triathlete, and an incredibly decent person. Over time, she became like a sister to me. A small group of us, including Billy a retired marine officer who was apparently sick of the strict military lifestyle and could never get anywhere on time, and who was now competing professionally, was part of that crew. Brandon (a guy I called Brando) was our comic relief. He'd grown up as a runner and competed at a very high level in college. I don't know if all the years of intense discipline had taken their toll on him, but by the time I met him, Brando's drive to succeed athletically had waned a bit. I think he could have been one of the top athletes in the country if he just applied himself a little more.

I gravitated to Brando because he was really quick-witted and sharp, but I sensed that his humor was a kind of defense. We talked a lot on our runs, and he confessed that, like me, he didn't have a whole lot of confidence in himself and his abilities. Brando was openly gay, and had a hard time accepting the truth about himself as a teen. He confessed that life wasn't very easy for him back then. I could understand how being outside the "norm" can create a real dissonance in your life. I let him know about what I'd done to myself, some of the conflicts I still struggled with. Not only was Brando a great friend, but he was also a good technical run coach. He helped me to think about timing and the rhythm of running. He told me that on our first few group runs, I sounded like a horse (more of a draft horse than a Thoroughbred) and I began to pay attention to the aural aspect of my running.

At the center of this little universe was Joanna. Because of her experience and accomplishments, we all gravitated toward her. We'd meet at her house, and for the most part, do whatever workout she planned on doing that day. This wasn't all about Joanna being magnanimous and dispensing her wisdom. She knew that working out with a group of really fit men was helping her as well. She was a strong woman in a lot of regards, and at times she could be quite intense. When it came to route choices or the structure of the workout, Joanna wasn't very flexible. It wasn't quite her way or the highway but she was definitely the leader of our little pack.

I don't know if it was because I was a newcomer in the community or what side of Joanna's personality I brought out, but Joanna and her husband, Mark, were like family to me. They took me in and she shared a lot of her experience with me. The same is true of Dave and Jane Scott. To improve my performance in the swim, I attended their masters swim classes. The first session, one thing became clear. I may have thought I was working hard in the pool, but the intensity of their workouts had me damn near drowning at first. Nearly everything they did was done at greater distances—3,300–4,000 meters in 60–70 minutes. I was used to shorter intervals and more rest in between, but they had us in the pool and going nonstop and at a pace much quicker than I was used to. The swims overwhelmed and discouraged me the first few weeks. To see how the other swimmers didn't seem to struggle as much as I did during the workouts was deflating. The intensity and duration of the swims were so much that I felt as though at the end of the workout I had swum back in time.

They also helped a great deal with my swim mechanics. Jane would pull me aside and tell me that I needed to be longer in the water or Dave would say that my hands needed to be closed more. All the little tweaks and the attention to detail they provided paid off. When I entered the class, I was swimming 1:50–2:00 for 100 meters. That's a common baseline distance used to evaluate your swimming. By the end, I was down to 1:30 per 100. That may seem like a slight improvement, 20 seconds, but over the long distances of the Ironman, distances measured in kilometers, those seconds turned into minutes.

More important, Dave Scott answered any question I had for him. How many miles should I be running in the off-season? How much should I ride? How should I organize my days and workouts? It didn't matter how inane the question might have been, Dave gave me a thoughtful response. To that point, Dave was by far the most knowledgeable person in regards to training that I'd met.

Despite all the great people I was surrounded by and the plethora of advice I was given, I still wasn't nearly as strategic about my training as I should have been. With our core group of four, I'd do whatever workout Billy was doing. Then the next day, I'd tackle whatever hell Joanna had in mind. I never took the time between to rest. I was always tired and strung out. I had heard them talk about *easy* days, but because I always seemed to catch them on their hard days, I had no real frame of reference.

Since running always felt like it was my weakest area, I decided to put some of my newly gained knowledge to the test at the Austin Marathon/Half Marathon. I ran the shorter of the two distances—the 13.1-mile half marathon. The half drew 6,200 participants, and I managed to finish 29th overall. Besides the Hill Country, much of Texas is flat, but the state's capitol is definitely not that. I felt great about that performance, and 6:03 per mile pace was definitely the quickest I'd ever run. This was a huge boost in my confidence. Every time I started the run in a triathlon, my head was full of doubts. This proved that I could hold a respectable pace. All I'd learned about cutting down my stride length, increasing my cadence, and now paying attention to the rhythm of my footfalls and arm swing was starting to pay dividends.

With the run coming at the end of every triathlon, the point at which you are the least fresh, being able to hang on to good form and execute proper and efficient run mechanics is especially critical when your brain and body are not functioning optimally. I was especially pleased that I kept a 6:07–6:08-per-mile pace for the first 10 miles and then picked it up to a 6:01 per mile for the last 3-plus. This wasn't a case of me bringing home a wounded aircraft and skidding across the finish line. I was flying at the end with some still left in reserve. I savored that feeling of not being on the verge of total collapse at the end of a race. I also stored it away in my memory banks, hoping that I could draw from that experience again down the line.

I would have loved to be able to duplicate the half marathon time in May when I competed in the Wildflower Half Ironman in Bradley, California, again. The Debbie Downer in me looks back at that race and thinks about the fact that I ran a 6:53 pace for the half marathon, almost a minute slower per mile than I'd run in Austin. On the positive side, that effort brought me home in 18th place overall out of a field of 1,650 men and the run course is one of the toughest in the country. I came out of the water in 61st place overall—not bad for me—and had a solid day in the saddle, and wound up in 9th, hanging on to finish in that top-20 position. I finished well enough to qualify for my professional card, though I chose not to pursue that option.

At this point in my career—less than three years in—I chose to pass, because I didn't have nearly enough time under my belt. I was working full-time, and often injured. Most of the pro men grew up running or swimming, many of them had been professional cyclists. Few of them worked at all. At the time, I just didn't stack up, and wouldn't want to be one of the last pro men crossing the line. We all race the same course so I figured it wasn't practical at the time. Certainly wouldn't have done my self-confidence any good.

What those numbers don't reveal is how much I struggled in the transition zones. Yes, I came out of the water in 61st place, but it took me 2 minutes and 26 seconds to get onto the bike and back out on the course. In that span, I was now in 85th place. Despite having the 9th fastest time on the bike overall, I was in 85th position by the time I made it out onto the running course. I had a lot of room for improvement in that area. Paying attention to details was never my strong suit and my slow transitions made that painfully clear. I was losing free time. I'd wanted to crack 4:30 as a finishing time, and I'd missed that by 3 minutes. I probably couldn't have made up those 3 minutes by speeding my transitions, but it would have put me a lot closer, and if I had known that I was so close, maybe I could have picked up the pace a bit in the run.

Still, I finished first in my age group, and that felt amazingly gratifying given that Wildflower is such a big race with a deep field.

I experienced another breakthrough at the Boise 70.3-mile race the following month. My swim was slower than usual—for some reason I couldn't stay on course. As a frame of reference, I finished the swim in 27:34 at Wildflower and in 32:23 in Boise. That's one of the things about triathlons that fascinates me and keeps me going. There are so many variables. Why on that particular day, in a body of water in which I'd trained, was I struggling so much to just go straight? I was 51st out of the water (better than at Wildflower despite my slower swim time). Miraculously, I maintained that same position when I got onto the bike. I guess I wasn't the only one with slow transition times. By the end of the ride, the last 8 miles, I had nothing left in my legs. It was like there were two logs attached to my hips. Still, I'd managed to climb to 30th overall, and 3rd in my age group.

With even a decent effort on the run, I had a real shot at finishing under 4:30, which was one of the milestone times for me. First my goal was to finish the Half Ironman distance race in under 5 hours, then 4:45, and now 4:30. At about mile 7 of the run, the inevitable happened. The week before the race, I'd been experiencing some severe pain in my right foot. I didn't get it checked out and hoped, stupidly, that whatever was wrong would magically heal itself. In the race, with every foot strike, a jolt of pain shot up from the area near my arch. I ignored it, but just past the halfway point of the race, I felt another shock of pain and heard and felt a kind of snap. At that point, those sharp sporadic pains turned into an intense, searing, and continuous jabbing that made each step agonizing. I knew that I'd broken my fourth metatarsal—the bone that makes up the second smallest toe.

Using all the old techniques of mental mastery—reminding myself that I'd felt worse before, I was late to the party and needed to catch up, and quitting wouldn't do me any good—I finished the race.

I'd actually completed the run portion faster with that broken foot than any Half Ironman I had run (1:25) previously, and I'd easily broken that 4:30 by finishing the race with a time of 4 hours and 23 minutes.

This race was supposed to be my lead in to Ironman Coeur d'Alene—my next attempt to qualify for Kona and which was only three weeks later. Instead, I had to rest for a couple of months to let that foot heal. Rest is a relative term here—I didn't stop training completely, but I couldn't put myself through the paces I needed to in order to race the full Ironman distance. I tried to make up for not running by riding and swimming more. Because of the popularity of the sport, most of the races fill their entry quota a year in advance. That means that you have to register early, have your upcoming season figured out well in advance of that, and target and tune in your training for those events that will help you qualify for the World Championship. Unfortunately for me, Coeur d'Alene was my last shot to qualify for 2008. I'd been doing well, steadily getting faster, fine-tuning my training (less weight lifting and more dynamic and global movement patterns to effect more tissues and create movement in more joints), and developing routines (thanks to all those aforementioned people) that were more specific to Ironman Triathlons.

At the time, I took pride in gutting it out, and to an extent I still look at it as an achievement, but hammering it all the way to the end wasn't the smartest thing I could do. That race was emblematic of the major problem I had in my first few years of training—I just kept going after it so hard day after day because I didn't trust myself. I was past the idea that I would one day just stop entirely and go back to my old life, but I lacked confidence in my abilities as an athlete. I didn't have faith in the training plan that I was executing—if I can really call it a plan at all.

The injury did allow me to thoroughly enjoy a family trip we all took to Alaska in mid-September. My mom and dad; my mom's brother John; my brother, Trent, and his wife, Carrie; and I all headed up there. My dad was still doing well, and he had always wanted to go to Alaska to enjoy its natural wonders. For him this was a bucket list trip. He and my mom chartered a boat that would take us on a ten-day cruise up and down the Inside Passage. This wasn't a giant ocean-going cruise ship, but a smaller vessel in which Uncle John and I were scheduled to be bunkmates while the other couples each had a room. A small crew would cook our meals and navigate the boat. I don't think I made the best impression on the captain when I showed up in Juneau with my bike and a portable indoor trainer. I still planned on getting some riding in, as well as some swimming. I had the Great Floridian Ironman coming up on the twenty-fifth of the following month. I also brought my wet suit and fully intended to swim in those frigid waters—seal populated, jellyfish infested, orca patrolled they may be, but nothing was going to stop me.

I spent some hours spinning away while the boat was docked, and I did swim, though my dad wasn't too happy about that thinking this was a little extreme. He was mostly joking with me when he said that he would be there to beat away the killer whales and salmon sharks that might get me. He also was genuinely concerned about my safety, so he insisted on paddling a kayak alongside me in the numbing waters. I had enough sense—after everyone told me absolutely no, I could not—not to swim along with my family when they went out in a motorized raft to get near a glacier that was calving. The huge chunks of ice that fell churned up the water, making mini-tsunamis and icebergs. It would have been like swimming in a margarita on the rocks, which appealed to me at the time.

I loved every minute of the trip. My dad was in his element. We went fishing and caught salmon and halibut. When we weren't kayaking along the shoreline or hiking, we hung out and played cards periodically looking out the windows at the enormous beauty we were immersed in. I was awed by the scenery with its contrasting vibrant greens and dreary grays and imagined that much of the landmass that made up these islands hadn't ever been set foot on by a human being. I loved paddling as close in as I could to the bears. I was amazed by how quick they could move for such a large animal. It was clear that it would be wise to not ever mess with one of them—something about their cold, malevolent eyes was chilling and made the hair on my neck tingle.

This was the first time we'd really been together as a family doing something like this since I was a kid. I could tell my dad loved it. He could go off tromping around in the woods—the area was as green and lush as anything I'd ever seen, and he'd come back with a huge smile on his face. After a while we lost count of the number of wildlife sightings we made. There were a few moments of tension between my dad and me. We were two men out doing things, and, of course, we each had our own way of doing them and thought the other's was the wrong way. Typical family stuff this time, not the kind of thing that ended up with me punching a hole in the boat's deck.

There was something about the contrast in the environment that made me understand just a bit better how much progress I'd made. Not every day of the trip was bright and sunny. In fact, there were more cloudy and foggy, damp days than those filled with sunshine. Somehow that appealed to me. I remember being struck by the contrast between the pervasive colors of the evergreen and the grayness of the sky, the rocks, and the water. Even though we were all together as a family, a pleasant sense of isolation and reflection crept in with the low clouds. Even with the lowering of the skies, you couldn't escape the sense that this was a vast environment and that you as an individual played a very small part in it. I found myself becoming even more reflective as the days went on. I liked the idea that we were all sitting on a boat playing cards and outside the window, Mother Nature in her most raw state was spread out around us. I felt both separate and somehow united—a part of but apart from the landscape and my family. Also, for the first time in a long time, the only baggage I brought on the trip was the physical stuff I carried. My past was out there, obscured and undifferentiated, a part of the vast wilderness.

Seeing that glacier calving and watching its effects, made me think that a little bit of me and my brittle and frozen past was being eroded and melted as well. My uncle John, everyone called him Farm because he'd never left Iowa and had worked the land his whole life (with the exception of a few trips to Arizona) was quite a revelation to me. I don't remember ever spending anytime with him when I was a kid (though I had) and by the time I was fifteen, I was out of the house and not really living with my parents. I wanted nothing to do with my family let alone extended family. Farm and I stayed up late at night, the boat rising and falling gently in the slight swells. We talked about a lot of things—women, work, and his friends. Every now and then he'd stop trying to make me laugh and he told me a bit about his lost years. Like my dad, he'd come back from Vietnam. He'd struggled to adjust, gotten into drugs and drinking while he tried to sort through it all. Eventually, he set all that aside and worked hard to pull himself together.

Hearing his story gave me some more insight into my dad. I always had a lot of respect and admiration for war veterans, though obviously I didn't extend that fully to my father, and I regretted that. I liked seeing the two of them together, my dad giving Farm shit because he came all the way to Alaska and he didn't eat fish or shellfish.

Farm was a meat and potatoes kind of guy, a solid citizen. He wore his hard-working life well, just as my dad had, and I didn't think it would be the worst thing in the world to end up like them at their age. Only when I really thought about it did I realize what that meant. It may have been their last trip together. My dad had cancer and even though he had really gotten the jump on it, somewhere it remained lurking inside him.

Returning to Boulder after that trip wasn't easy, but the memories and images of the things I'd seen and the sensations of the things I felt, a sense of belonging with these people who shared my name and my history, stuck with me. I can't say that the feeling of that freezing water stayed with me all the way to Florida where I finally cracked the 10-hour barrier (9:37) at the full Ironman distance. I was used to the heat, but the humidity of Florida was something else entirely. In Boulder, if the relative humidity is above 40 percent, that's a damp day. Factor in the 96-degree temperatures and no matter what the humidity, it would have been a hot one. Most of the run was exposed to the baking sun. I distinctly remember running along a busy stretch of road on the course where several landscaping trucks went by, and I kept thinking that I should just quit and hop on the back of one of those trucks so they could take me to the finish. The thought of quitting entered my mind at several points during the race and I was very, very close to caving in. I would run the scenario over in my head. I would flag the truck down and hop in the back and just jump out when I was closer to the end so I wouldn't have to walk the 9 miles back to the start/finish. I was really hot and felt as though I wasn't moving at all during the run. I had to force myself to keep moving moment by moment as I was unraveling mentally.

This race showed me that I was getting closer to having a performance that would qualify me for the big island; it was also the first time I ran under 3:30 on the marathon. It also reminded me of how close I could come to pulling the plug or giving in. I finished 3rd overall, but since it wasn't a race sanctioned by the World Triathlon Corporation and wasn't a true Ironman race (though it was the full Ironman distance it wasn't organized by the Ironman organization) that really didn't matter. Had I finished that high and with that time, I might have qualified for Kona. As it was, 2008 was a good but disappointing year. Nothing seemed to be proceeding smoothly for me, but I still had my eye on that prize, and it seemed to be getting nearer and nearer but it certainly wasn't coming easy.

Just when you think you've got this triathlon thing nailed, it comes back to bite you in the ass. I had every reason to believe that 2009 was going to be my year. That is, until the year actually began. My foot had healed, and I was really looking forward to the Oceanside 70.3 at the beginning of April. I took what seemed to me to be a step backward. Again, not having enough rest, or tapering off my workouts in the days prior to the race, took its toll. I was pushing myself really hard because I felt like this needed to be my year. At one point, I had to get off the bike to stretch my lower back because it was spasming so bad. Halfway through the run, I thought of just walking off the course. I didn't, but my 4:47 was nothing to write home about. I still had that goal in mind of finishing in the top 2 percent, but I'd only managed to make it into the top 9 percent. Not nearly good enough.

I thought I'd redeem myself in the Wildflower, where I'd done so well the year before, but I was 8 minutes slower than in 2008 and finished nearly 40 spots lower in the field. Was there such a thing as a junior year slump? If so, I felt like I was in it. I knew that I somehow had to pull my head out of my ass and do better. I trained even harder in anticipation of Ironman Coeur d'Alene in the third week of June.

If I was going to qualify, this was the race I really targeted. All I needed to do was to finish 6th in my age group, and I would punch my ticket for Kona. I finished 7th. As heartbreaking as that was, I really didn't need to have raced any faster to make up the 2 minutes that would have made the difference between my 7th place finish and *5th* place. That's a lousy 120 seconds. What cost me was that I had taken 8 minutes and 1 second in the two transitions. Eight minutes! My transitions should have taken less than half that amount of time.

The weather was cold that day and I took the time (which I had never done, nor will I ever again do) to put on compression socks and dry shorts. Again, it was my lack of attention to detail that killed me. Just as it was with nutrition and hydration in the past. Just like it had been with my failure to train systematically and adhere to logical workloads and intensities—it was my scattered brain that had cost me. There was really no excuse for it. It took me until Ironman Wisconsin to get over this one.

The gods did smile down on me. Two of the other competitors in my division had already qualified for Kona. That meant that the spots available in Coeur d'Alene "rolled down" two spots. That meant that the next two guys in line (one of whom was me) would be allowed in. I looked at that as backing into the race. I didn't really earn it, so I refused to take that option. I felt it important to get my spot legitimately and feel like I had really achieved it on my own. A roll down slot wasn't the way I wanted to get to Kona.

I needed to race again to get that monkey off my back after coming so close. My last shot at redemption in 2009 wound up costing me $1,100. I hadn't planned on entering Ironman Wisconsin in mid-September. When I sat down at the end of 2008 and figured out my race plans, I assumed that I'd have a spot in Kona all sewed up at Ironman Coeur d'Alene. Because I didn't, I needed to make a late entry into the Madison field. For that privilege, I paid that $1,100 dollars for what is called an "Ironman Foundation Slot." The entrance fee was double the regular cost, but if I spent any time thinking about all the money I'd spent on gear, bikes, entrance fees, travel, etc., over the years, I'd have to join that chorus of nonparticipants who wonder, "Why do you put yourself through all that?"

The answer to that question is a tough one. Unless you've ever raced you haven't experienced the sense of supreme satisfaction that comes from crossing the finish line knowing that you've done something that a relatively small percentage of the population has ever done. Sure, in time, just finishing one didn't give me the same surge of pride that the first one did. Those races were also very frustrating at times, but I wouldn't have continued to race if it weren't for the feeling that comes from setting your mind and body and soul on an objective, an ideal, and then having execution match expectation.

I'd raced Wisconsin before and knew what I was in for. I always hated the fact that the transition from the swim to the bike portion involved running up to the top of a parking structure. It just seemed to add insult to injury, but I had accepted the ups and downs of the sport a long time ago. For me, the 2009 full Ironman in Madison, was maybe the highest of the highs and the lowest of the lows I'd ever experienced racing.

After those early disappointments in 2009, I was even more focused than I'd ever been in my training. I went into Madison with high hopes. I'd come so close in Coeur d'Alene that I figured with the same effort, and slightly better transitions, I could make the cut and get to Kona. Unlike my previous experience in Wisconsin's capital, the swim didn't turn out to be a scene from the movie *The Perfect Storm*. The waters remained calm, and I exited Lake Monona in 58:58 and in 80th place in my age group and 96th overall. I didn't have a great swim, but for once a transition worked in my favor. It took me 5:36 to make the transition to the bike. Normally, that's a very slow time but with that run up to the parking lot it wasn't so bad. In fact, it actually pushed me ahead of a few other competitors. Those first few strides, when you ask your legs to stop kicking and start running are always a bit wobbly, but at Madison that 1,200-meter stretch from the beach to the bikes is a bitch. I clipped into the pedals in 74th place overall, leaving more than 20 competitors behind me who had actually swum faster than I had.

That was a good omen, but the temperature was 89 degrees and the Midwest humidity was a monkey on all our backs. I drank as much as I could and downed energy gels at regular intervals, but by mile 80 or so, my stomach started to feel queasy. I kept my effort level the same, but I could feel my gastric juices churning. Fortunately, what had to come out of me decided that the easiest way out was up and not down. I weaved toward the road's shoulder and spewed out a thin stream of vomit. For the next 5 miles, I rode along with the nasty taste of bile and vanilla Gu coating my mouth. Rinse and spit. Rinse and spit. I gagged down another gel packet, and by the time I approached Madison and the next transition area to the run, I was feeling better. My 5:07 bike wasn't near my best performance, but it was good enough to be the 24th fastest of the day.

Still feeling pretty good, I went out hard for the first 4 miles, at or near 7 minutes per mile and was pleased with how strong my legs felt. I eased up a bit, and cruised through the first 13.1 miles in well under 1:40. If I managed to do equal splits, I'd be in the range of 3:15 for the full marathon. As it turned out I ran 3:20. I had only gone faster once, a few months before, at Ironman Coeur d'Alene (3:16), which is a much faster run course. For my racing career to that point, I'd always thought my run was my weak point, but on that day, it would prove to be my strong point. You just never know how these things are going to shake out.

To that point on that September 13 in Madison, Smart Shane had been carrying the day. But, Stupid Shane was seldom very far behind, and at mile 14, shortly after doing those race pace calculations, Stupid Shane elbowed his way past Smart Shane in excitement. He said, looking over his shoulder, "Hey, dude! Follow me. I've got a great idea." So I did and the two of me raced right past the aid stations at mile 14, mile 15, and 16. Stupid Shane convinced me/us, that we shouldn't slow down to take in any kind of nourishment. We were doing so well, and that great time in the run was just a few more miles down the road. Better to keep the speed up and sail on.

By mile 17, Stupid Shane and Smart Shane were joined by another Shane—Angry Shane. If I was sometimes a Debbie Downer after a race, I could sometimes be a Raging/Ranting Randy in the middle of one. When my blood sugar level dips, like many people, I get edgy and irritable. Well, that dip in blood sugar, compounded by the fact that I was at 8-plus hours of incredible exertion, had me on the verge of total meltdown. I kept pushing myself, and then I went over the cliff. I entered Mother-Fuck Mode. The state of mind I have when EVERYTHING pisses me off. A crack in the road—motherfucker. A spectator ringing a bell—a motherfucker. The wind, the trees rattling, the smell of backyard barbecued bratwurst, any stimulus gets run through the mill and comes out a motherfucker.

In my light-headed and agitated state, the mill also produces ratio-nalizations, existentialist explorations of man's foolish struggles in the face of certain annihilation, and a chorus of voices encouraging me to just quit.

Before any of the *me*s knew what I was doing, I stopped running, took off my race belt, threw it aside, and began to walk off the course. I removed my hat, emptied my pockets of any remaining gels (motherfucker flavored), and stood there for a few moments muttering, "I quit. I'm done."

Thankfully, an older couple, both of them in floppy hats and sunglasses, encouraged me. I was off the course at this point, and the combination of their encouragement, my embarrassment, and the fact that I had sucked in a few calories prior to ridding myself of those pseudofoods, my brain began to function better. I started to walk toward the course, my new fans still clapping and shouting encouragement, and I stooped to pick up my belt. Not feeling any nausea or dizziness when I dipped my head, I thought, "Okay. I'll walk a bit." I ambled along for a while, then started to walk faster, next I lifted my feet up a bit and did a dainty little dog kind of trot, and before I knew it, I was back running. In a little while, when more of that sugar I'd ingested kicked in, I got back in rhythm.

When the finish line in any race comes into view, there's a bit of elation that sets in. When that view includes the timer telling you that you are running at a pace that will most likely qualify you for Kona, that bit of elation rises from the pit of your stomach, and a few moments later, has you feeling like you've levitated and are no longer fully in contact with the ground. As I ran down North Pinkney Street, the capitol building rising on my right, an enormous crowd howling and whooping, I could feel that something special was going on. I rounded the bend onto East Main, knowing that I had to take a sharp left-hand turn onto Martin Luther King Jr. Boulevard, with only a little more than a city block to go.

When I saw that the first digit was a 9, I was like a lottery player feeling pretty good about his chances. When I saw that the next one was a 3, I was really psyched. Going under 10 hours was great, but having something in the 9:30s, considering the puke fest and meltdown was beyond the beyond. I'd had tunnel vision before, that feeling when you're about to pass out—of the periphery closing in and then, the darkness. I'd experienced that as a drunk, an addict, and as an undernourished and underhydrated wannabe triathlete. Then, I was experiencing it as an athlete. My focus narrowed but it didn't close in and my vision didn't go dark. Instead I saw those Day-Glo yellow dots that made up each of those digits, which read 9:34 and put me 18th overall.

As I crossed the line, I threw my hands up in the air. I couldn't believe it. Four years of blood, sweat, and tears, and there I was, not bloody but certainly sweaty and tearful.

I'd done it. My finishing time and where I fell in the finishing order were enough to get me to Kona.

A mixture of utter joy and relief coursed through my veins. I walked through the post-race lines like a giddy zombie, shaking my head at the wonder of it all.

I didn't call anyone until much later. This was a very personal thing to me, maybe in some way, I could say it was a spiritual journey of sorts. I had been on this odyssey since reading that article in my prison cell. I had done my time, all the while keeping this dream on my mind. All the hours of training. All the cold days, hot days, wet days—days I didn't want to get out of bed or out of the door, but I did it, spurred on by this dream. This was my own thing to hold and process for a while. I didn't really want to talk to anyone. I didn't call anyone until much later. Everyone knew I had qualified and they left me messages. I just wanted to sit with it and hold it to myself.

That night, I got another reminder of how fortunate I was, how life always has its ups and downs, and most things wind up tasting bittersweet. A couple of days before the race, I got a phone call from my old friend Ryan Hornby. We'd met in Bloomington and had become best friends. Ryan was the first guy I ever got drunk with, the first person I smoked heroin with, the first one I'd snorted a line of blow with. When my parents couldn't put up with me anymore, I'd lived for a year with him and his family in high school. We were like brothers. We'd kept in touch sporadically, but I'd drifted away into a life of addiction and homelessness and then prison. While I was on my path of self-obliteration west of the Mississippi, he was doing much the same on the other end of the country.

Ryan was living in a halfway house in nearby Appleton, Wisconsin. Things hadn't gone so well for him since high school. He told me about how he'd been shot during a drug deal gone bad and how he'd lost a bunch of jobs. He had tried to get clean, and had bouts of sobriety only to be followed by more substance abuse. Still it was good to see him. Though he looked haggard and worn, I could still see the devilish light in his eyes that had made him so popular. This guy was my brother, and I was glad that he was there to share my big day with me.

We shot the shit, and it was so funny that on this day of all days, my past had come to revisit me. Mostly, Ryan had avoided the criminal justice system, and now after a decade, we were seeing one another again. I couldn't say any of this to him, but I had just fulfilled a huge dream, overcome so much even in just those last ten hours of competing, and here we were ten years removed from our days of wreaking havoc.

A question lingered long after we'd done our bro' hugs and back pats, and Ryan ambled off down the street to catch a bus, a wounded and wobbling presence receding from view.

Why me? Why me? Why was I the lucky one?

I had a sense, and it proved true, that I would never see Hornby alive again.

TWELVE

Anyone who's ever studied biology and chemistry in high school is likely to remember the chemical abbreviation ATP—that's the basic source of chemical energy that powers our muscular contractions. Those with really great memories may recall that much of this energy production and conversion involves the addition and subtraction (chemical bonds—phosphates—being broken and new ones being formed) with the resultant release of energy as ADP gets converted into ATP and AMP.

Our bodies are miraculous machines and we have three different metabolic systems that activate our muscles depending upon the duration of our effort/need—the phosphagen system for short-term power surges, the glycogen/lactic acid for activities lasting between 30–40 seconds, and the aerobic system, which has no time limit and will keep our muscles active as long as nutrients last.

Why this basic and simplified lesson in chemistry and kinesiology? Several reasons. First, I would sometimes think about these facts and other lessons I learned in becoming a personal trainer and how they applied to my workouts as I was in the gym, the pool, or training on the road. They helped to distract me from the monotony and discomfort of those hours and hours spent training. Second, 2010 was all about the breaking and forming of bonds.

Cellular reproduction and energy transfer were very much on my mind that year. I entered 2010 feeling very good about myself and my place in the triathlon universe and where my head was generally. Life was good. I was steadily and happily employed, free of drugs and alcohol, and in a comfortable relationship with my family, a woman I was dating, and with myself. For a long time, guilt and shame were the energy sources that fueled my efforts. Given that I was an endurance athlete, I frequently had to employ that long-term aerobic system to compete and train. In time, I realized that guilt and shame could only carry me so far in this life and in my chosen careers. I was going to have to find new sources of energy, healthier ones really, to fuel my desire to continue to compete at a high level. I'd qualified for Kona, but just getting there and finishing wasn't going to be enough. I wanted to kick ass and prove I belonged there.

I also wanted to continue to evolve and grow as a person. It was becoming clear that the feelings I had toward myself and the things I had done in the past were anchoring me and holding me back. I was going to need to let go of my past so that I could move forward as a man. In 2010, I learned another painful if clichéd lesson—be careful what you wish for.

Since we spent time together as a family in Alaska in 2008, my relationship with my parents was good and steady. I was never one of those talk-to-them-everyday kind of guys, and now that I was in my thirties, working, consumed by triathlon, I talked to my parents every now and then and saw them regularly but not frequently—not because of any tension but because we all had busy lives. Unfortunately, just about the time I was pointing toward a tune-up race in Galveston, Texas, at the end of April, my dad was very busy dying.

I don't know if there is a chemical formula to explain how a cancer cell mutates and then multiplies, how the drugs that cancer patients take into their bodies arrest that development. I certainly know that there is no formula for how to get your mind and spirit to optimally process the fact that one of your parents is dying. I was so used to seeing my old man strong and strong-willed. I don't think I could have admitted it at the time, but when I finished that race with a snapped metatarsal, I was drawing on the genes I'd inherited from him. Seeing him with those cancer cells running rampant through his body was shocking. I noticed that he had lost weight, that his clothes seemed to billow around him rather than cover him, and it was as if the disease was turning him inside out—his skin seemed to be receding, exposing vessels, ligaments, and tendons. The latter two were soft tissue, and I thought of that and all the vulnerability that implies. When my dad smiled, as he often did bravely trying to put everyone at ease, I noticed how much more of his gums showed, his drawn and pale face turning into something signaling his retreat. It was as if his body was drawing all its resources closer into its center, circling the wagons for one last and futile stand.

I hated seeing him deteriorate. I spent more and more time with him through April and May, trying not to notice the further decline. I had had a bunch of friends die, and I never went to any of their funerals, didn't know how to process the grief and the sadness. In the old days, I just added alcohol or drugs to the mix, diluted those emotions or altered them chemically. Though I was still feeling a lot of guilt and shame, I added sadness to the mix and used my workouts to try to process the painful reality we were all facing. I flogged myself in my workouts, hoping that staying focused on the training would help. It did to a certain extent, but like my dad's, my body was tearing itself down. I had a stress fracture in the same foot that I'd broken in 2008 but I kept doing the miles, and in that race in Texas, I really paid the price the last 4 miles. I told myself that the pain didn't matter. Think of what your father is going through. Think of what you put your father through. All the stress, all the anxiety, all the disappointment he must have felt because of me.

In my mind, I had given my dad pancreatic cancer. There were no two ways about it.

No longer working so that I could be available to my mom and dad at a moment's notice, the only outlet I had was my training. My hip had been bothering me for quite a while, but after returning from Galveston, I didn't let up even though I'd torn my labrum and my psosas. I was limping through the first 20 minutes of my runs until the muscles heated up. Afterward, the stiffness returned.

To give you some idea of how bad things got, over Memorial Day weekend, I really trashed myself. A few months earlier, I had a conversation with Dave Scott. He told me about one of his favorite workouts. He would ride for 3–4 hours, much of it at race pace, and then come off the bike and run 13–14 miles "swinging" the pace. For me, my target pace for a full Ironman was 7:10 per mile. So that meant for Dave's workout, I would run 7:40 for a mile, then swing up 60 seconds to a 6:40 pace, and so on and so on throughout the run. I decided to make the workout my own and rode the bike 80 miles as hard as I could, and then as close to 7-minute miles (the halfway point between the upper and lower limits of the swing) for 15 miles. I didn't go into that workout with any kind of rest. I was in the middle of a big block of training, and doing that workout really tipped the scales against me.

The next day, Billy, Brando, and I went on a 5-hour ride. We went to Joanna's house to change and then ran 2 miles to the track. As soon as we got there, I went to one of the portable toilets. I looked down at my urine stream and thought it looked funny. I had on reddish tinted glasses, and figured that was the reason why my piss looked odd. Done, I hopped onto the track and began to run 1,200 meter repeats on a 4:25 pace. I did four of them and then felt like I had to relieve myself again. This time, I took my glasses off. I was definitely pissing red. The sight of it made my stomach turn, but I was in no pain.

I went to the doctor the following day, and he told me that I should get myself checked into the hospital and get on an intravenous drip. I had developed a case of rhabdomyolysis—the breakdown of muscle fibers that leads to this cellular waste being released into the blood-stream. Myoglobin (an iron- and oxygen-binding protein) is harmful to the kidney and often causes kidney damage. I was obviously over-stressing my system and not getting enough fluids into me. I told the doctor that I wasn't going to go to the hospital. My training was too important. What I didn't tell him was that I'd just spent the night before in the hospital with my dad. He was in a very bad way, the pain really getting beyond the reach of the drugs. I'd had enough of hospitals.

I was a couple of weeks from racing Ironman Coeur d'Alene; the only thing that was helping me keep my shit together was thinking of that race and continuing to train. That same night, I got a call from Joanna asking me to meet at her place the next day before we rode. When I got there, I saw that Billy was there as well. We all sat down in the garage on lawn chairs, awkwardly looking at one another. I could tell something was up, because there was a somber feeling in the air.

Joanna began by saying that she knew that I was hurting. She could see me limping around. Billy added that they both knew that I was struggling emotionally as well. I had to agree. I was strung out and my soul was worn thin watching my father wasting away. To that point, I didn't really see that I was unraveling in a big way. I was angry and sad most of the time. I was abusing my body, hoping that I could make the other anguish go away.

"You'd be a fool to race CDA," Joanna said.

That was her—bluntly cutting to the chase.

I told them that the race meant a lot to me, it would be good for me to use the race as another way to process my dad's situation, and all the rest. I was doing what I did in races when my head told me to quit. I just kept fighting it, pressing on and on, but this was different, it was breaking me.

"You can't abuse your body enough to make this kind of hurt go away," Joanna told me. "It's okay to just be, to live with the pain. It's going to catch you sooner or later."

I saw the light and withdrew from the race. I was really grateful to the two of them for their intervention. Brando was also extremely helpful during that difficult time. I hadn't had real friends for a significant portion of my life, and their expression of concern and their support made them true friends whom I will always love.

Another bond of friendship had begun thanks to Joanna. I was at the pool, walking out of the locker room onto the deck in anticipation of another Joanna aqua-ass kicking. Ahead of me was this woman I'd never seen before. I was still dating a woman named Alison, but something told me to pay attention to what was going on here. Alison was wonderful, and the fact that we're still friends proves that, but she wasn't so into my triathlon obsession. Rightfully so, she deserved a guy who was into her and put her at the top of his priority list, and for me, to that point, my sport was number one.

I wasn't thinking about those things in that moment when I saw this incredibly well-put-together woman walking ahead of me. Her long hair, dark and wet and shimmering like an otter's fur, cascaded down her back. She was lean and muscular, with a lithe body that seemed like it had been copied from a textbook illustration of what an athlete should look like. She was walking with Joanna when she turned to smile, and something in the pit of my stomach went *whoa* and my adrenals got busy. After Joanna worked us down to a nub in the pool, I was glad that I was too wasted because I would have followed that woman wherever she was going. I couldn't get her out of my mind, and when, three days later, I walked into Joanna's house to meet up for a ride I was more than pleased to see that same woman sitting on the couch. She was sipping a cup of coffee, and when she saw me standing there, she smiled and dazzled me again with her teeth and the way her green eyes seemed to hold all the light in the room.

I felt like I was gawking at her like some mouth-breathing moron and that she was probably figuring I was just some creep like the dozens of other d-bags who had hounded her at some point in her life. As much as I was attracted to her without even having said a single word to her, I had two thoughts simultaneously: I have got to get to know this woman and I was so far out of my league here, that it ain't even funny. Then she slid over on the couch to make room for me, probably hoping that I'd sit so that no one else would notice me standing there with my mouth hanging open.

"Hi, I'm Mandy." Her voice came out all-kind-of caramelly, sweet and thick and with a lilt that let you know that she was from somewhere in the South.

We talked for a bit, and then it was time to hit the road. If you were to ask me the route we took on that training ride, I wouldn't be able to tell you. For all I know, we attached pontoons and outriggers to our bikes and rode up Boulder Creek, then took them off, rode to the top of Trail Ridge Road in Rocky Mountain National Park, attached wings to our bikes, and flew down from the top of Longs Peak back to Joanna's place. I knew that I was flying. I couldn't stop thinking about her. I was worried about how I came across. I don't have any kind of functioning internal editor, that voice in your head that tells you what's appropriate to say out loud and what you should keep inside your head. Mandy was just about the most self-assured person I ever met, so comfortable in her own skin that she even put a fast-twitch guy like me at ease.

Mandy McLane was a former pole vaulter and heptathlete from Clemson University. She lived and worked in Florida, where she ran her own business as a certified speech-language pathologist. Her primary focus was on working with young children, and she exuded the kind of nurturing patience that is necessary to do that work. When she talked about her clients, she was clearly passionate about them and their needs. She was also an accomplished triathlete and was in town for just a few days, working with her coach, Joanna.

We worked out a couple of more times, and we exchanged contact information, but with her living in Florida, the wise (well, really the stupid) thing to have done was to just chalk this all up as a nice experience to have met such a great woman who *clearly* had a plan for her life that didn't include someone like me. Then, completely out of the blue, a few months later I decided to e-mail her. What ensued was the kind of stomach-thrilling sensation you experienced when you were young and a girl slipped you a note. At first e-mails were flying back and forth, not really flirty at all. Then the phone calls started, and things got a bit deeper. I felt so comfortable with her that I told her about my past, and she was so open-minded and empathetic. Every time I paused or said that she probably didn't want to hear anymore of this, she encouraged me to go on. She opened up about her past, a remarkably normal and uneventful one in comparison to mine, but still filled with its own challenges due to her determination to earn her way through college.

I know that attraction is based on actual chemical responses between two people, and we are drawn to them inexorably and in some cases without thinking. That was true of our initial interactions, but as the weeks went by and Mandy talked about her desire to race triathlon professionally and move to Boulder, something deepened in a way that simple chemistry can't explain. I didn't want to analyze things too much then or now, but something out of the ordinary was happening between us. One night, toward the tail end of a marathon phone session, I told her that I loved her. She told me she loved me, too.

I saw in Mandy the possibility that all kinds of good things could happen in my life, that I deserved to be happy in all phases of it, not just out on the course competing. I'd dated my entire adult life, but I never really felt like I was willing or able to commit to anyone. Relationships were supposed to be fun. They weren't something you worked at. That was what I was doing in my sport. That was *serious* business to me and so was my work as a trainer and coach. The personal stuff, the social stuff, the relationship stuff—I could barely even stand to use that word—weren't really.

With Mandy our interactions were both fun and serious. We laughed a whole lot and enjoyed our time together, despite the electronic nature of it, immensely. I stopped thinking about my days in terms of how many hours I was going to spend at work and how many working out. Instead, I switched over to Mandy time. When was I going to get another e-mail from her? When were we going to be able to speak on the phone again? How long had it been since I last was in contact with her? When are we going to be able to be together in the same place at the same time?

I sometimes wondered if my personal successes figured into all of this. Work was going well, I had great friends, and I had been racing well. I was feeling pretty good about myself and things I'd accomplished, maybe it was the positive vibes I was generating that attracted someone so incredibly good for me into my life. The year, 2010, was proving to be a pretty good year for Mandy as a competitor, and as the spring events made the turn into summer, she was on a roll, winning her age group in several events and qualifying to race professionally. I was training and doing some running races but no triathlons. My focus was on two things: my dad and Kona at the end of the year.

I not only wanted to be with Mandy during this period, I really needed someone like her.

My dad's decline was precipitous. Cancer is a motherfucker. I spent a few nights by his side in the hospital, sleeping curled up on the windowsill. I had never seen someone in so much pain—certainly not my old man, the strongest SOB I had ever known. It somehow reduced him. We were able to talk a bit, but he was either in so much pain or so dimmed by morphine and I was so full of anxiety that I sometimes wondered if either of us made any sense at all. I knew that he didn't want to prolong the pain he felt he was putting us through, so when he told me that he was discontinuing treatment and opting for home hospice care for his final days, all I could do was support his choice.

Following the last of those nights I spent with him, he was released to home hospice the next day. I went to see him. They were celebrating my brother's birthday, and relatives were in town sensing it was near the end for my dad. Something about being home had rattled him. He looked more vital than he had for weeks, laughing and smiling. He was fine when I left the house. Early that next morning I got a call from my mom, telling me to come to the hospital. My dad had been writhing around on the ground in agony trying not to wake her. He had to be rushed back into the hospital.

The last time I saw my father alive, I walked into the semidarkness of the room. He was in a hospital bed, canted up at an angle, his head levered back in what looked to me to be a painful angle. He'd been transformed overnight from someone still vital to something completely enfeebled. In that position, his eyes could only really scan the ceiling. His skin was like parchment; his hand as I took it was oddly both warm and cold—the veins on the back were distended, swollen rivers, a relief map that offered no relief. His eyes were lazy from the pain meds. I wasn't prepared for the dramatic change. It was in that moment and the moments that followed when my heart cracked and split. It was one of the most transformative moments I would ever know.

I had a hard time believing that I was really there, spending the last moments I would ever spend with him. I shut my eyes and tried to take in a breath, release the tension in my jaw.

"Hey, bud," he said.

There was a chair beside the bed, and I sat in it briefly. When I saw my dad's eyes roll to the side, I realized that he couldn't really see me. I half stood and half sat on the bed.

My dad smiled and I tried not to think about how strained and stretched it was, how skeletal.

Stupidly, I asked him how he was.

His thumbs twitched, a fluttering gesture that told me that he wanted to let me know that he was okay, that all was good, but his body stated the obvious.

I held his hand and tried but failed to keep the tears at bay. One slid off my face and landed on his neck. I moved to wipe it away, telling him through a half-clenched jaw that I was sorry.

He shook his head. "It's okay," he said, his voice distant and strained.

I returned the gesture, "No, it's not. I'm sorry for everything. I was a horrible piece of shit. I am sorry for every single time I fucked up. Thanks for everything you ever did for me. You were always there no matter what. I don't know how you guys ever forgave me. You're a good man. I'm not one yet, but I'm going to be."

I felt as if a dam had burst, and my tears flooded along the canyon of my face. I held my dying father's head cradled in my hands. I was standing there holding him and crying and shouting. I was angry at life, at myself, and at the cancer. I was overwhelmed with the sadness I felt. I felt both emptied, and as if a surge of angry current was running through me and out of me. I was so wired that I couldn't keep my feet still.

He told me that it was time to let all that go. Let everything go, and it was time to move on with my life and make peace with myself. Forget about all the things that happened between us and let it go.

Somehow I just knew this was going to be that last time he was lucid and really alive, that it would be the last moment with him.

We talked for a while longer. He asked about how my training was going, let me know that he had hoped that he could have made it until Hawaii.

At that point I lost it again. I held his head in my hands and was nearly yelling through the tears pouring down my face and onto his. I told him again that I was so sorry.

He told me, "I love you. You need to break with the past and just let it be. If you don't lay all that down, it's going to consume you."

"Take care of your mother. She's the love of my life and the most special woman in the world. I'm a damn lucky man to have had her. Look after your brother, too."

He was exhausted, and I could see that the pain was getting worse.

He needed another dose of morphine and my being there was preventing that.

"I will. I will. I want to be as good a man as you are."

I walked out of the room to find the hospice nurse. He administered the dosage and my dad seemed to settle a bit, his breathing slowed, his muscles relaxed.

"Take care of the women in your life," were his last words to me as I walked out of the room.

His eyelids fluttered briefly and then stilled. His breathing remained shallow and regular.

As the nurse worked at her laptop updating my dad's chart, she said, "Your father's a good man. Much loved, too." Later, after he passed, that same woman would tell my mom how much she admired my dad.

I nodded and then remembering both that the nurse couldn't see me and that my father, despite the drugs in his system, could hear me, said, "He is. He really is."

How true to form, when he knew that his tumor was wreaking havoc and the end was near he stopped eating and drinking so the transition would happen fast, and we wouldn't have to suffer in seeing him like that. That was who my father was. Strong. Realistic. Truly great.

That was the last time I ever saw my dad alive. Something uncontrollable broke loose deep inside me, and I sat outside my car in the parking lot as great wracking, heaving sobs stuttered my breathing and snot and tears fouled my face. I don't know how long I sat there, but when I finally managed to calm down enough to get into the car, I had never been so drained. I drove around in a daze. I understood that was good-bye to the man who had raised me. I understood that, in so many ways, I was my father's son and now he was gone.

I knew I was done with hospitals and social workers and counselors and that whole fucking scene. I needed to get out of there and just go away someplace to sort it all out. I hadn't wanted to drink for a long time, but I remember thinking some whiskey on the rocks would salve the pain. That thought withered.

Later, I thought about what I knew were going to be my dad's last words to me. I called Mandy and I asked her if I could come and see her. She said, "Of course."

I left for Orlando later that night. Mandy was there to pick me up at the airport, and she held me for a good long time. I guess it's a good thing that she was used to working with kids who had difficulties with speech and language. All I could do was hang onto her with all my might.

When my brother's phone call came, Mandy was with me. I walked outside and fell to my knees and cried. Two days later, I was back in Colorado speaking in front of a small group of friends who'd gathered at the Devil's Backbone to celebrate Ralph Niemeyer's life. I thought of my dad's last words to me again, and I knew how proud he was of the fact that he and my mom had managed to ride out the rough patches and stay together. That a remarkable woman like her had seen fit to be with a man like him astounded and humbled him, made him wonder how it was that despite all the things that he may have done, she had chosen to spend her life with him.

As I stood to talk about being my father's son, I could hear the Big Thompson River whispering from a stone's throw away. I was truly back at the place where I had been born and raised, a thin line of cloud hairline fracturing the blue plate of a Colorado sky.

I already had another plan to run away and start fresh in motion. The day after the service, I flew back to Orlando. Two days later, the sound of a tape gun dispenser still ringing in my ears the boxes all loaded into the U-Haul, Mandy and I set out for Boulder and our life together. Mandy was willing to take a chance on me, and as we made our way north and west, we talked about how we were going to plan and prepare for the challenges that lay ahead of us. I was enormously grateful that my coach had given me those last words of advice before he went on his way.

THIRTEEN

My first experience in Kona in 2010 served as a microcosm for this phase of life. Mandy, my mom, and I were fortunate that a family friend who works for Sheraton offered all of us a place to stay in Waikaloa, about a half hour north of Kona and the start of the race. We spent a pleasant first four days—not the Aloha Hawaii travel brochure kind of pleasant, but triathlon pleasant. That meant that every day, since I was in taper mode (in other words cutting down on the duration of my workouts in anticipation of the upcoming event) I lightly worked out in each of the three disciplines. I didn't want to risk riding in the heat or in the traffic—to have an accident and injury at this point would be devastating not just physically but emotionally and financially, so I decided to get out early and beat the traffic and heat of the day. I'd do 90–120 minutes on the bike, run for 30 minutes, and swim for another 30. I'd do just enough to keep the muscle fibers enervated, but not enough to overtax them and produce micro tears. That meant that, compared to a normal day of training and working with my clients, I had a shitload of time on my hands. I was still consuming my usual diet and caloric intake—a bowl of oatmeal for breakfast, some Thai pasta or rice noodles for lunch, and spaghetti for dinner. Mandy was helping out by doing most of the food preparation, so that left me with more time to obsessively watch The Weather Channel to see how hot it was going to be on the Saturday of the race.

I also spent those first few days in Hawaii practicing my transitions—getting out of the water, sprinting to my bike, getting rid of my goggles and cap, putting on my helmet, getting into my biking shoes, getting out of those and into my running shoes.

But I didn't factor in how heavy a heart could become in an instant, how much it could weigh me down, how a few words tapped onto an alphanumeric pad, bounced off of cell towers and satellites, could create such a drag coefficient, slow me down to such a degree that I'd be transported back to another place and time. On October 6, my phone waveboarded across the tabletop.

CRAIG DIED YESTERDAY. SO SORRY TO TELL YOU. THOUGHT YOU'D WANT TO KNOW.

My old Bloomington buddy Woody sent the text. I was sitting in the living room, trying to read Thomas Pynchon's *Vineland* while listening to the Avett Brothers' "Head Full of Doubt/Road Full of Promise" when the message came in.

"Jesus Christ. No fucking way."

I forgot about the headphones being on, and cluster bombed the words. Mandy came running in from the kitchen, a paring knife in one hand and concern carved into her features.

"What? What is it?"

I leaned back in the chair, pinched the bridge of my nose right between my eyes, gripping the spot where the news hit me.

"Craig. He's gone. He's dead."

I walked over to Mandy and wrapped my arms around her. I'm struck again by how fortunate I've been, how the death toll has climbed and my name been spared.

Craig was my best friend from high school, a kid who never let his epilepsy get in the way of taking a bong rip, shotgunning a PBR, and approaching life with a fuck-it-all-anyway-'cause-it-ain't-never-gonna-last-no-way-anyway attitude that I admired and shared. He was my running buddy the time I was fifteen and sixteen and dashed out onto Veterans Parkway, looking to play chicken with a few cars. I lost.

I was doing enough crazy shit to make people think I was the one seizing, the one with the faulty electromagnetic regulator in my head.

A few phone calls later, and the tale was told. Craig was still doing drugs and drinking, still living in his parents' basement. The interaction with his seizure meds may have fucked him up and he died.

With all this time on my hands pre-race, I didn't really want or need any more input into thoughts about mortality. The fact that my father wasn't here with us, something we'd all hoped that he would have been able to live long enough for, had already cast a bit of a pall on the event. I'd finally accomplished the goal and was now supposed to get the reward for all my efforts. I felt shitty about what happened to Craig, told myself that I was one lucky bastard and shouldn't dwell on the past and just focus on the race and doing my best. Still, it seemed like I could never get to the point where I could fully leave my past behind.

I'd asked around, of course, and the consensus was that Kona was different. Though I'd done the distance before, the Ironman World Championship wasn't like those other races. It would be best to go into it with no expectations, no real time goal in mind. I should just go and do my best on that day and accept it. I nodded and thanked them, all the while thinking, so, okay, then a bad day there means 9:30. I was thinking I would race well, just three weeks prior I had gone 4:14 in the Half Ironman distance at altitude as my lead into Kona and a PR to that point. Why ask for advice if you're not going to pay attention to it? That's the Niemeyer Method at work.

I was so amped up at the thought of just being in Kona and having realized my dream that I couldn't contain myself. My swim was okay, and I got on the bike determined to just haul ass from the get go. I got so caught up in things that by mile 56 I was cooking my brain. I decided to go with the aero helmet, which meant fewer vents. Fewer vents meant less air circulating to cool my head. The negative effects of that could have been offset by drinking more, but typical of me, despite my pre-race reminders to myself, I was only consuming about 12 ounces an hour and not the 40–50 I should have been.

By the time I got off the bike, I felt like I was going to fall over. I walked aid stations. I sat on ice. I dunked my head. I soaked myself. At mile 5 of the run, I made my big move and sprinted for a nearby toilet, the sound of my rapidly evacuating bowels only a momentary distraction from the smell that seared itself into my memory. I hobbled out of there and made it through the next couple of miles, feeling a bit better, mostly because I'd already made the decision that I'd drop out at mile 10. This was some bullshit. My dad dies and can't be here. Craig's gone. This was all just bullshit anyway. As I neared the mile marker I spotted Mandy. I started walking toward her, shaking my head.

"Get your ass back out there and finish. You can't quit! You worked too hard for too long to just stop." Mandy's tone was a mix of an order and a plea.

Her eyes flashed that angry kind of love that we all sometimes need, the version of it that lets us know that someone really cares about us.

By mile 18, the NBC camera crews found me. I'd done a brief profile with them pre-race and I was now grateful that they were there filming me again. No way I was going to let them capture me pissing and moaning or walking. The last 8 miles were much better than the first 8 had been—kind of appropriate given my history—and the middle 10 were a hazy blur. As I came down Ali'I Drive, I felt grateful for the final downhill section to the finish line and regretted my earlier meltdown. I should have just been grateful that I'd made it to the start line. Why was my memory so short?

I had completed the Ironman World Championship in 10:07:11 to finish 512 overall. Initially, I was very disappointed. I knew that I could do better. But my time wasn't a date to be carved into a tombstone. I was going to have other chances at this thing. I knew I would keep going until I raced to my potential. I had to refine my training and my racing, and I was determined to do both.

What had been a lifeline I'd grabbed turned out to be a way of life for me.

Since qualifying for Kona that first time in 2009 and competing in 2010, I've qualified every year since. My 2011 Ironman World Championship time was worse than in 2010 thanks to two flat tires. For the second of the two, I didn't have a spare tube (most of us only carry one spare) and wound up *clippety-clopping* along, running in my bike shoes, with my bike hoisted on my shoulder for nearly a mile. I was so hot from running in those shoes with that helmet on that I strongly considered just not even going out on the run and calling it a day. I'd lost as many as 20–25 minutes with my tire mishaps.

I knew that I had to just leave the bad bike experience in the transition zone, but I didn't. I let it affect my run, and if it wasn't for Mandy being there to once again really support and encourage me, I would have DNF-ed for the first time in my career.

I am proud to stay that I continue to make progress: 2012 was my best year yet. Not only did I qualify for Kona in the full Ironman distance, I also qualified for the World Championship in the Olympic and 70.3 (Half Ironman) distances. It felt like a Triple Crown for me. Experience is a valuable asset, and I was making the transition from punishing myself in my training and my racing to actually refining some techniques and working toward mastering the most important—and in my case most stubborn—element of racing: my mind.

In qualifying for the Ironman World Championship at Ironman Texas in May 2012, I managed to tame some of my worst impulses. I had a strong swim and a good bike, but at the start of the run, I began puking. I'd made some adjustments to my nutrition during the race and had added too much caffeine. Apparently, that didn't agree with my stomach. My legs felt great, but it was hard to fully utilize their strength when I was vomiting every half mile or so. In the past, I would have gotten all bent out of shape, thought of quitting, but I kept my cool, kept moving, and wound up with a qualifying spot in Kona. I was getting to the point where I didn't have to have a good day to qualify; I just needed to hold it together.

I also decided to race an Olympic distance event, and was reminded that racing could be fun. The race felt like it was over in an instant—in fact it was over in 2 hours and 8 minutes—and I realized that I was taking myself and my training far too seriously. I was always letting myself get wrapped around the axel about the most trivial things. I was so tightly wound I'd lose some of my humanity and regress as a person if I didn't ease up a bit. This was true on the course and off the course. Fortunately, Mandy is much more laid back (but still an intense competitor) than I am, and I've seen her eyes go wide at some of the inappropriate responses I've had to what to her were meaningless slights.

Three World Championship qualifications for 2012 felt pretty good to put it mildly. Always one willing to add more to the calendar, I was thrilled that I qualified for another, though very different kind of event, in October 2012. Following my fastest time yet in Kona (9:36), Mandy and I got married in Kauai.

We're both still racing, I still have a cadre of clients who I value as friends, and most of all, I'm starting to strike a better balance and not be as obsessive in my pursuits. I still want to go faster, of course, that will never change, but now that I have a partner from whom I can learn even more, my focus isn't so much on the finish line as it is on all the moments leading up to it.

That's not to say that I don't have goals; it's just that I've refined them and incorporated them into a larger plan for my entire life. I want to win my age group in Kona and crack the top 40 overall. I'm realistic enough to know that at my age, thirty-seven, the next two or three years will be crucial to my success on the course. I plan to really step up the training one more notch and really go after it. I want to be able to walk away from competing knowing that I did everything I could and not have any regrets.

I also know that I can only go on being this selfish for so long. Ironman is an intensely selfish pursuit, and I presently work out 2–4 times a day, 7 days a week, totaling 20–30 hours of training. Training and racing fill my days and my thoughts like scoring drugs used to, and despite the health benefits of being fit, I know that too intense of a focus and obsession with any activity can't be good. I know that I've gone from one extreme to another. That means that I understand that change is possible, and I know that I can't keep up this pace forever. Change is coming and I want to be prepared for it.

That said, I know that exercise will always be a part of my life. As much as I've mentioned all the pain I've gone through in being injured, the truth is that I LOVE training and racing. I love the sensation of propelling my body forward through the water and along the ground. The human body evolved into a motion machine, and I'm convinced that the more we separate ourselves from that essential nature, the more problems we have physically, emotionally, and spiritually. Mandy and I have talked about the eventual transition we'll have to make, and mountaineering, kayaking, backpacking, snowboarding, and skiing always seem to figure in our conversations. We're both people who need to keep moving, and for me, I know that exercise and physical activity have become the medication I've needed.

Mandy and I are fortunate that we share these interests. We spend more time together than most couples we know, and we both feel best about ourselves and the world when we are together, whether its doing a training run or going shopping. There are times when I have to laugh. I think about all those times when I walked into a store intent on walking out with some swag that I could sell to fund my drug use. That makes me think about who I hung out with, how obsessively I craved those drugs, and the chaos that was my life back then. I don't know if I even considered the possibility of having the kind of life that I have now. I do know that back then I thought that I had no real choice. I was an addict and as a result that necessitated that I do all the things I did in order to maintain that lifestyle—there was an inevitability to it all that I was powerless to change.

I now see that the most fundamental power that we have as humans is our ability to choose and to effect change in our own lives and in the lives of others. I made a lot of horrible choices and continue to be sorry for hurting other people as a result. I wish that all my past actions had existed in a vacuum and had no negative consequences for anyone other than myself. I also realize that's a completely unrealistic view of how the universe operates.

I've spent a lot of time reforming myself and focusing on my goals and dreams. At times, I've taken a few steps back and thought about ways that I can contribute to the greater good. I've spoken to groups on college campuses, and at conventions, and I will do more and more of that as my career winds down as a competitor. In some ways I'm giving back by working as a coach and trainer, but I know that I've not assisted others in any measure that's equal to all the help that I've been given. Despite my worst efforts, I'm still alive. Somewhere inside of me, not a part of my conscious will, I found a way to survive a day when I thought that all hope was gone.

Hope never abandons us and we can never abandon it. As long as our cells have enough energy to perform their millions of processes each day, we can always go on. I hope that no one ever has to face the choice that I had, that they never have to stand on whatever ledge and say to themselves, I can't go on. I quit.

At any moment, any day, we can always choose to start over no matter how bleak things may seem. Some days it feels like it's a struggle just to get to that starting line. But once you do, the collective energy of others can help sweep you along. Just when you think you're out, someone will come along and say just the right thing to get you going again. You just need to keep looking ahead and moving forward never stopping and seeing the day through to its end. At least the next day you have another chance to do it all over again. In time, a plan forms and a set of ideals replaces the negativity, and your will helps you find your way.

It took me years and years to finally find my way, and a bit longer than that to finally stop beating myself up for having taken so long to do it. What matters is that I crossed that finish line, regardless of what it says on the clock. I've won.

Acknowledgments

Our actions and words always influence the people we interact with. Thanks to all those who helped or tried to help me when no one was looking. These are just a few among the many: Mom and Dad for always being there through everything and never giving up. My little brother, Trent, for acting like my big brother and for always sticking with me. Carrie. Marleene Woodruff for treating me like family. Chad Overton. Sarah Dunn. Ryan Murphy. Kristin Smith. John Flynn. Joe Mintus. Mike Flynn. My other brother, Woody. Lynne and Gary Stott. Andy Slagel and Matt Brundage for my introduction to the world of fitness. Bobby Croft—you tried, but we were both too far gone. Dave Barnes and the Barnes family—models of conduct. Judge Thomas Neville for truth in justice. Brett Fox for saving my ass over and over and a true friend in tough times and the finest attorney. Ma Keller and the Keller clan. Susan Schulte. Brad Seng. Zoot Sports for taking a chance and keeping me clothed and shod. Rob (doctor) and Susan (counselor) Centeno. Ann Sabala an unlikely sounding board. Bob's

Bicycles for the help. Mike Akana for the setback. Erin Carson. Missy Swajkoski. Nick Moore. Deputy Freeman (Ada County Jail). Jeff Gasser. Flatiron Athletic Club. SRAM for the power meters, wheels, and groupos keeping me on the road and making me faster. Doug Lamott for showing me what *not* to do in training and life. David Snitman. Julie Imig. Mandy McLane the love for my life. Corrections Officer Jarrod Cash for showing the value of exercise in prison. John Carter. The Entire Crew at Colorado Multisport. Jason Messamore. My POs Tad Tadlock and Erica Hamm for not busting my balls too much and giving me support when I needed it. Dr. Jeff Menzner. Craig Alexander for being an athlete to look up to. Dave and Jane Scott. Brando and Billy Edwards. Ryan Hornby and his family for putting a roof over my head in the early rough days. Dave Bigelow. Joanna Zeiger. Adam Young—proud of you for turning the corner. Dr. Ian Davey for guidance and friendship. Dr. Jill Beck and Dave Beck. Brendan Synnott and Justin Gold for demonstrating what is possible as young men. Charlie, Lisa, Cathy Cooper. Ginny and Joe Mello. Barbra Arnold. Kelley Brupbacher Synnott. Judy Goldman. Lacey Mendenhal (Josh and Nicole) for providing a port in the stormiest days of my life. Karen and Steve Meyers. Renee Shires—a kick in the ass and great lady. Tina Bianca and Diana Duncan for being great ladies. Dr. David Saintsing. William Littlejohn. Julie Joffrion. Chris Goolsby. Josh and Shannon Garner: for keeping me safe and trying to hold me together. Peter Genuardi. Rena Kirkland for believing in me and giving me confidence to spread my wings. Corissa Ferricks. Linda Wild. Larry and Sue. Tom and Sherry Altfillisch. Alison Steele. David Anderson. Greg Plavidal (and Plavidal clan). Uncle John (Farm). John Stone. Tommy Simmons. Kelly Williamson. Pat Marsaglia. Abby Baggs. Mark Hamilton. Billy Thiel. Jeff Hoobler. Michael Stone. Dennis Meeker. Tim Hola. Lisa Pederson. Justin Daerr. Sylvia

Hampel. Greg and Laura Bennett—true champions and models of conduct. Joseph Dabbs. James Carney. COACH: Curt Chesney for helping me develop into a better athlete and reminding me that nothing is impossible. Marcus Allen Hille—a great friend and a healer who has kept me healthy through all the miles.

Thanks to all our men and women serving at home and abroad. Thank you for protecting and providing our way of life, and for all the sacrifices.

Huge thanks to my superagent Steve Ross for all the help through the process, and to Gary Brozek my writer, friend, and master wordsmith. Both of you took a huge chance on this project and I will be eternally grateful for your help and support in making it happen. Lastly to my editor Rob Kirkpatrick and everyone involved with the book at Thomas Dunne—many thanks.

I miss my friends who left too early: Craig Sweeney, Ryan Smith, Ryan Hornby, Roger Hubbel, Julio Barquero, Brian Krull, Jeff Hammer, Jamie Boring, Mary Beth Olinger. . . .